Eternal Curriculum
for Wisdom Children

Eternal Curriculum for Wisdom Children

Intuitive Learning and the Etheric Body

DOUGLAS GABRIEL

Our Spirit, LLC
2017

2017
OUR SPIRIT, LLC

P. O. Box 355
Northville, MI 48167

www.eternalcurriculum.com
www.ourspirit.com
www.gospelofsophia.com
www.neoanthroposophy.com

2017 Copyright © by Our Spirit, LLC

All rights reserved. No part of this publication may
Be reproduced, stored in a retrieval system, or transmitted,
in any form or by any means, electronic, mechanical,
recording, photocopying, or otherwise, without prior written
permission of the publisher.

Library of Congress Control Number: 2017955152

ISBN: 978-0-9906455-5-9 (paperback)
ISBN: 978-0-692-95356-3 (eBook)

Contents

Foreword ix

A Brief History of Waldorf Education 1

Child Development and Age-Appropriate Education 7

The Waldorf Curriculum Recapitulates Human Development . 19

The Waldorf Curriculum by Grade Level 27

Grade One: Saturn/Polaris 37

Grade Two: Sun/Hyperborea 59

Grade Three: Moon/Lemuria 73

Grade Four: Earth/Atlantis 87

Grade Five: Jupiter/Post Atlantis 115
    Ancient Indian Cultural Epoch 120
    Ancient Persian Cultural Epoch 134
    Egyptian/Chaldean/Babylonian Cultural Epoch 150
    Greco-Roman Cultural Epoch 162
    Anglo-Germanic Cultural Epoch 187

Grade Six: Venus/Sixth Epoch 221

Grade Seven: Vulcan/Seventh Epoch 249

Grade Eight: New Octave. 267

Appendix. 277
    Source of the Force: Secret Behind Star Wars Inspiration. 277
    The Enduring Legacy of Han Solo and Indiana Jones 291
    The Tree of Life 305

Become

Foreword

Worlds collided when we met. My deep longing to find someone who could hold the spiritual imaginations that constantly swirled in my head was satiated when I met Douglas, the deepest and most profound student of Rudolf Steiner I had ever encountered. It made perfect karmic sense that we would not meet until later in our lives, after the household duties of rearing children and going to work were behind us, leaving us totally free to explore and create our spiritual legacy.

Imagine how intriguing it was to form a relationship with a person whose life experiences included being a cryptologist for the NSA, a Jesuit for Rome, a Waldorf teacher, monk, world-traveler, clairvoyant, exorcist, writer, poet, theologian, and friend to some of the most interesting people in the world. I didn't hesitate when he asked me to marry him, as I had finally found a mate who had the capacity to perceive the being of Sophia as I had through many years of anthroposophical studies.

As we began our spiritual journey, Douglas would tell me marvelous stories about himself that sounded more like a Forrest

Gump character than an actual person. As he would describe his encounters with the Dalai Lama, Mother Teresa, Marcia Lucas, Mark and Claire Prophet, Oral Roberts, Kathleen Kennedy, Nancy Raegan, David Spangler, Robert Bly, Gelek Rinpoche, Joseph Chilton Pierce, Manly P. Hall, Alan Ginsberg, and so many other intriguing people, not to mention all of the anthroposophists trained by Rudolf Steiner himself, I would stand back with discernment until I realized that these stories were authentic and that my new husband was a remarkable student-teacher of spiritual science who had much to share with the world.

    Indeed, just his contributions to the movie *Star Wars* alone made him my own personal legend. I had now come full circle from being a young woman enthralled with the deep spiritual metaphors of the first *Star Wars* movies, to the anthroposophist who had heard rumors that *Star Wars* was inspired by Waldorf teachers, to the wife who encouraged Douglas to publish his story online so that others would see the profound effects that a striving spiritual student can make in the world. In return, Douglas helped me understand my own spiritual experiences, which are described in *The Gospel of Sophia* trilogy. Now that this series has been published and our websites are overflowing with articles and lectures, we set out to share Douglas' spiritual insight of human development, particularly the education of the etheric body and his *Theory of Everything*, which offers a profound understanding of how spirit becomes matter, and matter becomes spirit.

    Douglas Jude Gabriel was a Waldorf school teacher and teacher training instructor for forty years at a variety of schools and colleges, but one day, an innocent and naïve set of questions from a budding Waldorf teacher brought new light to the overall scheme of why and how the Waldorf elementary curriculum replicates the development of collective humanity. Dr. Rudolf Steiner, the founder of the Waldorf school movement, believed in the theory that *ontogeny recapitulates phylogeny*—that the development of the child retraces the stages of growth and development of the intellect and consciousness that collective humanity has experienced over time. Steiner taught that the child develops the etheric body, or the life-body that sustains the physical body, between ages seven to fourteen. The etheric body is filled with the memories of collective humanity and holds the template for how humanity will evolve into the future.

During this sensitive period of seven years when the etheric body is developing, the same teacher stays with the growing child from first through eighth grade to mid-wife the birth of the etheric body in the child. The etheric body needs developmentally appropriate education to align itself with the stages of humanity's development. These first seven years of education are the only time in the child's life when the etheric body is open and sensitive to this development. Each elementary grade's curriculum is specially chosen to directly meet the needs of the child, who is changing and evolving quickly through the stages of mental, psychological, and physical growth that humanity has undergone.

In a way, the evolving child is calling out for the specific nourishment that past cultures took centuries to experience and develop. The wisdom of each culture is shared with the child as nourishment until he or she grows into a *wisdom child* who has been fed a curriculum that is alive, and in many ways, somewhat *eternal* as it replicates the past and points towards future human evolution.

Though I had personally studied Anthroposophy and Waldorf for decades, I was always puzzled about why specific sequences of literature from other cultures were arranged in a seemingly hodge-podge manner in the Waldorf curriculum. It didn't make sense to me that the literature did not follow a chronological sequence through history. The teaching of German fairy tales came before ancient India and ancient Persia in the curriculum, which seemed chronologically incorrect. It just didn't make sense, so I simply accepted Steiner's ideas and stopped asking Waldorf teachers about the discrepancy—until I met Douglas.

He cleared up my confusion and shared his interpretation of Steiner's curriculum in a scheme that resolved the discrepancies I had noticed. After his elaborate explanation, with accompanying Steiner quotes, references, and diagrams, I understood the overall intent of the Waldorf curriculum, and it became clear to me that the mysteries surrounding Steiner's educational revelation were no less than the very core of what I had been relentlessly pursuing throughout my life.

The wisdom of the Waldorf curriculum was clearly the Being of Wisdom who I had experienced and would later write about in *The Gospel of Sophia*. The Being of Wisdom is Sophia, and Steiner's Waldorf education was a direct experience of the Being of Wisdom, who Steiner called AnthropoSophia. The Waldorf curriculum introduced the student to Wisdom (Sophia) through the different cultural periods as She evolved alongside of the collective evolution of humanity's consciousness. The mystery of ontogeny recapitulating phylogeny became the path of AnthropoSophia as She evolved together with humanity. Finally, the Waldorf curriculum made sense to me and became a revelation of Sophia found in yet another aspect of Steiner's teachings.

I was amazed how simple and yet completely hidden the Waldorf curriculum had been to me throughout the decades of study of Anthroposophy and Waldorf. At long last, my intuitions about Waldorf education became confirmed, yet I insisted that we write *The Gospel of Sophia* series first before we started *The Eternal Ethers* and *Eternal Curriculum for Wisdom Children*.

Douglas' first book, *The Spirit of Childhood*, sold thousands of copies and is available on our website for free. As many people have downloaded a copy of the book, as it has become a standard in the Waldorf teaching community. Douglas taught thousands of teachers over the years, and his insights led him to create a restatement of Steiner's teachings in a movement called Neoanthroposophy. He has also participated at all levels of Anthroposophy and Waldorf education, from the Pedagogical Section of the High School of Spiritual Science to earning a B. A. in Anthroposophical Studies and an M. A. in Waldorf Education. During those studies, he became friends with many of the older anthroposophists who had personally known Rudolf Steiner. He studied with some of the great anthroposophists throughout the world and became lifelong friends with many.

He was a class teacher and school administrator, taught courses at most of the Waldorf teacher training schools in America, and was an educational consultant for Waldorf schools worldwide. Eventually, this led him to create a foundation to fund the printing of Steiner's books, including the Foundation of Waldorf Education Series and many other Steiner titles. During his decades of fundraising for Waldorf education, Douglas helped raise millions of dollars for the advancement of Waldorf education.

One of the little-known facts about Douglas's Waldorf teaching credits is his participation in rewriting the movie treatment for the first three *Star Wars* movies at the request of Marcia Lucas. Marcia came to the Waldorf Institute seeking help to make her husband's movie a better story. Her husband at the time was George Lucas, and this original movie treatment had been rejected twice before Marcia and Douglas met. Douglas tells the story as though it were just another day at school writing stories for the children. He believed, at that time, that what he was doing was writing an adult fairy tale in a science fiction genre that appealed to the child in each of us. He made sure to add many of the teachings of Dr. Steiner to the characters and plot. For those who know both Anthroposophy and *Star Wars*, the similarities are strikingly obvious.

In the few days he was working with Marcia, he was just being Douglas: an amazing spiritually gifted young man who was allowing Sophia to work through his capacities of Imagination, Inspiration, and Intuition. He gave little thought about what would happen to his contribution. Today, he is in awe of the billions of people who have gleaned the spiritual wisdom in *Star Wars*. However, he is not surprised that the being Anthroposophia can use any of us in this way once we allow Her to fill our human capacities and capabilities with Her Wisdom.

Like the character Forrest Gump, Douglas always seems to show up at key moments in history through the flow of synchronicity. This is just one of those stories. His *Star Wars* connection to Marcia Lucas prompted Kathleen Kennedy to call him and ask questions for George Lucas and Steven Spielberg throughout the early *Star Wars* movies, and also during the creation of the Indiana Jones movies. Douglas spoke with Kathleen on the phone many times, giving her ideas for the Indiana Jones movies. He sent her boxes of spiritual and historical books, answering questions and providing ideas for the movies. Douglas continued to embed Steiner's spiritual ideas into storylines, inspiring another blockbuster movie. At the time, he had no idea that these ideas would touch the lives of so many people.

The *Eternal Curriculum for Wisdom Children* began as a way to answer a question Douglas' son Rhys had when he was a young boy. Cuddled up with his dad in their favorite oversized reading chair, young Rhys said, "Dad, you are a very wise being. You have read all these books in the den: hundreds and hundreds of books. I don't think I will have the time to read them all, but I want to be wise like you." Douglas lovingly told Rhys that he would go through all of the books and extract every bit of wisdom that he could find and put it in one book that would be dedicated to him and could be passed down to his children. The book was originally entitled *Wisdom for My Children*.

As Douglas ploughed through his books for research, he realized that the wisdom in world literature is also contained in the Waldorf curriculum, the very focus of his lifework. The wisdom of the world and the Waldorf literature curriculum were one and the same, and that wisdom was the Wisdom of Sophia.

While researching *Wisdom for My Children*, he began to see the wisdom of how the Waldorf curriculum is presented in class lessons. He explained the idea to his colleague Eve Hardie, and she was so excited that she made him promise to write it down and share it with the Waldorf education movement. At first, he was reluctant because the idea was so radical, but Eve was persistent. Now Douglas had to please two people: Rhys, who wanted to glean wisdom from all the world's greatest literature in one book, and Eve, who wanted the Waldorf community to see the spiritual profundity of the Waldorf curriculum.

Waldorf Education and the Etheric Body

It is almost impossible to understand the Waldorf curriculum without understanding the nature of the etheric body. Waldorf education essentially is teaching and nourishing the etheric body of the child for seven years. The main problem with this is that most Waldorf teachers and Anthroposophists can't really tell you much about the etheric body, let alone how to nourish it and midwife its birth. Most studied Anthroposophists can throw out a few concepts about the etheric body, but none that I had known could present its full meaning in the way that Douglas did for me.

"The etheric body," he explained, "is the most mysterious aspect of the human being and seems to have no limit to its importance in all aspects of creation. The ethers create the world, and they feed the etheric body, which is supposedly the body that is made up of memories and images, and is essentially the blueprint of life." He described the magical qualities of the etheric body and showed his deep understanding of the mystery of the ethers. As a Waldorf teacher-trainer, he explained that the best way to understand the etheric body is to grow a garden and watch the etheric work in the growth of plants. He encouraged his student teachers to learn a type of movement art Steiner created called Eurythmy. He pointed out that everywhere you look in Anthroposophy, the ultimate inspiration for every branch of study leads to the etheric formative forces.

One thing that Douglas never tires of talking about is the etheric, in any of its many forms. In his efforts to understand the etheric worlds, he studied bio-dynamic gardening, Eurythmy, veiled painting, Steiner's Christology, architecture, and Waldorf education. His research into the history of the ethers showed me that to whisper the sacred names of the ethers—tattvas, quintessence, Fohat, akasha—is to speak the name of the gods. The magic of the theurgists, the alkahest of the alchemists, the pranayama of the yogi, the four elements of the Greeks, the harmony of the spheres of Pythagoras, and the luminiferous ether of Einstein all tell part of the story of the mystery of the ethers.

The Greek god Aether was seen as the highest creator god who brought all things into existence. Throughout history, the highest praise and honor is given to the ethers, which are also called the Mothers of Creation. The highest ether, the Akasha ether, is seen as a mother who has four sons. The mythologies of the world provide us with unending images that describe these fundamental forces of Mother Nature that we call ethers. Often these Imaginations from mythologies help us understand the profound nature of the archetypal ethers.

Through the comprehensive understanding of the ethers that Rudolf Steiner provides, a complete cosmology can be developed that encompasses the entire evolution of the Earth and humanity. The creation of time, space, matter, and consciousness is intimately connected to the evolution of the ethers, the etheric body, and etheric cycles of time. One can literally say that inside the etheric body of the human being is the past, present, and the future in a microcosm. The etheric body transcends time, holds memories, and controls rhythmic functions that are connected to the etheric bodies of the Earth, Sun, and planets. For example, the "music of the spheres" is created by the Sound Ether, which came into manifestation during the Moon Incarnation of the Earth. The four incarnations of Earth manifested the four ethers of warmth, light, sound, and life. These same ethers manifest in the four temperaments found in the characterological dispositions of children: choleric, sanguine, phlegmatic, and melancholic. These same forces, elements, and ethers manifest in fire, air, water, and earth. The macrocosm of the etheric formative forces manifests in the microcosm of the human etheric body and creates the foundation upon which a modern cosmology can be built.

The Philosophy

In preparing this book for publication, we decided that elucidating a comprehensive overview of the *Eternal Curriculum* would be difficult without providing a comprehensive overview of the ethers and the way they work into the human etheric body, especially in the years from age seven to fourteen. This is why the book is divided into two print volumes, with a third section on the website www.eternalcurriculum.com for the everyday application and practicalities of the curriculum.

The Eternal Ethers: A Theory of Everything provides a comprehensive presentation of the ethers and their exact functions in nature, nutrition, and human evolution. It provides the philosophical foundation for an understanding of the etheric formative forces.

The Content

The second book, *Eternal Curriculum for Wisdom Children: Intuitive Learning and the Etheric Body,* is a master curriculum that provides the parent or teacher with applications for each grade and age of the child, including literature suggestions and bibliographic references. We wanted this book to be a tool that parents and teachers could easily use to incorporate the curriculum into home schooling as well as traditional, Waldorf, charter, or alternative schooling. We also made it thorough enough that it could stand alone as a curriculum for any elementary educational setting.

The Application

A third section of the curriculum, entitled *Intuitive Learning*, provides parents and teachers with the application of teaching the etheric body. This section, located on our website, will grow and expand as we develop videos and content. We hope that it will become a resource library for the best applications that we can create and gather from best practices in the field. The two print volumes, enhanced with the online application resources, offer a path to comprehending the great mystery of Anthroposophy, the etheric formative forces, and their work in the etheric body of the human being.

When we teach a child from ages seven to fourteen, we witness a wondrous birth of intellect and consciousness that is strengthened by repeated, rhythmic activities that enrich, enhance, and nourish the human etheric body. The rhythmic activities in a classroom of wisdom children are enriched by the cultural experience of songs, literature, poems, and games used by other cultures who embodied the wisdom of the past.

You do not have to be in a Waldorf school to experience the Eternal Curriculum, because the etheric body itself is the content of the lessons. You just have to listen to what the students are inwardly calling out to be taught. Teachers throughout America learned on their own that fifth graders love studying Greece, sixth graders love Rome, and seventh graders love the Renaissance and the Age of Exploration without knowing that the Waldorf curriculum recommends those same lessons for the same grades. There is something in the student that is longing to be fulfilled through the lessons they study. In "becoming" a Greek while studying Greece, the student embodies the intellect, feelings, and daily life of a Greek philosopher or peasant. By truly "living into" the cultural experience, something comes to birth and is nourished at the same time. This experience is thoroughly fulfilling to the students, who seem to "become" whatever they are studying.

There is much to be said about the benefits of dramatizing scenes from history to develop deep knowledge of a subject. When you add a full-emersion experience of a culture to that, including language, literature, song, dance, mythology, philosophy, and daily routines, then you truly can "become" a Roman or Greek or an Egyptian in a microcosmic fashion. The wisdom children who are being presented with the Eternal Curriculum experience the lessons deep in the memories of their own etheric body and build each step of conscious human development again as a living task, like building a Gothic cathedral in Europe or the Hagia Sophia in Constantinople. Each perfectly hewn stone is essential to building a sound structure. Each cultural emersion is a lost key to the builder's plans of the child's own temple.

Every teacher or parent who wishes to accompany the journey of the wisdom child through the *Eternal Curriculum* can become a contributing member by immersing themselves in the culture that is taught at the appropriate grade level. Adults going through the curriculum can take their literature inspiration from sources other than the children's sources of literature. The point is that most parents and teachers have not gone through this sequence of lessons in the right order or at the right time during their own childhood, and can use the enrichment. Teaching these lessons to a child at the right time can provide a window to view what we missed if we were not treated as wisdom children during our own educational experience. Working through the material can also provide the reader with a view of what the etheric body can teach a person who is willing to listen.

This book's original interpretation of Steiner's universal curriculum is an attempt to accomplish the task that Dr. Steiner gave to Americans: to develop a cosmology that highlights the wisdom of the Cosmic Christ. Steiner indicated that what we need most at this time of evolution is to understand how Christ is part of every aspect of human development, from standing upright, speaking, and thinking to the modern challenges of developing the Consciousness Soul aspects of the human being. Without a spiritual cosmology that places the human being in the center of all scientific, religious, and psychological considerations, an individual can become lost, alone, and hopeless in these asocial times. The dignity of the human being needs to be raised above all scientific inquiry, and education needs to become a sacred act that can connect children with their spiritual foundations. A cosmology that embraces the Eternal Curriculum that is written into the etheric body of each human being can provide the spiritual insight and substance that is needed by the wisdom child in each of us.

Tyla Gabriel

A Brief History of Waldorf Education

Instruction and education must not proceed from applied knowledge but rather from a living abundance. With this abundance, the teacher deals with the children as though he were an instrument enabling the world itself to speak to the child. Then there will be an inherent life-stimulating quality to the instruction and not mere external pedantry.

Looking back on the achievements of those teachers, one can only describe them as outstanding. I have known no other body of teachers so unreservedly devoted to their education tasks as the original College of Teachers.

Rudolf Steiner (GA 307)

    After World War I, Emil Molt, an industrialist and the owner of the Waldorf-Astoria cigarette factory in Stuttgart, Germany decided to establish a private school for his employees' children. He asked a man he very much admired, the renowned scientist and philosopher Rudolf Steiner, to design and set up this school. Hence, the first Waldorf School, based on Steiner's wisdom and insights, came into being.
    The inauguration of the first Waldorf school was a landmark in the already formidable career of Rudolf Steiner that, from then on, channeled his creative genius to the creation of high-

quality education for children. The project intrigued Steiner because he had long been concerned about the need for cultural transformation, and he recognized that all effective social transformation begins with the education of children. The request from Molt came at a propitious time for Steiner, as he was at a point in his philosophical development where he was looking for a way to demonstrate the effectiveness of his philosophy in an environment where his pedagogical theories could be verified with scientific accuracy. Steiner designed a curriculum for the Waldorf-Astoria School, a title later shortened to Waldorf, based on the anthroposophical view of the developing human being as body, soul, and spirit. He blended the creative arts with applied sciences and designed a comprehensive curriculum that met the developmental needs of the maturing child.

The life and career of Rudolf Steiner (1861–1925) is a remarkable one. Born in 1861 on the Austrian border near Hungary, he went to school in Vienna by commuting on the train from the station where his father worked. He graduated with honors from both the Technical College and Realschule. At age twenty-one, Steiner, who was a scholar of Johan Wolfgang von Goethe (1749–1832), the great German statesman, poet, and scientist, was offered a prestigious assignment by the Goethe-Schiller Archives in Weimar, where he was asked to edit Goethe's monumental scientific work. He subsequently wrote several books on Goethe, including *Goethe's World View*, *The Goethean Conception of the World*, and *A Theory of Knowledge Implicit in Goethe's World Conception*.

Steiner finished editing Goethe's scientific work, but—true to his pattern of prodigious work—while he was editing Goethe's papers, he also earned his Ph.D. at Rostock University. In his thesis for this degree, *Truth or Knowledge*, Steiner developed his own unique theory of knowledge. He later created an epistemological basis for a spiritual source of thinking in what some consider to be his most important philosophical work, *The Philosophy of Freedom*.

Steiner first became publicly active in the dissemination of spiritual knowledge through his association with the Theosophical Society, which was founded by H. P. Blavatsky, Henry S. Olcott, and others in New York in 1875. Until the turn of the century, Steiner lectured widely in the Theosophical Society; however, he eventually left this organization, and with the many followers he had gained during his years with the Theosophical Society, formed the Anthroposophical Society. The name was derived from the Latin "anthroposophia," which means "the wisdom of humanity."

Steiner had turned away from the leadership of the Theosophical Society because he felt they were becoming too eastern in their philosophy, leaving out what he referred to as the "turning point of time," or the incarnation of the Christ into the being of Jesus of Nazareth at his Baptism in the Jordan River. Annie Besant, the President of the Theosophical Society, had quite other views on Christianity, including the notion that J. Krishnamirti was the new incarnation of the Christ. This point of contention led Steiner to withdraw from further participation in the Theosophical Society after the International Congress of 1905. Steiner's own clairvoyant perception of such matters never failed him, as he continued to shed new light on many such subjects.

In his books and lectures, Steiner demonstrated his scientific knowledge of both the seen and unseen worlds. His clairvoyant vision led him to disseminate broad ideas of reform in virtually every field of knowledge, including science, architecture, art, philosophy, medicine, agriculture, religious renewal, and, ultimately, education.

True to the title of the society, Steiner established Anthroposophy as the nucleus of the philosophy of the schools he later founded in Stuttgart, Germany in 1919. The human being is the central figure of all the lessons taught in these "Steiner" schools. Thereby, the dignity and place of the human being in relationship to the whole world is brought before the growing child out of Steiner's comprehensive Anthroposophy. His philosophy is never taught to the children outright, but rather is a spiritual source of inspiration that enlivens the teacher.

Waldorf education puts the image of the developing human being into a comprehensive theory of developmental stages that matches its holistic curriculum. Implicit in Steiner's Anthroposophy is a theory of knowledge and learning that encompasses the most complete psychology of the stages of the growing child available. The Waldorf curriculum, as it has come to be known, is an encapsulation of the wisdom that runs through Steiner's books and lectures.

After the founding of the first Waldorf School, Steiner was able to experience a validation of his educational philosophies based upon the fine results of the school. The transformation in the Waldorf student's academic and artistic progress was so phenomenal that the first Waldorf School became the spark that enkindled hundreds of other Waldorf schools. The Waldorf Movement, as it came to be known, flourished and swept over Europe and North America.

While some educators who think of education as job training for industry might be critical of Waldorf's artistic approach, research conducted in Germany has indicated that Waldorf students have a definite advantage in passing achievement tests and accomplishing their goals in life. "Number of years in a Waldorf school" was found to be directly proportional to higher achievement scores—the longer the student spent in a Waldorf school, the higher his or her scores. After ninety years of continuing research, the evidence indicates that Waldorf education successfully prepares students for life.

When one teaches first-grade at a Waldorf School, following Steiner's vision, the first-grade teacher is promoted to the next grade along with her students, staying with a class as they progress from first through eighth grade. This procession not only creates a strong bond between teacher and student, but also creates the opportunity for better follow-through from grade to grade and promotes consistency in a child's educational development. The class, as well as the teacher, grow together as the entire elementary curriculum is worked through year by year in a fresh way by the class teacher, who must teach a new curriculum for each new grade.

There is no need for standardized textbooks in a Waldorf school because the students make their own workbooks that reflect the daily presentations of the teacher. All lessons integrate art into an enriched curriculum that works from the idea that we need to proceed from the whole to the parts to develop the imagination of the child. The intent is to illuminate the subject so that the child can encounter the living being behind the phenomena of nature. While studying math, science, and humanities, Waldorf students learn to be artistically expressive and develop confidence in their flexible thinking abilities that gain focus through regular performances of those skills in creative illustrations, music, poetry recitation, and other integrated classroom activities. For example, the teacher and class often co-write class plays that characterize the lessons learned each year from the variety of world literature found in the curriculum.

To help students feel good about what they are learning and to sharpen performance skills, the school year is full of program offerings where friends and family of the Waldorf community may come and see the students' work displayed and share in musical and dramatic performances. At these gatherings, the students' paintings, sculpture, crafts, and self-created textbooks are displayed to demonstrate their understanding of the lessons. The children perform in orchestras, choirs, dance troupes, and endless other activities that are shared with the school community. The students become quite comfortable creating and displaying their works of art in the celebration of learning. In this atmosphere, self-discipline and deep learning can take place, activating the different intelligences (cognitive, kinesthetic, musical, analytical, and others) that the child brings to bear in any expression or performance. There is also "no competition" involved in activities, so that self-esteem can develop instead of envy, pride, and shame. The students learn that what they do in the classroom connects them to the larger, outer world of culture and society. This integrates the individual's gifts and talents into a community where they are respected for their strengths and weaknesses.

Due to the desire to promote self-esteem and social integration, rather than competition, a teacher in a Waldorf school does not send out letter-grade report cards. The child is not compared to any standard or any other child, but only to his own growth and development in relationship to the curriculum material presented. Teachers handwrite a detailed account of each student's progress, giving examples to support the statements made about the child. After the parents receive the report, an interview with the teacher takes place. There, the conversation about the child's development continues. This happens year after year and fulfills a prime directive of Waldorf education, which is to encourage parental involvement in the child's learning process.

Steiner's insight into education is comprehensive, but he leaves the teacher free to present the curriculum in his own manner and with his own strengths and weaknesses. Each teacher can enhance and enrich the curriculum out of his personal skills, talents, and artistic nature, flavoring the presentations with individual interests.

The psychological and physiological stages of childhood are addressed in the Waldorf curriculum. Appropriate materials are available to integrate the thinking, feeling, and willing of the student into a balanced whole, but it is the love, devotion, and respect that a teacher has for each child that creates a true "Waldorf mood" in the classroom. Studying Anthroposophy will lead the teacher in the right direction of seeing his job as one of helping to integrate the body, soul, and spirit of the child into a balanced whole.

Child Development and Age-Appropriate Education

The task of the teacher is not to mold the mind but to enable it to grow to new dimensions, maybe beyond the teacher's own reach. It is thus [the teacher] serves the present for the future. Pedagogy must not be a science; it must be an art, but the feelings in which we must live in order to practice that great art of life, the art of education, are only kindled by contemplation of the great universe and its relationship with humanity.

Rudolf Steiner (GA 34)

Any attempt to achieve an Anthroposophically illuminated study of developmental stages of childhood in relationship to Waldorf pedagogical methods can only be sketchy at best, but hopefully the brief overview contained in this section will suffice as a philosophical backdrop.

In the oldest philosophical writings of the Hindus, we find a great dilemma. *The Upanishads* state that there are two things for humanity to know: first is the Atman, or that which is in the human being, and the second is Brahman, or that which is outside the human being. The dilemma is that the Atman and Brahman are the same being. Rudolf Steiner refers to the same dilemma in *The Philosophy of Spiritual Activity,* when he states that all religion, art, and science come from the desire of humanity to bridge the gap between his I, or self/ego, and the world. Even though the names are different, the principle is the same.

Clearly, the resolution of conflict between the inner person and the outer world is an old and great task. This is the central theme of Waldorf education. In Steiner's terms, this task can be accomplished in a pedagogical atmosphere that engenders a wholesome relationship between the I (or ego) of the child and the world.

The awakening of this I (or ego) in a child can be seen in an especially pronounced fashion at the ages of three, nine, and eighteen years of age. At three, we often find that children are eager to attempt deeds in which they assert their egohood. "I can do it myself" is quite a common phrase at this age. While the three-year-old child's mother might refer to this stage of fanciful and aggressive tendencies as "the terrible threes," a Waldorf teacher sees these inclinations as the child's eagerness to attempt deeds through which she can assert her egohood. This phase can be imagined as the *dawn of memory* beginning to be impressed into the child's etheric body (life body) and is the first sign of the development of a sense of egohood.

At the age of nine years and four months, we often find that children have a powerful experience as they begin to realize that their I is bound and limited by their physical body. Before this revelation, the I finds its home more in the head—the human representation of the starry heavens. The "nine-year change," as Rudolf Steiner called it, has now been documented by recent brain research. It seems that the corpus callosum, which connects the right and left sides of the brain, doesn't finish its development until after nine years of age. Some brains that were studied didn't finish development until age twelve, or in rare cases even as late as age fifteen. Before age nine, the child is used to the right-brain activity of a kinesthetic, spatial, geometric, holistic, or full-bodied experience. As the corpus callosum finishes growing, left-brain activity becomes easier, and going back and forth between the two becomes easier. During the nine-year change, the I/ego begins to descend from the head into the rhythmic system centered in the chest, and then later even further into the metabolic processes (digestion, limb movement). The child becomes more agitated as she encounters the strong, rhythmic impulses of the heart and lung systems. Subsequently, the sense of oneness that the child had felt so strongly until that time begins to disappear. The child becomes more controlled by strong, new emotions. Time and space, once integrated in the child's consciousness, become separated in a linear fashion, causing her direct experience of archetypal forms to dissipate. She feels as if she is an orphan and asks tough questions about who she is and her limits. Talk of death, killing, or running away from home is common as the I/ego descends into the dynamic rhythms of the chest. It is at this point that self-consciousness develops and the child's need for music becomes paramount. Music provides harmony for these unsettled feelings. The various forms of music—singing, rhythmic movement, and poetry—are used to enhance Main Lesson blocks in which the teacher holistically presents the world through the kingdoms of nature, beginning with animals, plants, stones, and finally the human kingdom.

At age eighteen, another ego awareness experience usually manifests itself. The young adult becomes aware of her I in the stream of life, and out of this sense becomes aware of the need to direct her life's ambitions. Vocation choices and other major decisions are a direct result of this eighteen-year-old ego-consciousness transition. What teachers need to remember at this stage in the child's development is that she is becoming extremely aware of the authority of parents and other adults. Since we can teach little to an unwilling or rebellious child, we must always be aware that what we are—not only as teachers, but also as human beings—stands clearly before the student and is part of the world in which her I/ego develops.

We, as teachers, must know from our own experience where the I/ego of humanity truly dwells and be able to present this "Ego of Humanity" to the children by highlighting its dignity and purpose. In this way, teachers create a healthy environment in which the child can awaken to the part of herself that we are teaching about in the lesson. If there is any discrepancy between what teachers say and what they do, a child of this age will quickly discern it and may refuse to accept that teacher's authority and instruction.

By the age of twenty-one, the birth of the I/ego usually has taken place, but the young adult still must be helped and supported. "Ontogeny recapitulates phylogeny" is a phrase that speaks succinctly of the three "births" or developmental stages that an incarnating child passes through to become a young adult. The child must relive the metamorphoses that humanity has gone through, including the births of the physical body, the etheric body (age seven), the astral body (age fourteen), and the I/ego (age twenty-one). Each "body" has its birth, and each birth has unique characteristics surrounding it. But even at age twenty-one, the human I/ego is still a dawning experience, and the path beyond that point is also governed by further seven-year cycles that do not carry such powerful influences as we find in the three births of the physical body, etheric body, and I/ego. However, when a teacher is knowledgeable about these stages of development, he is in the position to give help, strength, and direction that may help the child pass gracefully into adulthood.

The cornerstone of a Waldorf education is a deep belief in repeated human earth lives (incarnations). Without this belief in life before birth and a firm grounding in knowledge that the prenatal world directly relates to the *conceptual life* of the child, teachers would be blind to the impact of that prenatal condition; consequently, they would have no grounded psychological understanding of the child's experience. We must also know, as a soul experience, that the deeds of a human being live on beyond death; otherwise, we can know little of the true nature of the "deeds of will" that, in fact, extend into that after-death condition.

From a contemplation of the birth/death continuum of life, we can begin to realize that the birth of the physical body must be understood in the light of reincarnation, which is a key element in the history of the spiritual evolution of humankind. We must be mindful that the child has chosen the body donated by her parents, and that with gestation and birth, the child passes through the cosmic evolutionary cycle of transformation from water (amniotic fluid) to air (first breath of life).

With the first breath, the child becomes a citizen of the present, but many forces are also rushing to meet her from the past. All that the child had as forces in prenatal life rushes forth to create her body out of the ether body of the earth. At birth, the child is given a model (hereditary) ether body which guides, forms, regulates, and enlivens the substances that constitute the physical body. As substance is constantly taken in, transformed, and excreted, the ether body (the memory of the bodily form) is performing the vital functions of the physical body during the waking hours of day and rejuvenating it during the sleeping hours of night.

In the donated hereditary etheric body, hierarchical spiritual beings are working to surround the child with love and hold this ether body together from birth until approximately age seven. Then the child's own unique ether body begins to take over these functions, and the ether body becomes more of a personal reflection of the soul-spirit nature of the child. The model ether body is donated by hierarchical spirit-beings as part of the activity in the first three years of life, when the *will* of the child is growing to a marked degree. In these primary years, the child learns to stand erect, speak, and conceptualize (make mental pictures). These deeds of will are intrinsically human and are essential to I/ego consciousness. The Being of Christ, through the combined forces of the Spirits of Form, is the spirit responsible for humanity's I/ego development and evolution. The Spirits of Form are essentially involved with the development of the I/ego because they have donated the forces that have created the possibility for the consciousness of the human I/ego. The child receives these gifts as part of the spirit of childhood, which leads her forward into adult life.

Through an understanding of this spiritual evolution from childhood to adulthood, teachers should be aware that everything that comes into contact with the young child has a powerful etheric, organ-forming influence over the child. Food, color, light, warmth, movement, sound, music, speech, forms, gesture, and all other aspects of the environment are the substances from which the child's organs are developed. Therefore, it is especially important that, during the first three years of life, the child has good nutrition and a healthy environment. A very important element of this healthy environment is acceptance of a child's natural development. One should not try, through clever means, to speed the processes of walking, speaking, or intellectual achievement. Parents and teachers alike, with loving acceptance and encouragement, must let the being of the child speak to them as her nature unfolds. This natural development from infancy to adulthood can be best understood in terms of certain predictable cycles.

From about two years, four months to four years, eight months, the child is in the middle part of the threefold division of the first seven-year cycle. Rhythm, repetition, and feeling are all-important during this time, as healthy feelings develop out of a regular sense of rhythm. Whenever possible, music should be soft and written in the pentatonic scale (a simple scale of five notes with no minors), and stories should be told "from the heart" (memorized). Important to the child's conceptual development at this time is her relationship to the rhythms of her mother's and father's speech patterns, because the forces in speech help create the convolutions of the growing brain. The simple repetition of a memorized story has a profound, magical effect on the young child. A lullaby can work wonders. All these elements are part of a healthy environment for a child and provide the necessary atmosphere that will engender a sense of awe and wonder towards life.

Implicit in this environmental design is the need to establish good models of healthy human relationships. From birth until age seven, imitation and example serve as the overall keynotes of child development. Whatever the child perceives during these years is observed and imitated. If the child experiences caring and loving relationships, this will engender a sense of reverence and devotion for people everywhere and enrich the path of healthy growth and development.

The natural tendency of the child to imitate what she sees and hears is an especially important consideration from the late fourth year until age seven. At this stage, the child is developing her thinking abilities. In order to offer examples of healthy, living thinking instead of dry intellectualism, teachers should use *lively imaginations* in their presentations. They must paint beautiful word-pictures for the child to live into with her whole being. The child can easily memorize when her own etheric forces are at work after the age of seven; until then, the child should not be made to crystallize her body with two-dimensional, abstract concepts or too much rote memorization.

The mental training of a child can be more properly started around the age of seven, when the etheric body of the child penetrates from the head downward. The signature of this occurrence is the eruption of the second teeth. After the second dentition of the teeth, memorization comes more easily for children. Even contemporary researchers know that this is a signal to begin a more formalized intellectual approach in a child's education.

When the thinking abilities that are associated with memory development start forming after the second teeth have erupted, strong will activities can be used to balance the new forces of permanent memory. The *birth of the etheric body* that accompanies memory appears from inside the organism and moves towards the periphery in an expanding, uplifting motion, much like the muscle activity that raises the child to the upright position. At this time, the rhythmic movement of eurythmy can help the forces of memory to be properly integrated into the child's muscular system.

The next critical phase of a child's development takes usually place around age twelve to fourteen, although this can depend greatly on geographic location due to the onset of puberty having such a wide variance in age. At this stage, the astral body, which has been hovering around the child, contracts into the body, marking the period known as adolescence or puberty. Marking the *birth of the astral body* and the onset of puberty are the dramatic changes of voice and the growth of the skeleton. As any parent or teacher who has witnessed this transformation from childhood to adulthood can attest, this period can be a chaotic one. The astral body, a vehicle used by the I/ego of a child, can be aggressive and animal-like; it can also be melodic, warm, and life-giving. To better ensure that the more positive aspects manifest, the child should be encouraged to play a musical instrument. Music can help tame and harmonize the more chaotic energies of adolescence.

Another calming influence during the stage from the birth of the ether body at age seven to the birth of the astral body at around age fourteen is having a central class teacher who develops a personal relationship with the child and becomes akin to an etheric/astral midwife. A Waldorf teacher is aware that the human is not a finished being at birth; the physical birth is but one of the births that must be carefully and thoughtfully prepared. The child must be nurtured and cared for throughout the birth of the etheric and astral bodies with all the loving care that the midwife gives to the birthing process of a newborn baby. Only when a teacher realizes his importance in this process of growth and development can he become the awakened, artistic teacher that is needed for the foundation of a sound educational process.

Steiner elucidates this crucial role of the teacher in the first chapter of *Study of Man*:

> The task of education conceived in the spiritual sense is to bring the Soul-Spirit into harmony with the Life-Body. They must come into harmony with one another. They must be attuned to one another; for when the child is born into the physical world, they do not as yet fit one another. The task of the educator, and of the teacher too, is the mutual attunement of these two members.

In using the term *Soul-Spirit*, Steiner is making reference to the threefold Soul (Sentient Soul, Intellectual Soul, and Consciousness Soul) and the threefold Spirit (Spirit Self, Life Spirit, and Spirit Man). The correct penetration of the Soul-Spirit into the Life-Body nature of man is accomplished through a proper sense of breathing, which, in turn, determines the rhythm of waking and sleeping.

This does not mean that teachers should empirically adjust the breathing processes of a child or try to alter his sleeping habits. This would be the worst of things that could be done. In presenting holistic, imaginative education to children, breathing is brought into harmony naturally, and the alternation of waking and sleeping becomes more rhythmical and filled with life and enthusiasm. This is what Steiner means when he speaks of the task of the teacher, which is to mutually attune these two polarities of the child's constitution: Soul-Spirit and LifeBody. Since breathing reflects the degree to which these processes are in harmony, it is important to understand this process in detail.

The breath mediates between nerve/sense processes and the will/metabolic processes. Breathing unites us most directly with the outer world as we take in life-giving oxygen and exhale the used carbon dioxide. All cells need this life-giving oxygen, including the nerves, the blood, and the metabolic processes of the will. The breathing activity of a class of students, from thinking to playing, should become a rhythmical process that allows each child to alternate between these poles in a healthy breathing rhythm. In doing this, we bring the child into proper balance so that the Soul-Spirit can harmoniously penetrate the Life-Body of the child.

If teachers have enriched the child's day with a proper balance of activity and thinking in a harmoniously rhythmic manner, they can know that they have also helped the child in the alternation of waking and sleeping. Each night, the child is renewed out of the spiritual world of sleep by what the child has taken into sleep. A healthy sense of involvement in the classroom is an indication that what you have taught is worthwhile and refreshing, instead of hardening and tiresome. What the child brings to class each day as renewed strength and energy is the indication of a healthy pedagogy.

The teacher must keep in mind that until the age of seven, the child is a citizen of two worlds. She is slowly penetrating the physical world but is not quite *on the earth* in her fullest capacity. From age seven to fourteen, the child becomes ready for school and begins to interact more fully with the environment. Eventually, by the end of this seven-year period, she reaches puberty. Only during this developmental stage can we begin, in a systematic way, to train the child's memory for concepts she will use in the exterior world. We must remember not to push the child into accepting things for which she is not quite ready. This is why the Waldorf pedagogy maps out the developmental stages of childhood. Understanding these stages helps a teacher understand each child more fully and work in harmony with the child's natural developmental processes.

There are signposts along the way that enable a teacher to predict what a child is ready to accept. For example, around age seven, we may see the protrusion of the child's second teeth. Before this time, the model etheric body formed the body of the child; after seven, the individualized etheric body of the child begins to take over the functions of the etheric body. The mobile world of archetypes in which the child has been living begins to fade. While this indicates that the child's memory is now able to hold the concepts used in grade school, it also marks the waning of earlier childhood. Two and one-third years later, at the "nine-year change," with growth and added weight, many changes come. Until now, the child has been enjoying feelings of levity and lightness and their recognition of the I/ego consciousness has been emanating from the head region; now the home of the I/ego drops from the head region through the chest/rhythmic region on its way into the metabolic processes. As the child begins to feel the limits of gravity restricting her body, the I/ego consciousness is also being limited by these same forces as consciousness drops further from the head into the throat, and then into the chest/rhythmic region. This change initiates a new experience of space in the child.

To accommodate these changes and help the child sort out her feelings in this new realm, the teacher can turn to the harmonizing influences of music again by giving the child an instrument to play. Other useful strategies to bring space into perspective are geography lessons and Norse myths, which use a hexameter meter that helps balance the breath with the heart-rhythm. All of these methods are only effective if the teacher is aware of these changes and responds to the child with warmth and guidance to help her live in harmony with herself between the forces of gravity and levity.

The "twelve-year change" is somewhat like the "nine-year change," but now the child has become more aware of time and her place in it. History can now be taught in imaginative pictures because the child is gaining the capacity to understand the flow of time. Roman and Medieval times are taught at this stage, and the lasting cultural, legal, and architectural influences of these periods can be seen and deeply felt by the child.

By age fourteen, the astral body, which has, until now, lived outside the body, starts to contract into the child, precipitating the onset of puberty. The voice changes, the limbs elongate, and the sexual glands develop and become active. The higher-level thinking skills concerning cause and effect are now taught in science classes and can readily be comprehended by the child in this phase of development. In fact, it now becomes possible to learn many subjects; before, the child had no inner experience to match the concepts. By this age, temporal sequencing is fully experienced, and modern history lessons begin. The child has learned about many civilizations of the past, and now they are introduced to modern history. The child has now descended from the archetypal realm into the space/time realm of Earth and modern-day consciousness.

An Overview of Child Development

Soul Capacity	Willing	Feeling	Thinking
Educational Realm	Psycho-motor realm	Affective realm	Cognitive realm
	Volition-action	Feelings-values	Analytical
Force in Education	Birth to 7	Age 7-14	Age 14-21
	Imitation	Imagination	Clear thinking
Reading Tactic	Storytelling	Retelling	Concepts
	Writing	Illustrating	Reading
Teacher Qualities	Reverence	Devotion	Music/Art
	Interest in the world	Enthusiasm	Sense of humor

Three Developmental Stages

	Age Seven	Age Nine	Age Twelve
Steiner	Birth of etheric	Nine year change	Limb/skeleton growth
Steiner	Second teeth	Inward/ independent	Causal relationships
	Imaginative pictures	Norse myths	Space and mechanics
Piaget	Pre-operational period	Conservation	Concrete operations
Pierce	Convolutions of brain	Corpus callosum	Cerebral cortex
	Subject/object merged	Subjective validity	Objective validity
Montessori	Reading by seven	Cosmology stories	Objective world citizens

The Waldorf Curriculum Recapitulates Human Development

What a piece of work is man! How noble in reason! How infinite in faculty! In form and moving how express and admirable; In action, how like an angel! In apprehension, how like a god! The beauty of the world, The paragon of animals...

Shakespeare, *Hamlet*

    The author was once asked a series of questions by a Waldorf teacher in training that prompted the insight that led to a comprehensive perspective about the Waldorf curriculum. The questions were the standard questions about why the Waldorf curriculum, which is purported to replicate the growth and development of humanity, is not presented in a chronological order. We were speaking specifically about the Waldorf literature curriculum for the elementary student from grades one through eight—the years in which the Waldorf *class teacher* teaches the same students as the principal teacher.
    This key factor in Waldorf education—having the same teacher grades one through eight—gives the teacher the opportunity to watch the same students grow year after year, deepening the relationship between student and teacher. Essentially, the Waldorf class teacher becomes a member of the student's family

through this extraordinary connection. Observing and interacting with the same students for eight years brings an unusual and unorthodox relationship that can shed light on the developing child and the way the Waldorf curriculum meets the needs of each developmental stage that the child is evolving through to become a "citizen of their own time" by grade eight.

The questions that the teacher in training asked were common ones, and they had been discussed many times, but this time, the manner in which the teacher asked the questions called forth an entirely new way of looking at the curriculum as the manifestation of the etheric body, or body of formative forces. As the questions probed deeper, trying to understand the seeming incongruences, I took colored chalk and added new elements to the chart that I had drawn on the blackboard for the class. As I gave my answers that were given to the questions, I drew new connections that I had not seen before. I illustrated my answers on top of the very complicated chart I had already drawn.

The teacher-trainee was on fire with his questions, and I could do nothing else but give him my best answers, which I drew from decades of Waldorf experience. In the end, a new theory arose that helps tie the loose ends of the curriculum into one comprehensive whole and highlights the nature and function of the etheric body as the focus of the Waldorf elementary school curriculum.

Essentially, what we discovered was that we are teaching the etheric body of the child from ages seven to fourteen. When Steiner refers to a first grader, he is referring to a seven-year old child. His indications on this point state that the child should turn seven during the first-grade year. In America, this already creates a large incongruency, because often children are only six years old when they enter first grade. Plus, many people believe that children are evolving faster than when Steiner gave the curriculum, and this may affect the seven-year cycles. But in the end, we imagined that the seven years of development of the etheric body are still needed for proper development in grades one through seven. In the years before elementary school, from birth to age seven, the education is focused on the physical body. The tasks of kindergarten and preschool are centered on the education of the physical body. From age fourteen to twenty-one, the focus is placed on educating the astral body, or body of desires. Therefore, the task of the Waldorf high school is centered on the healthy education of the astral body.

Developmental Stages		
Age	Focus of Education	School
Birth to five	Physical body	Mother School
Five to six	Physical body	Pre-school
Six to seven	Physical body	Kindergarten
Seven to twelve	Etheric body of formative forces	Elementary
Twelve to fourteen	Etheric body of formative forces	Middle School
Fourteen to twenty-one	Astral body of desires	High School/College

Rudolf Steiner's ideas about physical and spiritual history require a particular context to be understood. This context is a cosmology of correspondences used by Theosophists at the turn of the century. Essentially, it is an historical timeline that links time to spiritual beings, both through the spiritual beings' ('hierarchies') ancient donations of substances that comprise the human being's physical, soul, and spiritual bodies, but also through each individual's response to those donations as they play out in human states of consciousness in the future.

Humans have been the recipients of donations from the hierarchies: Angels, Archangels, Archai, Exsusiai, Dynamis, Kyriotetes, Thrones, Cherubim, and Seraphim. The Holy Trinity weaves the work of these ranks of hierarchies together. These hierarchical names are the traditional hierarchical categories of Dionysius the Aereopogite and the Catholic Church, among others. These beings are almost unimaginable to the modern materialist who uses earthly, sense-bound thinking. Through the writings of Rudolf Steiner, these beings are described as intimately involved in every aspect of humanity's evolution and spiritual development.

It is the intent of the Waldorf curriculum, created by Dr. Steiner, to recapitulate the developing consciousness involved in humanity's cultural development through the world literature content of the first eight grades in a Waldorf school. The Waldorf class teacher stays with the same class of students as they progress through grades one through eight. Steiner spells out a complicated progression of topics and themes for each of the grades.

For instance, in grade one, the world literature selections are taken from Grimm's Fairy Tales and are told using a detached, calm, non-dramatic mode of delivery. The children live into the images of the fairy tales, and the moral content of the story comes through with retribution for the bad and reward for the good. No judgments are passed on the content, and no commentary is necessary. Each fairy tale is a complete story unto itself that works as a holographic engram, symbol, or parable. All parts of the fairy tale are necessary to create the complete imagination.

The kindergarten child lives in her personal, subjective world that makes her feel like an integral part of the whole. The kindergartener is in an amorphous world, like the nature religions of the Atlanteans and Lemurians. They are part of their environment, and one with it.

The Waldorf curriculum for the eighth grade calls for some unusual subjects to be taught. By the end of the eighth grade, the student is supposed to become a "citizen of his own time." That is why modern history from the Reformation through to the present era, including American history, is taught in the eighth grade.

Scheme of the Developmental Stages

Grade	World Literature	Earth Incarnations	Eras
K	Fairy tales from all cultures	Atlantis/Lemuria	Outside of time (pre-natal world: past)
1	Grimm's Fairy Tales	Ancient Saturn	Polaria
2	Legends, fables, saint stories	Ancient Sun	Hyperborea
3	Old Testament	Ancient Moon	Lemuria
4	Norse myths	Earth	Atlantis
5	India/Persia/Egypt-Chaldean-Babylonia/Greece	Future Jupiter	Post-Atlantis (India/Persia/Egypt/Greece/Anglo-Germanic/Russian/future American)
6	Rome to Christian Middle Ages	Future Venus	6th Era
7	Renaissance to Reformation	Future Vulcan	7th Era
8	Reformation to modern times	Atlantis/Lemuria Revisited	Incarnated in time (after death: future)

What is often overlooked is Steiner's remark that we must begin eighth grade with a scientific and historical review of Atlantis and Lemuria. This usually baffles the eighth-grade class teacher, who ignores that element of the curriculum, since the scope of the grade eight history lessons is so demanding and covers such a great deal of history that is important to teach. Each teacher must choose what they can deliver from such a comprehensive curriculum.

No one teacher can *comprehensively* teach the curriculum of the Waldorf middle school. The curriculum is designed in a fashion that stretches class teachers to their limits and often makes them seek the help of high school teachers and others in the school to teach one course or another.

Another pedagogical component is that Atlantis and Lemuria are taught both in kindergarten and in eighth grade because both age groups stand outside the parameters of the seven stages of evolution, as described by Steiner in his fundamental books.

These seven stages are directly connected to the development of the seven cultural epochs that Steiner describes as the evolution of humanity. Steiner generally refers to these epochs as those of Ancient India, Ancient Persia, Egyptian/Chaldean/Babylonian, Greco-Roman, and our current cultural epoch of the Anglo-Germanic, which will be followed by the Future Russian and then the Future American Epoch. Each of these cultural epochs is approximately 2,160 years in length and corresponds to a respective astrological sign: Aries through Pisces, and on into the Aquarian Age, in the near future. Each of these epochs has a particular focus and develops a specific component of the human being. Humanity has passed through these epochs and developed certain characteristics individually and collectively. The human consciousness developed in each epoch builds upon prior development. Likewise, each child goes through a similar development in a sequence that is similar to that of the epochs.

The Waldorf curriculum was designed to meet the needs of the developing child at each age/grade and gives them a chance to develop their consciousness in the proper sequence and with the appropriate world literature that feeds their developmental needs. The Waldorf curriculum nourishes the developmental needs of the growing child with world literature that matches her evolving consciousness.

The evolving child recapitulates humanity's evolution. In Steiner's work, we can also find that each cultural epoch is related to a stage that the Earth itself has gone through in prior times. As described in the next section of this book, these great ages are called Incarnations of the Earth. The Earth we know now has gone through three prior "incarnations." These incarnations gave the hierarchy a chance to donate the substances that have become the physical, etheric, and astral bodies of humanity. We are currently in the fourth incarnation of the Earth, wherein the human I/ego has been donated for the free use of humanity. There will be three more incarnations of the Earth, which will develop the donations of the hierarchy into new spiritual capacities with which humanity will take control of its own bodies and the accompanying karmic responsibilities. Humanity becomes freer as development evolves.

Each cultural epoch develops an aspect of humanity that relates and corresponds to the previous development of the hierarchy. We can use the forces created in the past to recreate ourselves in the present. All prior donations of the hierarchy are actively available for us in the present incarnation of the Earth. The efforts of creation have built up to the point where humanity can now freely act as a conscious spiritual being among many other spiritual beings. Subsequently, the eighth-grade graduate stands as the outcome of all prior human evolution. Thus, ontogeny recapitulates phylogeny through the stages of human development.

If we tried to imagine a sequence of historical literature that could recapitulate humanity's development, it would be hard to make the selections chronologically sequential. This has been a lingering question for Waldorf teachers, who have noticed that the literature in the Waldorf language arts curriculum is not historically sequential. The author offers this new perspective as a way of thinking about the curriculum that matches the natural progression of Dr. Steiner's incarnations of the Earth and the cultural epochs. This idea is offered freely and is meant to aid in the further development of the Waldorf curriculum.

The Waldorf Curriculum in Relationship to Time and Space

From *The Living Being "Anthroposophia"* by Rudolf Grosse

Grade	The Flow of Time	The World of Space
	The Etheric	The Astral
	The Child's Relation to History	Child's Relation to Earth
1	Fairy Tales	Nature stories with personified characters
2	Fables and Legends	Animal fables and legends of places
3	Old Testament Stories	Basic human activities: house building, mining
4	Norse Myths	Local geography, man and animal
5	India, Persia, Egypt-Chaldean, Greek	World of plants, insects, birds
6	Rome to Middle Ages	Geology, astronomy, physics of sound and light
7	Age of Discovery	Physiology, chemistry, climatology, physics of heat and electricity, food, clothing, environment
8	Modern History	Anthropology, geography, physiology
9	Modern and Art History	Elaboration of eighth and seventh grade studies
10	Ancient History	Mastery of space through technology, power sources (atomic and electric), surveying
11	History of Music/Literature	Biological world of space and body
12	Overview of Religions	Evolution of nature, embryology

The Waldorf Curriculum by Grade Level

Anyone who says that anthroposophically orientated spiritual science is now founding the Waldorf School with the intention of establishing its outlook in this school is not—and: I say this on the opening day—speaking the truth. It is not our intention to teach the growing human being our principles, the contents of our world-conception. We are not aiming at education for the sake of any special dogma. Our aim is that what we have gained from spiritual science shall become a living force in education. All subjects should be taught in such a way as to be always related to man, so that man meets and recognizes man as a being belonging to the universe.

Rudolf Steiner (GA 298)

Grade One

- Introduction to the alphabet
- Simple spelling
- Introduction to reading
- Introduction to numbers (1 to 100) through rhythmic activities
- Elements of addition, subtraction, multiplication, and division
- Folk and fairy tales, nature stories— retold and dramatized by the class
- German and either Spanish or French
- Music: vocal and simple playing of wooden recorders
- Rhythmic and eurythmic exercises, games
- Handwork,* gardening

---

* In the early years, handwork progresses in the curriculum from simple activities such as beginning knitting, crocheting, wool crafts, practical and artistic stitchery, and nature crafts to more sophisticated work such as toy-making, hand-designed garments, woodworking and other crafts.

Grade Two

- Subjects in Grade One are continued
- Spelling, reading
- Arithmetic: multiplication tables
- Introduction to elements of grammar
- Fables, legends, saint stories, Jataka Tales, and nature stories—retold and dramatized, leading to composition in the child's own words
- German and either Spanish or French
- Music: vocal and recorder
- Rhythmic and eurythmic exercises, games
- Handwork, gardening

Grade Three

- Reading, spelling, writing (original compositions)
- Elements of grammar
- Arithmetic: continuation of the four processes, and multiplication tables continued
- Introduction to cursive writing
- Study of housebuilding and farming
- Old Testament stories (leading into history)
- German and either Spanish or French
- Music: vocal and recorder
- Playing orchestral instrument
- Rhythmic and eurythmic exercises, games
- Handwork, gardening

Grade Four

- Reading, spelling, composition
- Arithmetic: fractions and decimal fractions
- Grammar
- Local geography
- Comparative study of man and animal
- Norse myths and sagas
- German and either Spanish or French
- Grammar and reading
- Music: vocal and recorder, introduction to musical notation
- Playing orchestral instrument
- Rhythmical and eurythmic movement
- Handwork, gym, gardening

Grade Five

- Composition, grammar, spelling, reading
- Introduction to syntax
- Arithmetic: the four fundamental operations of common and decimal fractions
- North American geography
- History of ancient civilizations (India, Persia, Babylon/Egypt/Chaldean) culminating in
- Greek history
- Botany
- German and either Spanish or French
- Music: vocal and recorder
- Orchestra
- Choir
- Handwork
- Gym, eurythmy, games
- Gardening

Grade Six

- Composition, grammar, spelling, reading
- Literature
- Arithmetic: percentages, introduction to algebra, simple geometry
- Physics, earth science
- European and South American geography
- Roman and Medieval history
- German and either Spanish or French
- Music: vocal and recorder
- Orchestra, choir
- Handwork
- Gym, eurythmy, games
- Gardening

Grade Seven

- Composition, spelling, grammar
- Literature
- Algebra, geometry
- European geography
- Renaissance, Age of Discovery
- Physics, astronomy
- Chemistry
- German and either Spanish or French
- Music: vocal and recorder ensemble
- Orchestra, choir
- Gym, eurythmy, games
- Handwork
- Gardening

Grade Eight

- Composition, grammar, literature
- Algebra, geometry, business mathematics
- World geography, American history
- Physics, physiology, chemistry, mineralogy
- German and either Spanish or French
- Music: vocal, recorder ensemble
- Orchestra, choir
- Gym, eurythmy, games, handiwork, gardening

Throughout the curriculum, painting, drawing, and drama are used as part of the instruction. Woodwork is taught from fourth through eighth grade.

Grade One

Saturn Incarnation of the Earth
Stage One of Seven of the Eternal Curriculum
Planetary Influence of the Moon
The Mystery of the Abyss
Polaria

"Through Anthroposophy we ourselves learn once more to believe in legends, fairy tales, and myths, for they express a higher truth in imaginative pictures. And then our handling of these fairy tales, legends, and mythical stories will once more be filled with a quality of soul. Then when we speak to the child, our very words, permeated as they will be by our own belief in the tales, will flow over to him and carry truth with them; truth will then flow from teacher to child."

Rudolf Steiner (GA 307)

It is easy to see the kindergartner's consciousness as similar to the consciousness of the Atlantean. Taoism is the closest religion to the beliefs of the Atlanteans, according to Dr. Steiner. Ancestor worship and the worship of deities and nature spirits are major parts of the Taoist worldview, which directly connects them with nature. Similarly, the kindergartner's consciousness is outside the child, in the world around them. Taoist ancestor worship is strangely similar to the hereditary (ancestral) gifts and limitations that the kindergartner's body has been given as a foundation. The environment is essential to Taoists, as we see in their use of Feng Shui, or the art of placement, a type of expression using the environment and the primal elements in balance. So too, the environment of the kindergartner is a key element that is necessary for healthy education. The first-grade child wants to explore everything in the environment with fantastic interest.

The ancient folk stories of the Taoists often sound like fairy tales from a time before history. For instance, the question of human immortality is addressed in a story about the Jade Emperor who has access to the "peaches of immortality." Likewise, a kindergartner can play in a timeless land that is far, far away from the mundane world, much like the timeless fairy tales we tell them: "Once upon a time, in a land far, far away."

A first-grader is *one* with his teacher, as the Sun, Moon, and Earth were once *one* in the Ancient Saturn incarnation of the Earth, and during the Polarian Age of the Earth. The first-grader is not unlike the individual spheres of warmth that joined together to make the "raspberry clusters" of warmth on Ancient Saturn that Dr. Steiner describes. The first-grader is undefined, amorphous, non-individualized consciousness looking for the whole to merge into—to unite into the primal *one*.

Fairy tales and mythology are not childishly dreamt "pre-science" explanations of the world, but are, in fact, a realm of living archetypal beings. Humans have always had different symbols that represented what they could understand of these archetypal beings. When human beings "live into" a symbol, they can become aware of the nature and life of those symbols. Symbols "spoke" to ancient people and embodied powerful wisdom and cultural archetypes. Culture developed through the "gods" and the archetypes that were worshiped. One day, we may look back on the scientific theories used today and ponder the chasm that has been created between living forces and dead scientific theories. Overcoming the separation between the world of creativity (archetypes) and the world of scientific theory (dead thoughts) is an underlying purpose behind the inclusion of fairy tales and mythology in the Waldorf curriculum.

In the Waldorf first-grade curriculum, the reading, writing, and storytelling elements of the Main Lesson are drawn from Grimm's or Russian fairy tales. The colorful characters and dynamic, archetypal plots of fairy tales are particularly well suited to the first-grade child. There are also deep mysteries within the artistic form of these stories that have come from a living, mobile world of symbols and ideas populated by hierarchical and elemental beings. Often, the meaning of the fairy tale may not be understood in an overt, logical way, but the truth and meaning weave imaginative images into the child that later can become faculties of moral understanding that blossom into a healthy sense of truth.

In Waldorf schools, the Main Lesson is a morning block of instruction that centers on one subject for about four to six weeks and lasts approximately an hour and forty-five minutes at the beginning of the day. Movement, singing, reciting poetry, eurythmy (dance), speaking in response to questions, and repeating the ideas and stories that the teacher presents are all possible forms that the lesson may take. Extemporaneous speech by the teacher is essential, as is a mood in which the children can live with their whole being. The imagination of the teacher is the foundation for the art of education that Rudolf Steiner proposed.

Dr. Steiner speaks about the importance of the surroundings of the child. He says that the child literally *builds* himself from the forces and elements in his environment. This reasoning can make a teacher quite aware of the powerful forces involved as he creates imaginations from his words that can give the child either good or bad material from which to build his physical constitution. When a teacher prepares a Main Lesson, he should try to remember the profound stakes involved, and it is hoped that he can make the stories live in himself to such a degree that even in his soul state, there is a living example that is fit to be imitated by the child. Only a genuine involvement in the deeper meaning of fairy tales, legends, and myths can awaken in a teacher what is needed for him/her to be a proper example.

Steiner has created a new art of education that is centered on developing creativity, imagination, and flexible thinking in both the teacher and the student. There are many fairy tales from around the world, and the teacher needs to find the best tales that relate to archetypal issues that arise during the first-grade developmental stage. If the teacher's faculty of *Imagination* is filled with the wisdom of the eternal curriculum, then the path through that stage of growth and development is given the imaginative food that it needs to feel nourished and satisfied. Steiner tells us that the key is the teacher's personal self-development.

In the Torquay lectures (GA 307), Steiner says: "The child, especially in the age between the change of teeth and puberty, has a most sensitive feeling for whether the teacher is governed by his imagination or his intellect. The intellect has a destructive and crippling effect on the child, but imagination gives it life and fresh impulses."

The whole-language method of storytelling, retelling, and drawing (writing) is used in the Waldorf curriculum. Hearing and retelling stories supports the development of speech and the comprehension of content. This approach should supplant reading by rote, or the labored learning of the alphabet as something dead. There needs to be meaningful content linked to the presentation of the alphabet to create room for imagination. Fairy tales are used to introduce writing, reading, history, literature, and all other subjects because they are such graphic symbols that create meaningful content. Each fairy tale is a complete picture unto itself: a full paradigm, with each of its component parts. They can also offer endless wisdom that can take years to fully cognize.

The revelation of man's archetypal biography is found in fairy tales, as well as examples of the creative power and guidance that exists in the universe. The archetypal, symbolic realm of fairy tales is drawn from the Folk Souls (archangels) of ancient peoples and represents timeless truths and moral training through naive imaginations. The etheric body of the first-grader is still round, like the starry dome, and situated in the head of the child. Thus, the child can easily associate with the timeless, spaceless nature of fairy tales.

Additionally, fairy tales excite children's interest and enthusiasm for language and mental imagery, which ultimately result not only in writing, drawing, and reading, but also can increase vocabulary and verbal expression. This multi-level approach provides a basis for another important aspect of the Waldorf curriculum through the child's active involvement in stories that they can relate to and that are geared to their developmental stage of growth.

According to Waldorf methodology, space is considered a general category that combines all that is found in the total environment of the child. The "home" of a child is the Earth as a whole, living being, complete with all the forces that surround the child. In order to become an integrated part of this world, the child must relive each aspect of humanity's cultural and intellectual development in an imaginative, metamorphic synthesis of every cultural epoch through literature, song, architecture, dance, poetry, and stories about the aspects of different ways of life. These lessons also become the basis for further exploration and involvement in other associated lessons.

Since the microcosm of man is the focus of the activities in the macrocosm, a truly healthy picture of the world introduces the child to the parts of herself that are spread out in the wide expanse of space and over long periods of time. The task of the teacher is to responsibly introduce the child to her correlated aspects of human development through culture and nature. This type of space/time integration is the birthing process of human evolution, which follows in sequential stages from a world of archetypal images to the world of physics and mechanics implicit in the cause-and-effect laws of nature. Stage by stage, the child enters more fully into the understanding of the workings of nature. At every stage, a living picture can be brought before the child that matches their developmental needs.

The underlying object of this effort is discovery of the world, starting with the child's own body sitting at the desk or joined together with others in a circle. Beginning with their immediate environment, the classroom, and looking to the interconnected neighborhoods around the school, the children learn mapmaking and drawing to scale so they can properly find their place in the environment. The teacher continues these studies and leads the children into an introduction to cultural geography that expands from their personal desks to the entire globe.

Evolution of the Consonants

The order of the alphabet is not necessarily taught in the standard sequence in the Waldorf first grade class. There are natural forces behind each letter, and those forces work together to create a picture of the entire world as each letter of the alphabet evolved along with the forces we find in nature. Steiner's indications below were given to eurythmists so that they might fully understand the alphabet and its order of descent, or the order in which the natural forces came into being.

The following is a guide to the class teacher's meditation on the alphabet. It is not necessarily recommended for content or as an order of presentation to the children. Steiner's lecture entitled *The Alphabet* (GA 209) is highly recommended for the first-grade teacher to add to this meditation on the alphabet.

B-P	Man from his abode in heaven awakens to birth-Virgo-Soberness
M	More and more into matter he moves-Aquarius-Equilibrium in the human
D-T	Downward drawn he finds himself-Leo-Flaming enthusiasm
N	He is quickened by the knowledge of outer things-Pisces Destiny
R	Restlessly rushing he is carried onward (youth)-Taurus-Will, The still head forces
L	Until souls unfold from within (adolescence)-Capricorn-Coming to grips with the world
G-J-K	He grows and gains in inner strength (maturity)-Sagittarius Decisions
Ch-C-Q-K	Human by the breath of the spirit-Libra-The weighing process in thought
F	The fire of freedom is freed in the flow of air-Cancer-Motivation for future action
S-Z	Soothing the elements of unrest-Scorpio—Intellect
H	Heralding to new heights-Gemini-The capacity for doing
T-W	The light that streams towards him-Aries-Behold your deed

A (Ah) Venus   E (EE) Mercury   I (EI) Moon   A (A) Mars

Au (Ou) Sun   U (Oo) Saturn   O (O) Jupiter

The Alphabet for Grade One

The following examples of presentations of the alphabet show which fairy tale or story was used as the basis for the presentation of each letter. The short alliterative verses are examples of what the teacher or class might create to remind them of the story.

Examples of Individual Letters

Letter B—*Bearskin,* Grimm's Fairy Tales; *Silver Hair and the Three Bears,* from *Spindrift*

> *Rhyme:*
>
> The big bear has a straight brown back
> And a bumpty bump, and a bulge in the front
> And likes bees and bugs and big bear hugs
> And says b, b, b, b, b.

Letter C—*Dick Wittington's Cat; The Hungry Cat,* from *Spindrift*

> *Rhyme:*
>
> Dick's cunning cat curled and cuddled
> On the carpet mat.
> The creeping mouse with cold, cruel eyes
> Came crawling by.
> The crash, the clang, the cutting claws
> Clamored the mouse into his jaws.

Letter D—*The Donkey,* from *Grimm's Fairy Tales*

> *Rhyme:*
>
> The donkey dropped his dreaded disguise after the wedding was done,
> Darkening her doubting eyes.

Letter F—*The Frog Prince*, and *The Fisherman and His Wife*, from *Grimm's Fairy Tales*

Rhyme:
The friendly frog found the fair princess' fallen ball,
But a fright it was at first, for she failed to befriend him at all.

Letter G—*The Golden Goose*, from *Grimm's Fairy Tales*

Rhyme:
The golden goose got great giggles and guffaws
From the grumpy, grouchy princess.

Letter H—*The Seven Kids and the Wolf*, and *The Grey Brown Horse*, from *Grimm's Fairy Tales*

Rhyme:
The House (self-created story)
The house has high walls and long, handsome halls.

Letter M—*Semili Mountain*, from *Grimm's Fairy Tales*

Rhyme:
Semsi Mountain, Semsi Mountain called the man with might.
The mountain moved and made a mouth right before his sight.
Many mounds of money, and much, much more,
Millions of magnificent jewels to help the poor.

Letter R—*The Runner* (self-created story); *Rumpelstiltskin*, from *Grimm's Fairy Tales*

Rhyme:
The runner ran on the rim of the roaring river.

Letter S—*The Three Snake Leaves,* and The *Seven Swans,* from *Grimm's Fairy Tales*

Rhyme:

The snake makes a silent and secret sound
As she swings and sways and slithers on the ground,
And says s, s, s, s, s.

Note: During the second block of language arts, I began to teach more than one letter with each story.

Letters X, Z—*Brothers X and Z* (self-created story)

Letters N, V, W—*The Nixie of the Mill Pond,* from *Grimm's Fairy Tales*

Rhyme:

The naughty nixie nimbly snatched the miller's son.
Down he went, not to return 'til three deeds were done.
Never go near the mill pond for fun.

Verse:

Vanessa picked very beautiful violets from the valley.

Rhyme:

The wild waves whipped, whirled, and washed the waiting gifts away,
While the white Moon watched the wishing-maid wonder and pray.

Letters K, Q, J, L, P—*King Winter and Queen Summer* (self-created)

Rhyme:

King Winter casts cold, clear crystals over the frozen land.
It cracks and quakes as the crisp frost covers where you stand.

His splendid palace has powerful pillars of packed snow
And proud ramparts pouring piles of perfect crystals
On paths where he goes.

Verse:

Jack Frost jumps and jingles during the jolly month of January.

Verse:

The quiet queen is quite beautiful and never quits her garden.

Verse:

The golden lamp lights the world and brings life to leaf and flower.

Letter T—*Yggdrasil the World Tree*, Norse mythology

Rhyme:

The tall tree trembles as the tongues of Angels sound
Blowing tender twigs tumbling to the ground,
And the little birds twitter all around.

The Vowels

The vowels were presented as the five branches of the Norse World Tree, Yggdrasil. We transformed Odin's experience of finding the "runic letters" in the twigs that fell from the World Tree into a presentation of the alphabet. The wind in the branches made the vowels either *soft* or *hard*, depending on the strength of the wind. We always "sang" the vowels because they can be sustained like a musical note.

Rhyme:

A—Awake, awake and make your way, be brave and glad today.
The angels say A, A, A, A, A.

Rhyme:

E—Look and see, I am E, without me you can't be.
I see, I feel, I gladly greet the earth beneath my eager feet. E, E, E, E, E.

Rhyme:

I—My hand can fly high from the sky to the place where I lie.
I, I, I, I, I.

Rhyme:

O—Oh, we go slow and around we flow, so heart's gold can grow. O, O, O, O, O.

Rhyme:

U—You and I are truly too few to make a beautiful U. U, U, U, U, U.

Rhyme:

Y—Oh, Yggdrasil you youthfully spy, all the funny yellow twigs
That yonder, by your side do lie. Y, Y, Y, Y, Y.

Note: Because Y is the trunk of the tree, it also has the ability to sound like any of the other branches.

Literature for Grade One Teachers and Parents

The literature selections below are for teachers and parents of first-grade children. They are intended to be used for the personal development of the teacher or parent who wants to accompany a child's growth and evolution through this stage of development. The selections for teachers and parents are not to be used with the children. The selections follow the spirit and mood of the grade, but they are on a higher level than the child would fully appreciate or understand. For instance, *Cupid and Psyche* is not technically a story that would fit into the standard fairy tales generally used for first-graders. As an aid in understanding the archetypal nature of fairy tales, there is no better story than *Cupid and Psyche*. Conscious reflection on this story can open the mature mind to the archetypal forces shaping the development of a first-grade child.

As the reader reflects on the Selections for Teachers and Parents, the adult can have an opportunity to feel a bit of what the first-grade child experiences. The point of these selections is to attune the teacher or parent to the mood of the first grade that is accomplished through classical fairy tales that seem so able to feed and nourish the first-grade child. This "adult" example of an archetypal fairy tale is the Greek story of *Cupid and Psyche*, which is the basis of many other fairy tales found in a variety of cultures throughout the world.

A Retelling of Cupid and Psyche
Derived from *The Golden Ass* by Lucius Apuleius (124–180 AD)

Once, there was a king and queen who had three daughters, and the youngest daughter, Psyche, was so beautiful that people came from near and far to behold her beauty. The common people brought Psyche gifts as offerings to her beauty; they even said she was more beautiful than Venus herself, and the common people began to visit the Temple of Venus less and less. Some even said that Psyche was Venus in a human body.

Venus became angry with Psyche because her temples were empty and her renowned beauty was being challenged by a mere mortal. Venus called for her son Cupid, the god of love, who was feared by gods and mortals due to his golden arrows that inspired love at first sight. Venus ordered her son to use his arrows to make Psyche fall in love with the most hideous monster in the world.

Cupid prepared by taking two amber vases that he filled from the two fountains in his mother's garden: one of sweet water, and one of bitter. Then he suspended the two vases over his quiver and hastened to the chamber of Psyche, where he found her asleep. He sprinkled a few drops from the bitter fountain over her lips. He was then filled with emotion, and for a moment, he almost pitied the beautiful girl. He touched his arrow to Psyche, and she awoke and looked upon Cupid , even though he was invisible. Cupid was so startled that he accidently wounded himself with his own arrow. In his confusion, he did not know what to do, so he sprinkled the drops of joy from his mother's fountain all over Psyche's beautiful hair.

After this, no suitors came to ask for Psyche's hand in marriage, even though she was the most beautiful maiden alive. Everyone watched Psyche and talked about her, but none offered promises of love. Her two elder sisters had long been married to princes. Psyche sat alone in her room, sick of the beauty that had become a curse.

Psyche's parents were worried about her and consulted the oracle of Apollo at Delphi. They received an answer that said: "The virgin is destined for the bride of no mortal lover. Her future husband awaits her on the top of the mountain. He is a monster whom neither gods nor men can resist."

This decree filled everyone with sorrow. Psyche was upset and told her parents that they should have stopped the people from calling her Venus and treating her as if she were divine. She felt she was a victim of this betrayal and submitted herself to her dreadful fate.

When all things were prepared, Psyche took her place in the procession that led up the mountain to the summit, where her parents and the people left her alone. While Psyche stood on the summit crying, gentle Zephyr raised her up from the earth and carried her down into a beautiful valley. After she settled to the ground, she finally relaxed and curled up on the grassy bank next to a creek to slumber.

When she awoke, she was refreshed and calmed down, and she saw a tall grove of trees nearby. She walked over to the grove, entered it, and found a beautiful fountain sending forth crystal clear waters. Behind the fountain was a magnificent palace that looked like the home of some god. Psyche was drawn in by the wonder of the palace, and she ventured inside.

Every object in the palace was so wonderful and amazing that they each filled her with joy. Grand golden pillars supported the vaulted roof, and carvings and paintings displaying the wonders of nature were everywhere. As she walked from room to room, she saw that each was filled with priceless treasures and works of art. She heard a voice say to her that all of these things were now hers, and that anything she desired would be brought to her by invisible hands that were anxious to satisfy her every need. Her bath had been drawn and her clothes laid out for dinner, which awaited her in the dining room.

Psyche listened to the voices, did what they said, and had a restful bath and repose before dinner. When she sat down to eat, many invisible hands delivered the greatest delicacies of food and drink. She listened to the wonderful harmonies of instruments and voices that blended together like some heavenly music created just for her.

Psyche had yet to see her destined husband, for he came only in hours of darkness and fled before dawn. He told Psyche how much he loved her from the first time he saw her, and that his love was true. Psyche, too, gave pledges of love, and a great passion for her husband rose in her. Psyche often begged her husband to stay and let her look upon him, but he would not consent. He told her to make no attempts to see him and that his appearance must be kept from her. He said he worried that if she saw him, perhaps she would fear him or adore him; all he asked for was her love. He wanted her to love him as an equal rather than adore him as a god.

This reasoning quieted Psyche's concerns, and she was truly happy for a while, but after some time, she began to miss her parents and sisters. She wished to speak with them and let them know that she was well and happy and that all of her needs had been met. She began to feel that the palace was more of a prison than a home. Finally, she got her husband to consent to a visit from her sisters.

Psyche called Zephyr to the palace and told him of her husband's commands, and he flew off, gathered Psyche's sisters, and brought them to her in the valley. The sisters were very happy to see Psyche, and she invited them to come into her palace and enjoy all of the many wonders at her disposal. Invisible hands waited on the sisters and treated them to delights they had never known. Before long, the two sisters started to harbor envy in their hearts due to the spectacular wealth and wonderful life their sister enjoyed.

The sisters asked many questions about her husband and reminded Psyche that the oracle said he was a monster. Psyche admitted that she had never truly seen her husband. Her sisters convinced her that she should get a lamp and keep it by her bed with a knife. Then, when her husband was sleeping, she could get up, light the lamp, and see the true form of her husband. If he was a monster, she could then cut off his head and free herself from this bondage.

Psyche tried to forget her sisters' suggestions and put them out of her mind for a while, but they were too powerful, and her curiosity was too strong. She prepared her lamp and sharp knife, and hid them near the bed. When her husband fell asleep, she silently got her lamp and knife. Psyche was surprised that instead of a hideous monster in her bed, there was only the most beautiful and charming of the gods, complete with wings on his shoulders. As she leaned over to have a better look at his face, a drop of burning oil fell on the god. Startled and hurt, he awoke, and without saying a word, he spread his wings and flew out the window. Psyche tried to follow him, but fell from the window to the ground.

Cupid, beholding her as she lay in the dust, stopped his flight for a moment and said, "Oh foolish Psyche, is it thus you repay my love? After I disobeyed my mother's commands and made you my wife, will you think me a monster and cut off my head? Go, return to your sisters, whose advice you seem to think preferable to mine. I inflict no other punishment on you than to leave you forever. Love cannot dwell with suspicion." He then flew away, leaving Psyche in the dirt, with her tears and mournful lamentations.

When she recovered her composure, she looked around to find that the palace and gardens had disappeared. She found herself in a field outside her town. Psyche rushed to her home and reported all that had happened to her parents and sisters. The sisters inwardly rejoiced, hoping that now, perhaps, the god would choose one of them instead.

Both sisters had this same evil thought to replace their sister Psyche in the god's palace, so they went quietly up the mountain early the next day and called upon Zephyr to come and carry them down into the valley. As Zephyr arrived, they leapt into the air to be caught by Zephyr, but he was not able to sustain them, and they fell to their deaths.

Psyche, without food or shelter, wandered day and night in search of her husband and could not find him. After much travel, she came upon a lofty mountain with a magnificent temple at the top, and she thought it might be another home of her husband. She climbed the mountain and entered the temple to find that the many offerings of corn and barley to Ceres had been scattered about with sickles, rakes, and other instruments of the harvest.

Psyche immediately began cleaning up and ordering all of the confusion as a gesture of respect and love for Ceres, whose temple it was. Ceres looked down on Psyche's piety and devotion and spoke to her about her dilemma. Ceres could not intervene in a matter with another goddess, but she recommended that Psyche go to Venus, beg her forgiveness, and demonstrate her modesty and submission by surrendering herself voluntarily. Psyche obeyed Ceres and found her way to the temple of Venus. There, she would surrender her fate to her husband's mother in hopes of restoring his faith and loyalty.

Venus received Psyche in anger. She accused her of coming late to the very place she should have come immediately and being very slow to check on the terrible wound she had inflicted upon her husband. Venus told Psyche that she would have to pass trials before she could win the favor of her mistress. The first was to separate all the large piles of wheat, barley, millet, vetches, beans, and lentils that were used to feed Venus's pigeons. This task had to be accomplished before evening fell. Venus left Psyche with this overwhelming task.

Psyche sat silent and dumb, thinking about the enormity of the effort needed to accomplish the task. Cupid saw and took pity on her. He asked the ants to have compassion for her and help with the task of separating the grains. The ants got right to work and diligently separated the piles, sorting each kind to its parcel.

At twilight, Venus returned from a banquet with the gods. She saw the completed piles and yelled at Psyche that she was wicked and used trickery to accomplish the task. She threw a piece of black bread at Psyche and left her alone.

The next morning, Venus ordered Psyche to be called before her. "There, along the river, is a grove of trees where you will find golden, shining sheep feeding without a shepherd. Go there and fetch me a sample of that precious golden wool from each of the sheep," Venus commanded.

Psyche obediently went to the riverside to try to gather the wool. The river god inspired the reeds with harmonious murmurs that seemed to say to Psyche that she should wait until noon, when the sun was high and the river flowed less furiously. Then she should cross over and gather the wool from the bushes and trees, where the sheep had rubbed it off. Psyche followed the advice of the reeds and gathered armfuls of golden wool. She hoped that Venus would show her mercy, but Venus was again outraged and accused Psyche of trickery, saying that Psyche had not accomplished this task by herself.

Night fell, and Venus appeared, along with her retinue. Surprised and angry, she surveyed the work done and snapped, "Right, well, obviously this was not all that difficult. Tomorrow's task is harder. Here is a crystal bowl. Go to the river Styx and fill this bowl with the water of life. I shall be back by nightfall, and woe unto you if you fail to complete your task." Off she went again.

Psyche stood there with the bowl, despairing at the thought of the task at hand. It was too difficult. She fell asleep and set off the following morning. The Styx is the river that emerges out of Hades at an extremely high point and plunges straight down into a deep ravine without any protrusions or coves. Getting close enough to the edge to fill up a bowl is impossible. Again, Psyche had no choice but to simply get going. The sun was high and hot in the sky. Psyche held the bowl out in her hands, and it happened that a ray of sunshine reflected off the crystal bowl and landed right in front of Zeus's throne.

His curiosity piqued, Zeus looked down to see where the light beam came from. There, he saw Psyche making her lonely way. The gods tend not to interfere in each other's business, and this was between Venus and Psyche, but he took pity on Psyche and sent his eagle down to help her. The eagle landed in front of her and offered to fly past the river with the crystal bowl so it could be filled with the water of life. Grateful, Psyche handed the bowl to the eagle, which took it in its beak and flew off. A little while later, it returned with a full bowl. Psyche quickly made her way back to Venus to surrender the Water of Life.

Venus was not satisfied that Psyche was at all useful, and therefore gave her another task. She gave Psyche a box and told her to go to Proserpine and ask her to send a little of her beauty, for in tending her sick son, she had lost some of her own beauty. Venus told Psyche that she needed the beauty that very night so that she might paint it on her face before going to a banquet with the gods.

Psyche was now sure that she would die attempting this next trial of going to the underworld and returning. In despair, Psyche climbed to the highest tower to cast herself down. Then a voice spoke to her and asked why she would give up faith now, after fortune had protected her in the previous trials. The voice told her how to find the cave that was the entrance to Hades, pass by Cerberus, and prevail on Chiron to ferry her across the black river and bring her back again. The voice also warned her not to open the box and let her curiosity about the beauty of the goddesses overtake her.

Psyche was encouraged by the advice and did as the voice suggested. She traveled to the realm of Pluto and was admitted into the palace of Proserpine. She refused the wonderful delicacies offered at the banquet table and ate only coarse bread. Psyche delivered Venus's message to Proserpine, and the box filled with the precious commodity was shortly returned to her. Psyche returned the way she had come and was glad to return to the light of day.

Having come so far in success with the trials, Psyche convinced herself that she should put a little of the beauty in the box on her own face so that she might look more beautiful for her husband. When she opened it, she found nothing in it but the deep sleep of the underworld: a Stygian sleep that shrouds one with unconsciousness and a corpse-like slumber.

Cupid had recovered sufficiently to slip through a crack in his chamber's window. He flew to the place where Psyche lay unconscious, gathered up the sleep from her body, and returned it to the box. Then he woke Psyche with the touch of one of his arrows. "Again," said he, "you have almost perished by the same curiosity. Take this box to my mother and finish the task, and I will take care of the rest."

Then, Cupid flew like lightning to the throne of Zeus and presented himself in supplication and submission. Zeus was convinced enough to plead the cause of the lovers to Venus and win her consent. Then, Zeus sent Mercury to bring Psyche to the heavenly assembly, where he offered her the cup of immortality with the ambrosia of the gods. Zeus bound the two together in a perpetual knot. Thus, Psyche was reunited with Cupid at last, and in time, the two bore a daughter named Joy.

Rudolf Steiner's Curriculum Recommendations for Grade One

At the end of each section, we will offer the generally accepted indications of the original curriculum concerning the recommended literature selections for each grade. Karl Stockmeyer was one of the original Waldorf teachers. His summary of the curriculum is the most commonly used source for the Waldorf Curriculum.

Karl Stockmeyer's summary of the Waldorf Literature and History indications

History: Story material is drawn from fairy tales

Bibliographical References and Recommending Reading—Grade One

This Recommended Reading List is for teachers and parents to use as a guide to appropriate, grade-level reading content that can be read to the children (or by them, if they have already learned to read) or read by the parent/teacher. Teachers will use the two standard fairy tale books, *Grimm's Fairy Tales* and *Russian Fairy Tales*, as the foundation of their presentations of the letters of the alphabet and any other aspect of the curriculum for first grade.

Afanasyev, Alexander. *Russian Fairy Tales*. ADS Inc., 2011.

Asbjornsen, Peter Christen. *East of the Sun and West of the Moon*. Old Tales from the North. Doran, 1914.

Barnes. *The Golden Footprints*. Adonis Press, Hillsdale, NY.

Gmeyner & Russell. *The Key of the Kingdom. A Book of Stories and Poems for Children*. Anthroposophical Publishing Company.

Grahl. *The Wisdom in Fairy Tales*. St. George, New Knowledge Books.

Grim, Jacob & Wilhelm. *Grimm's Fairy Tales: Complete Edition*. Alpine Books, 2014.

Harrer, Dorothy. *Nature Ways in Story and Verse*. Mercury Press, Spring Valley, NY, 1996.

Harrer, Dorothy. *Verses & Poems and Stories to Tell*. Rudolf Steiner School, New York.

Koconda-Brons, Angela. *Jorinde & Joringel*. Anthroposophic Press, New York, 1981.

Koconda-Brons, Angela. *The Six Swans*. Anthroposophic Press, New York, 1990.

Macdonald, George. *The Complete Fairy Tales*. Schocken.

Magoun & Krappe. *Grimm's Folk Tales*. St. George.

Merry, Eleanor. *The Ascent of Man*. St. George.

Opie, Iona & Peter. *The Oxford Nursery Rhyme Book*. Oxford University Press, USA, 1964.

Peckham. *Nature Stories*. St. George.

Ranson. *Old Peter's Russian Tales*. Nelson.

Steel. *English Fairy Tales*. MacMillan.

Wyatt, Isabel. *Hay for My Ox*. Lanthorn Press, 1968.

Grade Two

Sun Incarnation of the Earth
Stage Two of Seven of the Eternal Curriculum
Planetary Influence of Venus
The Mystery of Number
Hyperborea

It is on fantasy then, on imagination, that our teaching and our education is built. You must be quite clear that before the ninth or tenth year the child does not know how to differentiate himself as an ego from his surroundings. Out of a certain instinct, the child has long been accustomed to speak of himself as "I" but in truth, he really feels himself within the whole world. He feels that the whole world is connected with himself.

Rudolf Steiner (GA 307)

In first grade, a strong bond is created with the teacher. In second grade, the teacher now becomes somewhat removed and is in a higher authoritative position above the children, somewhat like the Sun removing itself from the Earth during the Sun Incarnation of the Earth. The Hyperborean Age was one of drinking directly from the source. Second-graders drink in everything their beloved teacher gives them, like a suckling child. The Hyperboreans lived in happiness and harmony with nature, which was eternally blooming while the warm Sun was always shining on the youth of eternal summers. Eventually, differentiation started to take place, and this was the beginning of individualization and separateness. There was only one season in the Hyperborean Age, and the Sun was always shining. It was from the Hyperboreans that the Golden Bough was brought to Greece as a gift of Apollo from his sun-filled realm. The Golden Bough was the symbol of the Mystery initiation temples that surrounded ancient Athens and represented the wisdom of the past.

The second-grade transmission from teacher to student is much akin to the passing of the Golden Bough from the Hyperboreans to the Greeks. The Waldorf teacher "brings the entire world" before the student and shows the interconnectedness of all things in a process of natural growth and development. Like Apollo, the teacher is seen as a "god" who has come from a mysterious land where life is good and all things work together to make the true, the beautiful, and the good manifest in the world. Somewhat like a great world tree, the second-grade class teacher calls the students to sit underneath her shade and listen to the whispers of other worlds blowing through the branches.

In second grade, the story content for literature is taken from legends and animal stories. Saint legends are often told, as well as animal stories from fables, which often have accompanying morals associated with them. Legends and fables are, at least in part, based upon earthly experiences, and in these stories, one can sense a stronger relationship to the Earth, which the child is now becoming more aware of.

Legends tell tales of the origin of things, sometimes in quite fantastic ways. Nature stories personify beings that spoke to humanity in the past. The second-grader herself is beginning to question the nature of the world and seeks an answer from it. These stories bring the child further down from the timeless and spaceless lands they have lived in, down to the Earth and into the flow of time, as the child's etheric body descends from the top of the head.

Rudolf Steiner gives us a beautiful picture of the way to imagine that the second-grade child is connected to the kingdoms of nature.

> Just as the world of plants should be related to the earth and the child should learn to think of them as its offspring; the last, outward-growing product of a living earth organism; so should the animal world as a whole be related to man. The child is thus enabled—in a living way—to find his own place in nature and the world. He begins to understand that the plant world belongs to the earth. On the other hand, however, we teach him to realize that the various animal species spread over the world represent, in a certain sense, the path towards human development. The plants have a kinship to the earth, the animals to man—this should be the basis from which we start. (GA 294)

Literature for Grade Two Children

The following selections are a sample of what might be used to present fables, legends, and animal stories either in a classroom setting or at home with parents. Most Christian legends, Aesop's fables, and animal stories can provide the appropriate literature. The point is to take these larger-than-life stories and make them simple and imaginative so that their true meaning and intent shine through without having to explain the story. If the second-grader understands the story inherently, then the story is a good selection.

The selections below are examples of rhymes that second-graders help write to summarize a story, fable, or legend that the teacher told the class by heart. After retelling the story and "acting it out," each child in the class should be able to tell the entire story on their own. Putting the story to rhyme helps make it fun and creates the written material to copy and illustrate in the child's personal Main Lesson book, which is a record of what the student is learning.

The Fox and the Crow

A hungry fox did chance to spy
A crow with cheese that flew up high
And rested on a branch to have his meal
But the fox had in mind, another deal.
"Oh crow," said the fox, "you have beautiful eyes,
And what lovely wings upon which to fly."
The crow listened carefully to all this praise
And soon his chest with pride he began to raise.
"But what a shame such a marvelous bird
Doesn't have a lovely voice to be heard."
But the crow, being tricked, was anxious to show

That his voice is sweet, so he let go
Of the cheese in his mouth to sing from his soul
And the fox got his wish as he swallowed the cheese whole.

The Shepherd Boy and the Wolf, *Aesop's Fables*

A shepherd boy beside a stream,
"The wolf, the wolf," was wont to scream;
And when the villagers appeared
He'd laugh and call them silly-eared.
A wolf at last came down the steep:
The wolf, the wolf, my legs, my sheep,
The creature had a jolly feast,
Quite undisturbed, on boy and beast.
For none believes the liar forsooth,
Even when the liar speaks the truth.

The Wolf and the Stork

Wolves have a name for appetite
And one, upon a festive night,
Bolted his meat so greedily
They say he nearly breathed his last.
Far down his throat a bone stuck fast,
He couldn't even raise a cry.
By lucky chance a stork flew by
And saw him signaling.
She came in haste, and most professionally
Set about plucking the obstruction out.
The service done, she claimed her fee.
"A fee? You surely jest," said he,
"You poke your neck between my jaws
And get it back and talk of further pay?
Ungrateful creature, fly away
And keep your distance from my paws."

Earth Folk, by Walter de la Mare

The cat she walks on padded claws,
The wolf on the hills lays stealthy paws,
Feathered birds in the rain-sweet sky
At their ease in the air, flit low, flit high.

The Stag, the Hare, and the Donkey

A stag with beautiful antlers was once walking across the fields.

A hare ran past and when he saw him, stopped in amazement. Then, getting on his hind legs, he approached the stag, saying, "Look at me! I am a little stag, for if I stretch my ears, they are like your antlers."

A donkey heard this and said: "You are right, we are all one family."

The stag cast a glance at them and went back to his woods.

The Sheepdog

One evening an old sheepdog, the faithful guardian of his master's sheep, was on his way home. Little lapdogs yapped at him in the street. He trotted on without looking around. When he came to the meat stall, a butcher's dog asked him how he could bear such continual barking and why he did not take one of them by the scruff of his neck.

"No," answered the sheepdog, "they do not worry or bite me. I must keep my teeth for wolves."

St. Michael the Victorious, Old Gaelic Poem

Thou Michael the victorious,
I make my circuit under thy shield.
Thou Michael, of the white steed

And of the bright, brilliant blade!
Conqueror of the dragon,
Be thou at my back.
Thou ranger of the heavens!
Thou warrior of the King of all!
Thou Michael the victorious
My pride and my guide!
Thou Michael the victorious
The glory of mine eye.

The Rune of St. Patrick

At Tara today in this fateful hour
I place all Heaven with its power,
And the sun with its brightness,
And the snow with its whiteness,
And the fire with all the strength it hath,
And the lightning with its rapid wrath,
And the winds with their swiftness along their path,
And the sea with its deepness,
And the rocks with their steepness,
And the earth with its starkness:
All these I place
By God's almighty help and grace,
Between myself and the powers of darkness.

Michael and the Hermit

Once upon a time, there lived a hermit who had withdrawn from the world to contemplate God. But the more he pondered, the more he began to doubt whether God was truly just, so he set out to seek the justice of God.

He left his hut in the silence of the wood, and found his way to a road. He had not gone far when he met with a youth, and they journeyed on together. At the setting of the sun, they came to a lordly castle. Here, they were made welcome and led into the banqueting hall, where a feast was prepared in their honor. In the midst of the festivities, no one saw the young man steal a precious goblet and hide it beneath his cloak.

The next morning, as they journeyed forth, the youth showed the goblet to the hermit, who was filled with dismay.

At nightfall, with no other dwelling in sight, they knocked at the gaunt, gray house of a miserable miser. Begrudgingly, he granted them a night's lodging. He offered them neither food nor drink, and naught but the bare boards for their bed. On departing the next morning, the youth presented the miser with the precious goblet.

They wandered on until they came to a village. The youth stopped at the door of a poor cottage and asked for bread. A woman bade them enter. Her husband and children were gathering wood in the forest. There was but one small loaf in that poor home. The woman halved it, and gave the wanderers their share. The hermit thanked her and was about to depart, when he saw the youth slyly thrust a glowing ember into the thatch of the cottage. They hurried away into the mountains. Looking back, the hermit saw the house enveloped in flames.

Soon, the path they were following dwindled to a narrow track and finally disappeared, but in the distance, they saw a lonely hut. On nearing it, they heard the sound of moaning and weeping. Within, they found a young child lying desperately ill. His parents wrung their hands and cried aloud in sorrow. The youth brewed a drink for the child, but as soon as he had sipped, the child fell dead.

The hermit was deeply shocked by all that he had seen, and only with great reluctance remained in the company of the young man, who now asked the father of the dead child to guide them across the mountain. As they were crossing a narrow bridge, the youth pushed their guide into the abyss.

The hermit stood still, frozen with horror. As he gazed, the youth vanished from his sight. The Archangel Michael stood before him.

"Behold the justice of God for which you sought," he said. "The father of the child was a robber and a murderer. The child I took from the world would have lived to be a criminal. The poor people whose cottage I burned down will find, when they dig their new foundations, a buried treasure. The goblet I took from the friendly folk in the castle was poisoned, and in it, the miser will find his reward. Thus it comes to pass that what is just in the eyes of God often appears unjust in the eyes of men."

The hermit went back to his cell in the wood, and from then onward, he doubted the justice of God no more.

Literature for Grade Two Teachers and Parents

St. Augustine, extracts from *The City of God*

He that is jealous is not in love.

He who created us without our help will not save us without our consent.

It was pride that changed angels into devils; it is humility that makes men into angels.

Love, and do what you like.

Patience is the companion of wisdom.

Pray as though everything depended on God; work as though everything depended on you.

Seek not to understand that you may believe, but believe that you may understand.

Since love grows within you, so beauty grows. For love is the beauty of the soul.

The World is a book, and those who do not travel read only a page.

There is no possible source of evil except good.

To seek the highest good is to live well.

We make ourselves a ladder out of our vices if we trample the vices themselves underfoot.

What does love look like? It has the hands to help others. It has the feet to hasten to the poor and needy. It has eyes to see misery and want. It has the ears to hear the sighs and sorrows of men.

Will is to grace as the horse is to the rider.

St. Francis of Assisi, from *The Little Flowers*

Above all the grace and the gifts that Christ gives to his beloved is that of overcoming self.

For it is in giving that we receive.

Grant me the treasure of sublime poverty: permit the distinctive sign of our order to be that it does not possess anything of its own beneath the sun, for the glory of your name, and that it have no other patrimony than begging.

I have been all things unholy. If God can work through me, he can work through anyone.

If you have men who will exclude any of God's creatures from the shelter of compassion and pity, you will have men who will deal likewise with their fellow men.

It is in pardoning that we are pardoned.

It is no use walking anywhere to preach unless our walking is our preaching.

It is not fitting, when one is in God's service, to have a gloomy face or a chilling look.

Lord, grant that I might not so much seek to be loved as to love.

Lord, make me an instrument of thy peace. Where there is hatred, let me sow love.

No one is to be called an enemy, all are your benefactors, and no one does you harm. You have no enemy except yourselves.

Preach the Gospel at all times and when necessary use words.

Start by doing what's necessary; then do what's possible; and suddenly you are doing the impossible.

Where there is charity and wisdom, there is neither fear nor ignorance.

Where there is injury let me sow pardon.

While you are proclaiming peace with your lips, be careful to have it even more fully in your heart.

St. Thomas Aquinas, extracts from *Suma Theologica*

A man has free choice to the extent that he is rational.

All that is true, by whomsoever it has been said has its origin in the Spirit.

All the efforts of the human mind cannot exhaust the essence of a single fly.

Because philosophy arises from awe, a philosopher is bound in his way to be a lover of myths and poetic fables. Poets and philosophers are alike in being big with wonder.

Beware of the person of one book.

Happiness is secured through virtue; it is a good attained by man's own will.

Hold firmly that our faith is identical with that of the ancients.

How can we live in harmony? First we need to know we are all madly in love with the same God.

How is it they live in such harmony the billions of stars—when most men can barely go a minute without declaring war in their minds about someone they know?

Human salvation demands the divine disclosure of truths surpassing reason.

It is requisite for the relaxation of the mind that we make use, from time to time, of playful deeds and jokes.

Love takes up where knowledge leaves off.

Man cannot live without joy; therefore when he is deprived of true spiritual joys it is necessary that he become addicted to carnal pleasures.

Man should not consider his material possessions his own, but as common to all, so as to share them without hesitation when others are in need.

Perfection of moral virtue does not wholly take away the passions, but regulates them.

Reason in man is rather like God in the world.

Temperance is simply a disposition of the mind which binds the passion.

The test of the artist does not lie in the will with which he goes to work, but in the excellence of the work he produces.

The things that we love tell us what we are.

There is nothing on this earth more to be prized than true friendship.

Three things are necessary for the salvation of man: to know what he ought to believe; to know what he ought to desire; and to know what he ought to do.

To bear with patience wrongs done to oneself is a mark of

perfection, but to bear with patience wrongs done to someone else is a mark of imperfection and even of actual sin.

To live well is to work well, to show a good activity.

To one who has faith, no explanation is necessary. To one without faith, no explanation is possible.

We can't have full knowledge all at once. We must start by believing; then afterwards we may be led on to master the evidence for ourselves.

Well-ordered self-love is right and natural.

Wonder is the desire for knowledge.

Rudolf Steiner's Curriculum Recommendations for Grade Two

Karl Stockmeyer's Waldorf Literature and History indications for Grade Two

History: Story material (literature) is taken from stories of the animal world introduced through fables and the lives of saints.

Bibliographical References and Recommending Reading List—Grade Two

Barnes. *The Golden Footprints*. Adonis Press, Hillsdale, NY.

Butler. *Butler's Lives of Eminent Saints*. Murphy & McCarthy, Boston.

Colum, Padraic. *The King of Ireland's Son*. MacMillan, New York.

Farjeon, Eleanor. *Ten Saints*. Henry Z. Walck, Inc., New York

Green. *The Big Book of Fables*. Dobson.

Jacobs. *Fables from Aesop*. MacMillan.

Kingston, Henry Giles. *The Seven Champions of Christendom*. AMS, Inc., 2012.

Lagerlof, Selma. *Christ Legends*. Saint George Press, New York.

Lindholm, Dan. *How the Stars Were Born: Norwegian Nature Fables, Tales and Legends.* Henry Goulden Books, 1975.

McGovern, Ann. *Aesop's Fables.* Scholastic Books, New York, 1963.

Santore, Charles. *Aesop's Fables.* Jelly Bean Press, New York, 1988.

Streit, Jacob. *The Animal Stories.* Saint George Press, New York.

Tolstoy. *Fables & Fairy Tales.* Signet Classic.

Turnball, Lucia. *Legends of the Saints.* Lippincott Co., New York.

Voragine, Jacobus de. *The Golden Legend.* Arno Press, New York, 1969.

Grade Three

Moon Incarnation of the Earth
Stage Three of Seven of the Eternal Curriculum
Planetary Influence of Mercury
The Mystery of Alchemy
Lemuria

A complete pedagogy cannot be written out of the intellect alone; it must be the effluence of the whole nature of man: not merely of the nature that observes externally and intellectually but of the whole one that deeply and inwardly experiences the secrets of the universe. The curriculum must be a copy of what we are able thus to read in the evolutionary process of the human being.

The office of teacher becomes a priestly office, a kind of ritual performed at the altar of universal human life, not with the sacrificial offering that is to be led to death, but with the offering of human nature itself that is to be awakened to life.

Rudolf Steiner (GA 300a)

The third-grade child objectifies himself from the world when he "wakes up" and finds he has been separated from "Eden," just as the Moon was extruded from the Earth during the associated metamorphoses of the Earth and Moon during the Lemurian

Age. The Old Testament stories of Moses teach individualization and independence, just as the first Eden took place and certain individuals came to their own personal, individualized selves on Lemuria. Waldorf teachers can see that the stories they tell the children directly meet their developmental needs. It is easy to see the third-grade curriculum matching the stage of the Moon incarnation of the Earth and the Lemurian era.

The third-grade language arts material is taken from the Old Testament; the Biblical stories of Creation, Adam and Eve, Noah's Ark, and Father Abraham are archetypal images in which the child can experience the simplicity and devotion of the Hebrew nation. In preparation for the full experience of coming into a new awareness of space in grade four, we find that these Old Testament stories come down from the realm of mythology into a closer relationship to history, and thus help bring the child into a healthy accord with his imagination prior to fourth grade. Old Testament stories are wonderful paradigms of human relationships, and the struggle for personal identity through the trials that these bring to a person. At this age, the child needs to be made aware of his surroundings and those feelings and activities that can bring him into harmony with them. These imaginative motifs, which may not be considered historical fact, are perfect for students to truly have a chance to embody deep, personal feelings. The stories powerfully come alive in the child and meet the developmental need of the third-grader, who is looking for more objectivity and personal responsibility.

In the book *The Curriculum of the First Waldorf School*, Dr. Steiner tells us about this stage of child development:

> With the ninth-year there comes an important stage in the development of the growing child, and this should be carefully watched and considered in education and teaching. It is the age at which the child first really feels himself separated from the surroundings that he formerly took so much for granted. His self-consciousness become noticeably stronger, and his soul-life more inward and independent. All his powers of consciousness stir to life, and he wants to learn to know both teacher and world from a new angle.

According to Dr. Steiner, the experience of the ego prior to the second grade finds its home in the head, which is like the starry expanse of the heavens and is indicative of the spiritual world that the child has so recently left. The ego moves from the head into the rhythmic and metabolic will processes of the child, starting in the third-grade and continuing into the fourth grade. As the ego becomes more entangled in the body, the child becomes more aware that he is an ego and is limited by his body. He realizes that he experiences himself subjectively and, in doing so, awakens to the objective world. The child begins to question both the subjective and objective worlds in which he now finds himself. Space can now create a new perspective, and exploration in both directions is common. Objectively, the child finds a fresh need to question what stands behind the world. He begins to question his teacher's authority, whereas before, he would never have felt the need. The duality of subjectivity and objectivity presses in on the child at this stage, and the Old Testament as third-grade literature meets those needs.

Literature Selections for Grade Three Children

All the stories of the Old Testament can be used as literature for the second grade, and they are best when told in sequence and in shortened versions. Often, a childrens' Old Testament book is perfect for making the long stories of the Old Testament into short stories that still get the meaning and content across to the students. Numerous versions of abridged Old Testament stories can be found in the Suggested Reading List at the end of this section. The teacher has to be quite selective when choosing stories because there are so many important ones.

It is recommended that the Old Testament stories be dramatized to get the meaning across more easily and let the children truly "live into" the Hebrew culture. Stories may even grow into dramatic plays that can be co-written by the third-graders and their class teacher. Below is an example of a play based on the Old Testament story of Tobias, found in the *Book of Tobit*. The play shows the level of writing and storytelling that third-grade children can easily understand. This particular play was performed before the entire school as an end-of-the-year offering.

Tobias
A Third Grade Play
By Douglas Gabriel and the Third Grade

Chorus
Tobias was a man upright and just.
He helped the slaves of Israel as he must,
To ease their pain and give them rest.
In all the country, he was known as the best.

In the eyes of the king, Tobias was free
To help his neighbors justice to see.

He fed the poor and buried the dead.
He gave away his clothes, and even his bed.

But the old king died, and his son took his place;
He hated Tobias and shunned his holy face.
Tobias and his wife, with child in arm,
Escaped to the mountains to protect him from harm.

The new king was cruel, and his people were mad;
They rose up against him with a plan they had.
His death came quickly by their own hands;
They returned to Tobias his house and his lands.

Tobias again tended the people's great need;
They listened to his words and followed his lead.

One night, while he buried the dead,
He grew so weary he longed for his bed.
As soon as he entered his house that night,
He laid himself down and blew out the light.

He had chosen a new place to lay down to rest,
But it was under a little swallow's nest.
During the night, the angel of God did appear
To test his faith with a hardship so dear.
He rested uneasy, until the bright morning light
Startled him with the news of his lost sight.
His sight was now gone, and he was blind.

Old Tobias
Surely some trial is come, so that faith we can find.
To find God's purpose in this seeming plight
Is but a chance for us to seek his light.

Chorus
But now, Tobias could do no kind things
For his ailing neighbors whose pain still rings
Throughout the country, through every town,
The people were sad when his friends found

Tobias was blind; Who shall ease our growing pain?
There was no one to help them; this was plain.

Tobias' wife went to work and earned their bread;
She helped keep the house, and a place for their bed.
But Tobias would not accept gifts from others,
Neither a crust, nor a coin from his brothers.

Then one day, when all hope was past,
He called his son Tobias and told him at last
That there was a debt that was owed by a brother
That he would accept from him, but no other.
So he asked him to go to a faraway city,
And there to collect what was theirs without pity.

Old Tobias
The city is Rages where you must go,
And the brother is Raguel, whom you do not know.
A guide you must find to show you the way,
In the market you'll seek him; do not delay.

Young Tobias
Dear Father, look, I have straight away found
A guide for the way who knows the ground
Twixt here and Rages, he will guide,
And home again, 'til we're at your side.

Old Tobias
For your efforts we'll pay you well
When from your journey you can tell
The fate of this debt owed to my family here;
The curse of our poverty will then disappear.
God bless you on your way; may his angel alight
And guide you on earth with his heavenly light.
To you, my son, this blessing I tell;
Take it to heart and remember it well.
Keep God in your heart, all of thy days;
Walk without sin in his holy ways.
Keep his commandments, on his law you can lean;

Give to the poor; don't touch the unclean.
Do unto others as you would have them do unto you;
Then wisdom shall come, and your heart will be true.
So go with my blessing and listen to your heart,
Be ready at sunrise your journey to start.

Their journey the first day was quick and well known;
The guide was silent and the path was shown.
The travelers were weary by the end of the day;
They stopped by a river the night to stay.
Tobias went to the river, to wash his feet,
But out of the water, a great fish he did greet;
With startled fear he ran up the river's side,
But his companion told him he must not hide.

Guide
Go back to the river and catch it by the gill,
With your bare hands you must kill
And eat the great fish for dinner tonight.
And from his gall shall you return the sight
To your father who waits with patience dear.
Hurry! Your task is at hand; do not fear.

Chorus
Tobias did what his guide had said;
They ate the fish with their wine and bread.
The gall was saved for healing the eyes
Of his aged father so old and wise.

The second day, to Rages they came;
Inside was the uncle and his daughter of fame,
Who had married many men that suffered ill fate
And died soon after, before the marriage gate.

Guide
Sarah is her name, and for her hand you must ask,
Though it be a rough and difficult task.
If you pray and fast for three days without end,
To you and her God's grace will descend

To remove this evil which plagues her life
And make an end to your toil and strife.

Young Tobias
Of this, I am full scared to do;
But because of your words, I will be true
To this task so noble, to free her hand,
And make her my wife, and return to our land.

To the house of Raguel they both did speed
And told the whole family of their need.
Raguel was quite frightened, Sarah was scared;
Should they do what Tobias has dared?

For three days, they did pray and fast
Until God's mercy was given at last.
The evil spirit left Sarah in peace;
The spell was broken, the curse released.

Raguel
To you, my new son, half my possessions I give;
You have my lovely daughter and a good place to live.

Young Tobias
I must be going, for my parents await
Until I return to my own city gate.
My father is blind, my mother is poor;
They anxiously wait for my knock on the door.
Your daughter is my wife and half your goods my own,
To my family all these things must be shown.

Thank you for your kindness, and gifts so great;
They will add much to my father's estate.
Goodbye, and God Bless you, thank you again.
Come, my companion; let our journey begin.

Chorus
Tobias' mother had no rest in her heart
Ever since her son's journey did start.

She worried so much and cried bitter tears;
She sat on the hill and tended her fears,
Until one day she did chance to see
Her young son and all his company.
She sent for Tobias and ran to greet her boy,
She was so happy; the tears turned to joy.

Old Tobias was quickly led to his son;
He was so happy to hear the task was done.
Not only a debt was paid that day,
But many other gifts, and a wife, had come to stay.
Old Tobias was amazed and wondered at the guide
Who had led his son and stood at his side.

Tobias took the gall from his bag where it lay
And anointed his father's eyes that day.
In a while, his blindness went totally away;
His sight was returned, and his strength came to stay.
They rejoiced to see that Tobias' sight
Was now filled with the sun's great light.

Old Tobias
What gift can we give to your guide so true,
Who has led you to darkness and shown the way through?
The deeds he has done, the gifts he has earned,
Are help for us all, and lessons well learned.
Half our goods to you we will give
To pay our debt and help you to live.

Guide
No gift do I need, for God is my part;
I have been paid long ago by your kind heart.
When your tears fell like rain
Over those who had been slain,
And you found them a grave
By your deed, true and brave.
Then payment came plenty to God's throne on high;
To you I have come to bless by and by.

The Guide becomes Raphael

God's will shall be done on earth as in heaven,
His spirit shall reign, and his peace shall be given.
Bless you, Tobias, and all your ways;
Bless your children all of their days.

God's reward to you has been shared,
Because to others your heart has been bared.
Live thy days in peace and grace,
And God's mercy shall shine on your face.

Exodus, by Moses

Moses kept the flock of Jethro, his father-in-law and the priest of Midian, and he led the flock to the backside of the desert, and came to the mountain of God, even to Horeb. And the angel of the Lord appeared unto him in a flame of fire out of the midst of a bush: and he looked, and, behold, the bush burned with fire, and the bush was not consumed. And Moses said, I will now turn aside, and see this great sight, why the bush is not burnt. And when the Lord saw that he turned aside to see, God called unto him out of the midst of the bush, and said, Moses, Moses. And he said, here am I. And he said, draw not nigh hither: put off thy shoes from thy feet, for the place whereon thou standest is holy ground. Moreover, he said, I am the God of thy father, the God of Abraham, the God of Isaac, and the God of Jacob. And Moses hid his face, for he was afraid to look upon God. And the Lord said, I have surely seen the affliction of my people which are in Egypt, and have heard their cry by reason of their task-masters; for I know their sorrows. And I am come down to deliver them out of the hand of the Egyptians, and to bring them up out of that land unto a good land and a large, unto a land flowing with milk and honey.

Literature for Grade Three Teachers and Parents

The Wisdom of Solomon (**1500 BC**)

Wisdom is bright and unfading,
And she is easily seen by those who love her,
And found by those who search for her.
She forestalls those who desire her, by making herself known first.
The man who rises early to seek her will not have to toil,
For he will find her sitting at his gates.
For to think of her is the highest understanding,
And the man who is vigilant for her sake will soon be free from care.
For she goes about in search of those who are worthy of her,
And she graciously appears to them in their paths,
And meets them in every thought.
For wisdom is more mobile than any motion,
And she penetrates and permeates everything, because she is so pure;
For she is the breath of the power of God,
And a pure emanation of his almighty glory;
Therefore, nothing defiled can enter into her.
For she is a reflection of the everlasting light,
And a spotless mirror of the activity of God,
And a likeness of his goodness.
Though she is one, she can do all things,
And while remaining in herself, she makes everything new.
And passing into holy souls, generation after generation,
She makes them friends of God, and prophets.
For God loves nothing but the man who lives with wisdom.
For she is fairer than the sun, or any group of stars;
Compared with light, she is found superior; for night succeeds to it,
But evil cannot overpower wisdom.

Wisdom of Sirach (**1500 BC**)

I prayed and understanding was given me; I called upon God, and the spirit of wisdom came to me.

I loved her above health and beauty, and chose to have her instead of light, for the light that cometh from her never goeth out.

And all such things as are either secret or manifest, them I know.

For wisdom, which is the worker of all things, taught me; for in her is an understanding spirit, holy, one only, manifold, subtle, lively, clear, undefiled, plain, not subject to hurt, loving the thing that is good, ready to do good.

Kind to man, steadfast, sure, free from care, having all power, overseeing all things, and going through all understanding, pure, and most sublime spirits.

For wisdom is more moving than any motion; she passes and goes through all things by reason of her pureness.

For she is the breath of the power of God, and a pure influence flowing from the glory of the Almighty;

For she is the brightness of the everlasting light, the unspotted mirror of the power of God, and the image of his goodness.

And being but one, she can do all things: and remaining in herself, she maketh all things new: and in all ages entering into holy souls, she maketh them friends of God and prophets.

For she is more beautiful than the sun, and above all the order of stars: being compared with light, she is found before it.

I loved her, and sought her out from my youth, I desired to make her my spouse, and I was a lover of her beauty.

Rudolf Steiner's Curriculum Recommendations for Grade Three

Karl Stockmeyer's Waldorf Literature and History indications for Grade Three

History: Story material is drawn from Biblical, Old Testament stories as part of ancient history.

Bibliographical References and Recommending Reading List—Grade Three

Ben-Gurion. *Legends of the Jews*. St. George.

Birnbaum. *Bal-Shem*. Hebrew Publishing Co.

Bock, Emil. *Genesis*. Floris Books.

Bock, Emil. *Kings & Prophets*. Floris Books.

Bock, Emil. *Moses*. Floris Books.

Cohen, Lenore. *Bibles Tales*. Books 1 & 2. Union of Hebrew Congregation, New York, 1936.

Compton-Burnett. *And It Came to Pass*. Old Testament Reader. New Knowledge Books, 1964.

Hurlbut. *Hurlbut's Stories of the Bible*. Hebrew Publishing Co.

James. *Old Testament Stories*. Longman.

Keller. *The Bible as History*. Morrow.

Rapport. *Myth & Legend of Ancient Israel*. Greshan.

Steiner, Rudolf. *Genesis Cycle*. Anthroposophic Press, New York.

Streit, Jacob. *And There Was Light*. Anthroposophic Press, New York.

Streit, Jacob. *Sons of Cain*. St. George Book Service, New York.

Grade Four

Earth Incarnation of the Earth
Stage Four of Seven of the Eternal Curriculum
Planetary Influence is Mars
The Mystery of Death and Birth
Atlantis

Deep truths are embedded in the myths, truths more concerned with reality than those which are expressed through modern natural science about this thing or the other. Physiological, biological truths about man are to be found in the myths and origin of what they express rests upon the consciousness of the connection of man as microcosm with the macrocosm.

Rudolf Steiner (GA 202)

The fourth-grade child experiences the "Death of the Gods" (Ragnarok) from the Norse myths, wherein most of the gods and goddesses die battling frost giants and evil creatures. Only a few old gods and a few children of the gods cross the second rainbow-bridge into the newly created future land of the surviving gods. Likewise, the gods of Atlantis are silent (dead) and their lands are gone (like the first rainbow-bridge Bifrost), and the image of the rainbow is there to remind us of a previous world that is now out of reach.

The fourth-grader often reaches the stage of development that Piaget calls "conservation" and Steiner calls the "9/10-year change." The child now enjoys a certain objectivity and becomes more logical than they were before. Often, the past must be put aside before the new can be dealt with. Just as Atlantis (kindergartner) had a certain subjective connection to the natural world, a new, more objective thinking needs to arise so that the individualized personality of the child can come to birth. The fourth-grader needs this "sinking of the past" (Atlantis) and a birth of a new objectivity that is rational and logical. We can also see this previous stage of development as a sort of Biblical Garden of Eden. The fourth-grader is cast from the garden and must build their first house (objectified body) from the natural world around them. Illness, old age, suffering, and eventually death are the results of leaving the garden (subjective body) and entering the cold, hard, material world. This painful awakening is the typical emotional experience of the child at this age.

The fourth grade and the ninth/tenth year of age mark the real beginning of the use of mythology in the Main Lesson of the Waldorf curriculum. Throughout the year, the stories of the Norse myths are told to the children, and this material is used for reading and writing purposes as well as songs, plays, paintings, and other creative activities that may arise.

According to Dr. Steiner, the experience of the ego prior to this time finds its home in the head, which is like the starry expanse of the heavens and is indicative of the spiritual world. The ego moves from the head into the rhythmic and metabolic-will processes of the child. As the ego becomes more entangled in the body, the child becomes more aware that he is an ego and is limited by his body. He realizes that he experiences himself subjectively and, in doing so, awakens to the objective world. The child begins to question both the subjective and objective worlds that he now finds himself torn between. Space now has a new perspective, and exploration of the self and the world is to be expected. On the subjective side, he may find loneliness and doubt. The need to play music becomes important, as well as the human warmth of a devoted friend. Objectively, the child finds a new need to question what stands behind the world. He wonders about the world around him; therefore, the study of geography begins in this grade. He also feels more bound by his body, making this an ideal time to learn folk dancing.

Norse mythology has a powerful sense of duality that can be found in no other mythology. Fire and ice are the foundation of the Norse world-conception, which clearly shows the strong dual natures at war in the world, and thus in the fourth-grade child. The Norse felt themselves deeply in their bodies and souls. The cold, icy winds of the north seemed to restrict them to their bodies. Only strength, endurance, and valor could see them through their challenging lives. In the stories of the many Norse gods, the children have a chance to experience the full range of dynamic, polarized feelings that they come to know within themselves.

Myths consist of living archetypal beings that move and weave in nature and among themselves, performing the duties of their godly offices. One can even come to know and experience the gods directly through the manifestations of child development. Myths place man on earth in time and space and give him meaning to life and something higher to strive towards. The deepest wisdom of a nation can often be found in its myths.

"What prevails in the historical, the social, the ethical life is more or less dreamt, slept through by mankind, that in any case abstract ideas are not fitted to take hold of the impulses which must be active in the social life. In earlier times men were aided through older, what we call atavistic knowledge, through myths. They brought to expression in the form of a myth what they thought concerning the world, what entered their vision of the world secrets."

Rudolf Steiner (GA 202)

Literature Selections for Grade Four Children

Any good children's Norse mythology book can be used to present the stories to the fourth-grader. Good editions are in the Suggested Reading List at the end of this section. The Norse myths are usually presented sequentially, and it is not hard to cover the entire pantheon of the gods and goddesses during the year. The question comes when the class teacher has to ask if they will present the stories from the *Kalevala*, the Finnish National Epic, along with the Norse mythology, which is usually taken from the *Eddas*. Often, the *Kalevala* is laid aside, and the easier to get Norse myths are used as the only source of "northern" tales in the fourth-grade.

Fourth-graders love Norse myths, and once again, we can see that Steiner's ideas of appropriate literature seem to be quite correct. Watching the children unfold through each different grade and seeing the way they take up the grade-specific lessons is remarkable and confirms that the Waldorf curriculum clearly meets the needs of the child. This is especially obvious when the children choose the character they wish to portray in the Norse mythology play at the end of the year. The Norse gods and goddesses are such extreme characters that the students enjoy portraying these deities. Many of the Norse gods and goddesses die in a final battle, and students are happy to "battle to the death." This seems to feed a need to answer the death questions that come up so frequently in this grade.

It is quite common for the students to study the Norse myths while the class teacher studies the *Kalevala*. Rudolf Steiner recommended studying the *Kalevala* as an antidote to our modern age. Therefore, the students might not quite be ready for the modern relationship challenges presented to the heroes of the *Kalevala*. As a matter of fact, most Waldorf teachers never even read the secondary choice for fourth-grade literature.

We will present here a Norse mythology play compiled and written by a fourth-grade class and their class teacher. The *Kalevala* will be presented afterwards for the teachers and parents to study for their own edification and deeper understanding of the fourth-grade literature themes.

A Grade Four Norse Mythology Play

This play was written in part by the students and teacher of the fourth grade at the Detroit Waldorf School. Parts of the text are extracted from the *Poetic Edda*, the Icelandic Sagas that bring us the most comprehensive picture of the Norse gods and goddesses. Other parts of the play were adapted from Longfellow, Matthew Arnold, and others. The play is the aggregate result of ten weeks of lessons on the creation, life, and destiny of the Norse World.

The Twilight of the Gods

Recorder Song: *The Ash Grove*
Opening scene under Yggdrasil, near the Nornies' pond:

In rounds with choral speaking:

Chorus:
The Nornies with wise, foreseeing ken
Spin the lives of gods and men.
Warp and weft, they weave the thread
For joy and woe, for hope and dread.
Comes the hour the last of all
The thread is cut; the leaf must fall.

Urd:
I remember the past, before time began;
Nothing was except we three, tending the seed
Of Yggdrasil, the World Tree.

My name is Urd, the past I understand;
The thread of life I weave for gods and man.
We feed the tree with holy drink
To heal its wounds, renew the link.
The pond is ours where swans swim free;
Their songs of joy we understand.
Odin is our friend, good council we lend;
We join with the Aesir, Asgard to defend.
The rainbow bridge leads the way here
Under the branches for counsel so clear.

Verdande:
I am Verdande, I pull the string of life;
From my sister Urd I take the thread of time
And hand it to my sister Skuld who cuts the string.
Seven swans swim silently in the pond;
Their reflections show all realms beyond.
Nothing happens in the present and escapes my sight;
On every happening, my eyes turn their light.
My counsel is good, many things I see now;
I understand the why, the wither, the how.

I know men's hearts; the aims of the Aesir,
The Jotuns, the dwarfs, the elves do I hear.
The present I rule every moment I'm awake;
I sleep not for time's holy sake.
When Ragnarok comes, we Nornies will spin fast;
For the Doom's Day of the gods will have come at last.

Skuld:
I am the future Nornie, the thread of life I cut;
The lives of Gods, the lives of men I know and shut.
My name is Skuld, the future I see clear;
All things to come before my eyes appear
The fate of Midgard, Asgard, Jotunheim.
I share the future visions with Odin in rhyme;
My Counsel for the future is the gods' highest prize.
When my scissors cut, it is life's demise;
A person's thread of life will see no other sun

His life is over and all his deeds are done.
I listen to the winds blowing through the branches;
They speak to me and tell me what are the chances
For good or ill, for health and romances.
Even the fate of Baldur, the magic whispered word,
The hope of Gimli, the new rainbow bridge of Urd,
The treasure of Odin, and the hope that men have heard.

Odin:
Hail Nomies, thou three weird sisters,
The pool of Yggdrasil shimmers before thee;
Each day your kindness heals the tree,
And your thread designs the life of gods.
We seek your counsel, your help, your aid.
The past I remember as well as you,
So shed your memories like the morning dew.
I can see deeper than the elves;
My one eye sees all, including the nine realms.
I am kind hearted and sweet tempered, not like Thor;
In a hundred ways, I'll tell you more.
I, of all dwellers in Asgard, can see deeper than the seed itself.
I am called the one-eyed wanderer.
I travel into Midgard to visit earthly men.
I taught them to make and swing an axe.
Frigga, my wife, taught them to cook.
Good friends these humans were to me and my wife.

The Nomies hold the thread of life, and nourish Yggdrasil the
    Great Ash Tree.
When they cut the string of life, the time for life is ended.

The Dance of Urd and the Nornies accompanied by the Chorus

Chorus:
I remember the past when Jotuns were born,
They who in past times fostered the Aesir:
Nine worlds I remember, nine in the Tree,
That glorious Fate Tree that springs 'neath the earth.
'Twas the earliest of times when Ymir lived;

Then was sand nor sea nor cooling wave,
Nor was Earth ever found, nor Heaven on high;
There was the Yawning of Deeps: Ginnungagap.

The sun knew not where she had housing;
The stars knew not where stood their places.
Thus was it before the earth was fashioned.

Of Ymir's flesh the earth was created,
And of his sweat the sea,
Crags of his bones, trees of his hair,
And of his skull the sky.
Then of his brows the Aesir gods made
Midgard for sons of men;
And of his brains the bitter-mooded
Clouds were all created.

There are three roots stretching three divers ways from under Yggdrasil's ash:
'Neath the first dwell Hel, 'neath the second Mimir and Midgard 'neath the third.
An eagle sits in the boughs of the ash, knowing much of many things,
And a hawk is perched, Storm-pale, aloft betwixt the eagle's eyes.
Ratatosk is the squirrel with gnawing tooth which runs in Yggdrasil's ash:
He bares the eagle's words from above to fierce Niddhog below.

Odin:
Wounded I hung on a wind-swept
Gallows for nine long nights,
Pierced by a spear, pledged to Odin,
Offering myself to myself:
The wisest know not from whence spring
The roots of that ancient rood.
These things are thought the best:
Fire, the sight of the sun,
Good health with the gift to keep it,
And a life that avoids vice.

Loki:
Loki am I, swift and sly;
I can turn into a bird and fly.
With all the gods and goddesses around me,
Mischief I make when anyone's about me.
Some think I'm mean, some think I'm cruel;
But everybody knows Loki's no fool.
Sometimes I'm caught and pay the price;
To Jotun men, some look like mice.
I stayed in a dungeon for a .month or three,
Wondering what was to become of me.

Loki, (A second Loki):
Loki am I, mischief maker, working ill where I can.
It's always my endeavor to bring strife to gods and man.
Mischief can I ever boast of, working good is not my will.
Though I am a Jotun, my charm and cunning have
    tremendous skill.
After I, Freya's necklace did steal,
Heimdall himself blew his horn with a peal.

I and my Jotun wife three awful children did bear:
Hela, Midgard Serpent, and Fenris Wolf are children so dear,
But for others they are figures to fear.
Wherever I go in Yggdrasil, my honey tongue will prevail,
It can get me out of any mischief from Asgard to dark Hel.
Many tricks I have pulled and many will I pull yet,
For I am a match for the gods an enemy they'll never forget.

Thor:
I am the God Thor, I am the War God,
I am the Thunderer! Here in my Northland,
My fastness and fortress, reign I forever!
Here amid icebergs rule I the nations;
This is my hammer, Miolnir the mighty;
Giants and sorcerers cannot withstand it!
These are the gauntlets wherewith I wield it,
And hurl it afar off. This is my belt;
Whenever I brace it, strength is redoubled!
The light thou beholdst stream through the heavens

In flashes of crimson, is but my red beard
Blown by the night-wind, affrightning the nations!
Jove is my brother mine eyes are the lightning;
The wheels of my chariot roll in the thunder
The blows of my hammer ring in the earthquake.
Force rules the world still, has ruled it, shall rule it,
Meekness is weakness, strength is triumphant;
Over the whole earth still is Thor's Day!

I am great and powerful when Miolnir I have hurled;
My hammer is the strongest in the world.
My wife is Sif with the golden hair:
Together we make a handsome pair.
But the Midgard serpent and I are not friends at all.
We will battle at Ragnarok until we fall.
I have met him once and will meet him again
Miolnir my hammer, this time, will make an end.

Sif:
Sif am I, Thor's loyal wife;
I always calm his toil and strife.
But his friendship with Loki has caused me pain
For Loki stole my hair and replaced it again
With golden strands forged by dwarves so wise,
And with it came two gifts the gods do prize.
A ship for the gods, Skildbaldnir was made
And a spear that never misses, in Odin's hand was laid.

Thialfi:
I am Thialfi, the farmer's son.
My legs move like lightning for fun.
I am the fastest of all men
And maybe gods too—let's not pretend.
I am Thor's helper, a messenger of dread;
I ride in his cart or run on ahead.
I am fast and Thor is strong with might;
Put us together and we make a perfect sight.
The greatest of frost giants was made of clay;
We battled him fairly 'til we won that day.

No enemy can face us: Thor never misses;
Giants shudder at Miolnir's kisses.

Freya:
I am Freya, the goddesses of beauty and love.
I have a cart that is pulled by cats from above.
I and my daughter, Noss, ride together wherever we go
With my beautiful necklace that I will gladly show.

Noss:
I am Noss, Freya's only daughter.
My mother and I feel sad right now because
My father has gone, and we do not know where he is.
We live in Asgard in my mother's castle,
And other gods and goddesses dwell there too.
We ride in a cart pulled by cats and kittens.
Sometimes my mother cries golden tears because she is sad.
She has a beautiful necklace that makes her happy.

Freya:
I remember the days of long ago when Od and I would walk
 through the valleys.
We picked beautiful flowers, and Od would look at me and say:
"These flowers are beautiful, just like you are."
I remember the day when Noss was born.
I look at her now and mourn, "You are the only one who makes
 the tears go away."
Every day I cry golden tears waiting for my husband, Od, to
 come back.

One day when I was in my room, Loki turned himself into a fly and flew through the keyhole. He flew towards my necklace to take it, but I always hold on to it. He started to buzz around me. I tried to swat him, and I took my hand off my necklace. When I did, he turned back into himself and grabbed the necklace. Then he ran out of Asgard and turned himself into a seal, but Heimdall heard him. So, Heimdall turned himself into a bigger seal and chased after him. When Heimdall caught up with Loki, he put the necklace on a rock and sat on it like nothing happened.

Heimdall said to him, "I know that you are Loki. Now give me back the necklace!"

But Loki would not. So, they started to bite and smack each other. Heimdall won the fight, and he got the necklace and brought it back to me. Heimdall and Loki have been enemies ever after.

Heimdall:
My name is Heimdall, guard of the rainbow bridge.
I can see and hear a hundred miles away.
I and Loki are not friends at all
Because he is a thief and stole Freya's necklace.
He is quite a thief, and someday I'll make him pay.
I have strength beyond anyone's imagination;
That's why I don't need any weapons.
I put my horn in the well of Mimir until
The day of Ragnarok appears.
On the day of Ragnarok, I will blow my magic horn,
And it will be known to all that Ragnarok is here;
For the Day of Death is near.
Then, the gods will all come to the
Fields of Ida in Asgard for the last battle.

Mimir:
I am Mimir, the wisest of Frost Giants.
I guard the well of wisdom in Jotunheim.
Odin came to me and sacrificed his left eye;
Now he can see like the sun in the sky.
Good counsel I give to Odin, for I am wise;
No truth can hide, no lie disguise
The knowledge I can see in the well so deep
No secret is safe from me to keep,
For I know the well has Heimdall's horn
Which will not be blown 'til Ragnarok is born.

Baldur:
My name is Baldur. I am the son of Odin.
I have a wife whose name is Nanna.
We have a palace made out of gold.

Wherever I walk, flowers spring up around my feet.
I comforted my father when he started the first war in
Asgard against the Vanir and the Jotuns.
Come, my fellow Aesir, let us go to Peacestead;
There I shall give you wonderful mead and bread.

Odin:
Come, Aesir, to Peacestead we go, over the rainbow bridge
Except for mighty Thor, who Bifrost will not hold.
Thank you, Nornies, for your good counsel and far-seeing sight
Let us go while there is good morning light.

Loki's Dance: both Loki and the Other Loki dance before speaking

Loki:
These are my three children, evilest of kind;
The destruction of the world they shall find.
Under the ocean, under the earth
My three children came to birth.
Aesir Gods they hate with a rage
Until the ending of this Norse Age.

Fenris:
I am the son of Loki. I am a wolf; my name is Fenris!
I am the biggest wolf you have ever seen.

Nothing can bind me except the roots of a mountain and the sinews of a bear. The gods put chains on me, but I broke them, so the gods put bigger chains on me, but I broke those also.

So the gods said, "We will take the sinews of a bear and the roots of a mountain."

After they did that, they said to me, "We will bind you with this thin string." I laughed and thought, "Surely they can't bind me with this string. It is so thin."

But I thought there might be magic in it, so I said, "Only if one of the gods puts his hand in my mouth while you try to bind me."

Tyr put his hand in my mouth, and they bound me. I tried to
get loose, but I could not, so I bit Tyr's hand off. Now I am
still bound here in the iron forest until the day of Ragnarok.

Hela:
I am Hela, the child of Loki. I am black and white.
I am evil clear through. I rule the lands of the dead.
Darkness and sadness reign in my realm.
I am the sister of Midgard Serpent and Fenris Wolf.
When Ragnarok comes, I and my brothers and Black Surt
Will build a boat and bring the dead to the fields of Ida in
Asgard,
There to battle the gods.

Midgard Serpent:
I am the serpent; I entwine the Midgard plain.
I'll only rise up when the gods shall be slain.
I am filled with venom that flows out like rain.
Thor I hate for the blows he has dealt me.
I will arise like a bridge to ride on,
Stretching to the Asgard plains;
Evil will mount me to ride to that day
When all will be turned to fire and pain.

Loki's Dance, part two

T y r:
I am Tyr, I am the God of War:
A bright red sun beams from my sword.
The hound of Hela, I hate like a devil.
The life of the Aesir I protect from such evil;
My hand I have given, as ransom to fool
To bind evil Fenris, the Wolf so cruel,
In the forest of iron on an underground island,
There he is bound,'til Ragnarok is at hand.
I'll fight bravely, to defend all Asgard
From the fires of Black Surt and his hound.
Evil we shall fight, 'til our lives are no more.

Surt:
I am Black Surt of the fiery realm of Muspelheim,
I have a flaming sword of war.
I wait for the Twilight of Asgard
When I can rise and burn earth and kill the Gods.
The Aesir are brave, but my army is great;
Fire and destruction go before me, death and evil trail behind me.

Chorus:
I heard a voice that cried, "Baldur the Beautiful
Is dead, is dead!" And through the misty air
Passed like the mournful cry of sunward sailing cranes.
Saw the pallid corpse of the dead sun
Borne through the Northern sky.
Blasts from Niffelheim
Lifted the sheeted mists around him as he passed.
And the voice forever cried, "Baldur the Beautiful
Is dead, is dead!" And died away
Through the dreary night in accents of despair.

Baldur, the Beautiful, God of the summer sun,
Fairest of all the Gods! Light from his forehead beamed,
Runes were upon his tongue as on the warrior's sword.
All things in earth and air bound were by magic spell
Never to do him harm; even the plants and stones;
All save the mistletoe, the sacred mistletoe!
Hodur, the blind old God, whose feet are shod with silence,
Pierced through that gentle breast
With his sharp spear, by fraud
Made of the mistletoe, the accursed mistletoe!

They laid him in his ship with horse and harness,
As on a funeral pyre. Odin placed
A ring upon his finger and whispered in his ear.
They launched the burning ship!
It floated far away over the misty sea,
'Til like the sun it seemed sinking beneath the waves.
Baldur returned no more!

Behold there breaketh the day of doom,
Darkness descendeth the elements rage.
Thunder rolls loud, and lightnings flash fire
Earth splits asunder, heaven falls in flames.
Take courage my heroes now as of old;
Let mood be the mightier, blood burn with fire.
Rend Oh ye Nornies your weaving of runes
The gods' great ending dawneth at last.

Baldur, Hodur:
Through the stress of the storm,
Through the darkness of death
There flashes the flame of fire through the night.
Behold in his beauty there rises once more
A god in his glory of love and of light.

Vidar, Magni:
So perish the old Gods!
But out of the sea of Time
Rises a new land of song,
Fairer than the old.
Over its meadows green
Walk the young bards and sing.
Build it again, O ye bards,
Fairer than before!
Ye fathers of the new race,
Feed upon morning dew,
Sing the new Song of Love.

Entire cast sings The Ash Grove

Literature for Grade Four Teachers and Parents

The Kalevala
**Paraphrased from a synopsis
by Elaman Opisto and John Major Jenkins.**

Ilmatar, the virgin of the air, left the loneliness of the sky and moved down to the sea, where the wind impregnated her. She drifted upon the waters for seven hundred years, pregnant but unable to give birth. A magical bird flew by and laid several eggs on Ilmatar's upraised knee. As the bird sat brooding in the nest, the heat made Ilmatar jerk her knee, and the eggs begin to change. One broke open; the lower half became the earth, the upper part became the sky, the yolk became the sun, and the white became the moon. During her pregnancy with her son Vainamoinen, Ilmatar sculpted the cliffs, coves, beaches, meadows, forests, and other features of the earth and sea. Finally, Vainamoinen (the eternal sage) forced his way out of his mother and floated on the sea for eight years before he reached land.

After many years on the barren land, Vainamoinen asked Sampsa Pellervoinen to plant trees. They all thrived, except for the oak tree. So they found another oak acorn-seed and, for fertilizer, Tursas the sea ogre burnt some hay that had been gathered by five water nymphs. The acorn was planted, and the oak that grew from it was so huge that it blocked out the sun and moon. No one was able to chop it down. Finally, a pygmy emerged from the sea and suddenly grew into a giant. He confidently felled the tree with three blows of his axe. The sun shone again. Now there were trees, grass, and berries, but no barley. A little titmouse told Vainamoinen that no barley would grow until he cut down the trees. Vainamoinen did this, leaving only one birch tree standing. An eagle flew by and was so pleased that Vainamoinen left a tree to perch on that he struck fire to burn the fallen trees. Vainamoinen planted seeds in the fresh mulch, and barley began to grow.

Joukahainen, a young man from Lapland, heard of Vainamoinen's growing fame, became envious, and challenged him to a singing duel. Vainamoinen easily outdid him, and, angry at being bested, Joukahainen threatened Vainamoinen. However, Vainamoinen sung Joukahainen—that is, magically enchanted him—deep into a paralyzing swamp. Vainamoinen released him when he promised his sister Aino as a bride. Later, Aino was upset when she learned of this, but her mother was pleased at the prospect of Vainamoinen entering the family.

Vainamoinen happened upon Aino gathering sauna switches and told her to adorn herself only for him. Aino, upset, tore off her adornments and raced home, weeping. Her mother attempted to console her, but Aino was distraught at the idea of becoming an old man's bride. She went to the sea to bathe and was drawn into the water by a brightly colored rock. Sadly, she drowned and became a salmon.

Grieving for Aino, Vainamoinen asked Untamo, the spirit of sleep, to tell him where the sea maidens lived. He set out to fish for them and caught a salmon. However, it slipped back into the water and transformed into Aino, who taunted Vainamoinen for having lost her a second time. He went home heavy-hearted, where his mother, Ilmatar, advised him to travel to the north and court one of the daughters of Pohjola.

Crossing a river while journeying to Pohjola, Vainamoinen was ambushed and shot with an arrow by Joukahainen. His horse dead, Vainamoinen fell into the water and was swept out to sea, drifting at the mercy of the waves. After drifting for several days, Vainamoinen was rescued by an eagle—the same eagle who was thankful for the tree Vainamoinen had left for birds to perch on. The eagle left him in Pohjola, where a maid found him weeping on the shore. Louhi, the mistress of Pohjola, took him in and entertained him well, but Vainamoinen was anxious to return home. She gave him a horse to ride home on, and promised her daughter in marriage to the man who could forge the Sampo for her. Vainamoinen rode away, thinking he would get Ilmarinen to forge the Sampo, because he could not do it himself. As he departed, Louhi warned him not to look up on his way home.

However, riding home through the meadows, he did look up and saw the lovely maid of Pohjola sitting on the rainbow, weaving. He tried to persuade her to come down and ride with him, but she refused. They debated the merits of the single life versus the married life, and finally she made him do a number of tasks: split a golden hair using knives that have no edges, snare a bird's egg with an invisible snare, peel the sandstone, cut a whip-stick from the ice while making no splinters and losing no fragments. He did all of these, but the last task was to build a boat from the fragments of her distaff—from the splinters of her spindle that propelled itself. While working three days on the boat, during a moment of inattention, Vainamoinen gashed his knee with his axe. He tried to staunch the blood flow by singing magic verses, but he forgot the Origin of Iron blood-stopping rune. In pain, he sleighed off to find someone who knew it. Finally, he found an old man who claimed to have stopped worse bleeding.

    The old man also had forgotten some parts of the magical incantation, but Vainamoinen reminded him, and he completed the healing spell. The flow of blood from Vainamoinen's knee stopped, and the old man's son went into the woods to gather ointments and salves to heal the wound. Vainamoinen recovered, and warned listeners not to take up impossible tasks on a dare.

    Vainamoinen returned home and urged Ilmarinen to journey to Pohjola and forge the Sampo. Ilmarinen suspiciously hesitated and then refused, but Vainamoinen tricked him by singing into existence an enchanting fir tree with the Great Bear on its branches and the moon on its crown. Climbing up the tree, Ilmarinen was caught up in a whirlwind and magically delivered to distant Pohjola. There, he was well received, and set to work forging the Sampo, hammering the lid of colors from the tips of white-swan feathers, from the milk of greatest virtue, from a single grain of barley, and from the finest wool of lambkins. He looked for three days to find the place to make his forge and finally came upon a stone with rainbow-colors. There he built his smithy. He stoked the fire for three days and then began forging, and on the first attempt created a golden, silver, copper crossbow but found it was ill-natured, so he broke the bow and threw it back into the furnace. On the second day, he created a skiff of metals that was purple, golden, and copper, but it was a thing of evil, so he threw it back. Then a golden heifer arose from the furnace, with the Bear of Heaven on her head and the disc of sunshine on her brow, but she was ill-tempered. On the fourth try, a plow of beauty arose: golden, copper, and silver, but ill-mannered.

Then he stoked the furnace for three days, until it felt like mid-summer and flowers began sprouting, and the Sampo arose with the lid of colors: on one side the flour was ground, on another salt was made, on a third was money forged, while the colored lid rocked. It ground one measure at daybreak, then a measure fit for eating, a second for the market, and a third one for the store-house. When it was done, the mistress of Pohjola locked it up in Pohjola's Stone Mountain with nine locks upon the wonder and made three strong roots that reached nine fathoms beneath the mountain, the sandy sea-bed, and the mountain-dwelling around it. Ilmarinen then asked for the beautiful daughter's hand to wed, but was rebuffed. Dejected, he went home and told Vainamoinen that the Sampo had been forged and was busy grinding things for Pohjola.

Lemminkainen was very handsome, but was also a rascal filled with wanderlust. He heard of Kyllikki a beautiful island maiden much sought after, but disdainful of all her suitors. Lemminkainen went to the island to woo her, but she refused him too, so he carried her away by force. Resisting at first, she finally gave in to his love when he promised to never go off to war. Likewise, she promised to never go to parties without him or gossip around the village. Lemminkainen's mother was delighted with her new daughter-in-law.

While Lemminkainen was away gathering fish, Kyllikki went to a dance with her girlfriends in the village. Lemminkainen found out. His trust shattered, he angrily prepared to go off to war. His mother begged him not to go, protesting that he would surely be killed. He left his hairbrush, saying that if he died, it would bleed. Arriving in Pohjola sometime later, he defeated and scattered all the Pohjola wizards in a singing contest with them. He ignored only Wet-Hat, an ugly, blind, crippled cow herder, believing him to be beneath contempt. Angered, Wet-Hat ran to the river, where he laid in wait to get his revenge on Lemminkainen.

Lemminkainen asked Louhi for one of her daughters. She refused, saying he must first catch the Elk of Hiisi in a ski chase. He went to a ski maker but was secretly given skis made of bad wood. After an exciting chase through the snow-filled forests, Lemminkainen did momentarily catch the elk, but it bolted, and he broke his ski-staff and one of his skis.

With the help of Ukko's skis, hunters' charms, and forest spirits, Lemminkainen finally caught the elk. The mistress then demanded that he bridle the fire-snorting horse of Hiisi and shoot the Swan of Tuonela on the river of death. On his way along the river, Wet-Hat, lying in wait, killed Lemminkainen with a poison serpent. Forgetting the charm to cure the poison, Lemminkainen staggered and died, and was thrown into the river by the shepherd. He was chopped into five pieces by the son of Tuoni.

Back at home, Lemminkainen's mother and Kyllikki frightfully watched the brush begin to bleed. Rushing off to Pohjola to find her son, Lemminkainen's mother was led astray by Louhi, but the sun told her what happened. She asked Ilmarinen to make a rake for her, and then she retrieved all of Lemminkainen's body parts by raking through the river and fitting him together with the help of special charms. To restore him to life, she sent a bee to get an ointment from the Creator's storehouse. Lemminkainen was revived, and they returned home together.

Vainamoinen sent Sampsa Pellervoinen, the little man, to fetch wood for a boat he was building. Using a solid oak log that Sampsa found for him, he began singing the boat into shape, but forgot three magic words. He decided to journey to Tuonela, the land of the dead, to find them. After arriving at the bank of death's river, Vainamoinen pretended to have died in order to get in, but Tuoni's clever daughter would not ferry him across until he told her the truth. He eventually told her why he came, and she boated him across. On the other side, the old man of Tuonela tried to trap Vainamoinen, but he narrowly escaped back to the land of the living by turning himself into an otter and a serpent, and then he warned everyone never to attempt to go to Tuonela. He did not find the missing magic words.

Vainamoinen decided to seek his missing magic words from Antero Vipunen, a famous giant shaman who had been asleep for ages. Surviving dangerous trials along the way, Vainamoinen found him and, while prying open the giant's mouth, fell in. Once in Vipunen's belly, Vainamoinen tormented the giant shaman so much that he sang out all his magical charms for Vainamoinen to hear. Vainamoinen escaped with the verse he was looking for, returned home, and completed his boat.

Vainamoinen set sail for Pohjola to court the daughter of Northland. However, Ilmarinen found out from his sister what was happening, and he also set out. Seeing them both arriving, Louhi, the mistress of Pohjola, advised her daughter to choose Vainamoinen, but she wanted the forger of the Sampo, and told Vainamoinen as much.

Ilmarinen arrived at the house of Pohjola and was given four tasks to perform in order to win Pohjola's beautiful daughter: plough a field full of serpents, bridle the wolves of Mana, fetter the bears of Tuoni, and catch the gigantic pike in the river of Tuonela. With the help of the maiden, he was able to accomplish all of the tasks. He claimed his bride and was told to protect her. Vainamoinen left, disheartened, and advised older men to never compete with a younger man for a beautiful maiden.

While grieving for his wife, who was killed, Ilmarinen forged for himself a gold and silver woman, but she was icy cold. He could not fully bring her to life, and, distraught, tried to give her to Vainamoinen. But Vainamoinen told him to melt her down to make useful tools, and Vainamoinen urged people not to worship images, nor to seek happiness in gold and silver.

Ilmarinen returned to Pohjola to court the sister of the Northland maiden, but Louhi expressed regret at having given him her first daughter. She reprimanded him and vowed to not repeat her mistake. Ilmarinen asked the girl to come with him, and when she refused, he carried her off by force. Sleighing southward through the woods, she treated him to a tongue-lashing for being so foolish, and spent the night at an inn, laughing with another man while Ilmarinen slept. The next morning, disgusted with such behavior, Ilmarinen changed her into a seagull and continued on his way home. He met Vainamoinen and told him what he did to the girl, and that the people of Pohjola were prospering with the Sampo in their possession.

Vainamoinen urged Ilmarinen to come with him to Pohjola to retrieve the Sampo. They started out by land, but found a warship and took to the river. On the way, they came upon Lemminkainen, who jumped in with gusto, happy to be along for the adventure.

The *Kalevala* heroes came to a rapids and got stuck on the back of a huge pike. Lemminkainen and Ilmarinen failed to get them free, and finally Vainamoinen killed the pike. They made their way to an island. They cooked the pike and ate it, leaving only a pile of bones. With them, Vainamoinen mades a kantele—a five-stringed harp. All of the others tried to play it, but none could.

As Vainamoinen played his new musical instrument, all of nature flocked to listen and rejoice. The animals, the birds, the fish, and even the nature spirits wept for joy. Vainamoinen, overcome with emotion, cried, and his tears rolled into the sea. A duck went to fetch them and found they had turned into pearls.

The *Kalevala* heroes arrived in Pohjola. Vainamoinen first asked Louhi if she would share the Sampo, but she refused. He then said they would have to take it by force. Louhi, angered at such a threat, called her warriors to attack. However, Vainamoinen acted quickly, played his kantele, and enchanted all of Pohjola into a sleep-trance. Going to the copper mountain where the Sampo was kept, the three heroes worked to free it. Vainamoinen opened the doors with a chant, Ilmarinen buttered the hinges to keep them from squeaking, and Lemminkainen was chosen to heave the Sampo up. But its roots went down to a depth of nine fathoms, and Lemminkainen failed to lift the Sampo out by himself. He enlisted the aid of Pohjola's strong ox and plowed the roots up. Heaving the Sampo free, they carried it to their boat and departed. The third day on the water, Lemminkainen decided they needed some cheer and, against Vainamoinen's wishes, began to sing. His bellowing startled a crane, who flew off, squawking, to awaken Louhi from her trance back in Pohjola. Realizing that the Sons of Kaleva had taken the Sampo, she conjured up a storm and called upon a sea monster to kill the men of *Kalevala*. Though the *Kalevala* heroes overcame these obstacles, the kantele was blown overboard and lost.

Louhi gathered an army and sailed in pursuit of the Sampo. Vainamoinen, seeing they could not outrun her, conjured up a reef that wrecked Louhi's ship. Louhi transformed herself into a huge eagle, took her warriors onto her wings and tail, and alighted on the mast of the heroes' ship. Vainamoinen smashed her claws with the rudder, and her warriors fell into the sea. Louhi was able to claw at the Sampo, and it fell overboard, shattering into pieces. Vainamoinen saw a good omen in the pieces of the Sampo spreading over the ocean: some of them reaching land. As Louhi departed with the Sampo's lid and handle, she threatened to lock up the sun and moon and send diseases to *Kalevala*. Vainamoinen went ashore, gathered and sowed the pieces of the Sampo, and prayed to Jumala to protect the people of *Kalevala*.

Feeling that it was time to make music again, Vainamoinen asked Ilmarinen to forge a rake to search for the pike-bone harp. Unable to find it, Vainamoinen made a new kantele from birchwood, with tuning pegs of oak and strings made from the hair of a beautiful forest maiden. Again, all of nature responded to his playing with joy.

Hearing the rejoicing, Louhi bitterly determined to send a plague to the people of Kaleva. The origins of illness were invoked and cast over the land. In response, Vainamoinen warmed up the healing sauna, and with powerful incantations sent the aches and pains away to Pain Mountain, thus curing his people.

Hearing that Kaleva's people had escaped her plague, Louhi sent a bear to wreak havoc on their cattle. Vainamoinen killed the bear, and they held a ceremony and feast. The bear was treated with respect, as a welcome guest, and the feast was in his honor. Vainamoinen sang of the birth of the bear, friend and brother to man, born not on earth, but upon the shoulders of Otava, the Big Dipper. Vainamoinen played and sang, delighting the gathering, and concluded with an eloquent prayer for the welfare of the land of Kaleva.

The sun and moon came to sit in the limbs of a tree and listen to Vainamoinen's enchanting music. Louhi quickly stole them, hiding the sun in a steel mountain and the moon in a rock cave. Next, she stole fire from the people of Kaleva. Ukko, the highest god, wondered why it was dark, and struck up a new spark of fire from which he planned to make a new sun and moon, but the maid who was appointed to nurse the spark dropped it, and it fell to earth. Vainamoinen and Ilmarinen set out to find it. Ilmatar, Vainamoinen's mother, told them that the fire, after causing great damage, fell into Lake Alue, causing the lake to boil over its banks. The firespark was swallowed by a whitefish, which agonized until it was swallowed by a sea trout, which, in turn, was swallowed by a pike. Vainamoinen and Ilmarinen wove a fiber net to catch the pike, but were unsuccessful.

Vainamoinen had a huge net woven of fine flax linen, with which they succeeded in catching the pike. As the Son of Day cleaned the fish, the precious firespark popped out, badly singed Vainamoinen's beard, scorched Ilmarinen's face and hands, and burned down half the forests in the country. Vainamoinen finally captured the fire and returned it to its proper place in the hearths of *Kalevala*. Ilmarinen healed his hands with the help of a frost charm.

Ilmarinen forged a new sun and moon, but they gave no light. Vainamoinen cast lots and learned where the sun and moon were hidden. He went to Pohjola and defeated the guards, but could not open the locks and bars that imprisoned the sun and moon. He returned home and had Ilmarinen forge special tools to open the locks. While Ilmarinen was working at his forge, Louhi visited in the shape of a hawk and asked what he was making. He replied that he was forging an iron collar to chain up the mistress of Pohjola. Feeling she was doomed, Louhi released the sun and moon. Changing herself into a dove, she flew back to Ilmarinen and told him that the sun and moon were once again in the sky, where they belong.

* * *

Marjatta the Virgin lived a chaste and pure youth in the house of her father. One day while herding sheep, she swallowed a lingonberry and magically became pregnant. When the time came to give birth, she was shunned by her family and went off to a stable, where she gave birth to a son. She kept him away from other people, but had to bring him to the old man Virokannas so that he could be christened. As she was sitting with her little son on her lap, combing his hair, the boy suddenly disappeared. She searched for him everywhere. In vain she asked the Highway, the Star, and the Moon. At last she was informed by the Sun and found the boy in a swamp. Vainamoinen was called upon to question her, determine who the father was, and decide whether the boy should live or die. Vainamoinen decided that since he was conceived from a berry of the earth, he should be planted in the earth—that is, left to die in the forest. But then the one-month-old boy began to speak, and accused Vainamoinen of false judgment. Angry and ashamed, but recognizing that his successor had come, Vainamoinen sangs himself a brass boat and sailed away. The boy was baptized and made king of Karelia. As he departed, Vainamoinen said that a time would come when his people would need him again, and he left his kantele and his songs for his people behind.

Rudolf Steiner's Curriculum Recommendations for Grade Four

Karl Stockmeyer's Waldorf Literature and History indications for Grade Four

History: Transition from study of home surroundings to history lessons via local history.
Norse Mythology or The Kalevala.

Bibliographical References and Recommending Reading List—Grade Four

Colum, Padriac. *About Norse Gods*. MacMillan.

Column, Padriac. *The Children of Odin*. Macmillan.

Crawford, John Martin. *The Kalevala*. John B. Alden, New York, 1888. (Steiner recommended this English translation.)

Crossley-Holland, Kevin. *Norse Myths*. Pantheon, New York, 1980.

D'Aulaire. *Norse Gods & Giants*. Doubleday, New York.

Green. *Myths of the Norsemen*. Puffin.

Hollander. *The Poetic Edda*. University of Texas Press.

Hveberg. *Of Gods & Giants*. Tonum Publishing, Norway.

Steiner, Rudolf. *The Mission of the Folksouls*. Anthroposophic Press, New York.

Taylor and Auden. *The Elder Edda*. Faber & Faber.

Titchenell, Elsa Brita. *The Masks of Edin*. Theological University Press, Pasadena, CA, 1985.

Uehi. *Norse Mythology and the Modern Human Being*. AWSNA Publications.

Grade Five

Jupiter Incarnation of the Earth
Stage Five of Seven of the Eternal Curriculum
Planetary Influence is Jupiter
The Mystery of Evil Transformed through Alchemy
Post-Atlantis

The way man looks at the wonders of nature changes in the course of time. Our natural science is proud of its interpretation of nature. There seems little ground for this pride when we reflect that by representing the force hidden in depths of Nature as the female ruler of the wonders of Nature, the Greek system of divinities showed a far deeper wisdom than the science of today has any inkling of, or will so much as guess at until spiritual science is allowed into our civilization."

Rudolf Steiner (GA 129)

    The fifth grade is the golden age of childhood, just as the post-Atlantean age is our golden age. All new impulses come out of the fifth stage of development in the seven-stage system. Humanity is only as far advanced as fifth grade. The cultures of ancient India, ancient Persia, Egypt/Chaldea, Greece, and Anglo-Germania create the leading images that we offer the developing child through the fifth-grade curriculum. Alexander the Great stands between myth and history, just as our post-Atlantean age stands between the myths of Atlantis and Lemuria and the history of humanity, which gets very sketchy before 3,000 BC. We have yet to understand the previous epoch, let alone what Steiner has told us about ancient history and the distant future.

It will be hard for some Waldorf educational theorists to agree with this scheme from this point on. There is no complete picture to show us why the literature chosen for the curriculum matches the developmental needs of the growing child. Some aspects remain a mystery or are open to interpretation, but Steiner also didn't tell us that one source of the outline of the Waldorf curriculum comes from Aegidius Romanus, a student of Thomas Aquinas, whose expertise was education and the training of princes. In his work *De Regimine Principum* (*The Governance of Kings and Princes*), Aegidius lays out the model curriculum to train a prince to become a king. Everything from virtue development to games was laid out in the curriculum. Many of the ideas of the Waldorf curriculum can be found there, including the idea of the threefold nature of the human being's soul capacities of thinking, feeling, and willing, as well as the idea that ontogeny recapitulates phylogony. Aegidius's curriculum constitutes the highest moral development merged with the best sciences and arts of the day.

The fifth-grade curriculum goes back into ancient history that is not recognized by modern historians. Ancient India and Ancient Persia are beyond the normally accepted scope of history. Recently, archeological digs in India have uncovered highly civilized cities built by the Harappian culture that reach back to 9000–8000 BC and before. Previously, references in sacred texts to such ancient antiquity were considered mythological. Steiner was aware of these cultures before others because he could see into the past and read the imprint of these cultures in the etheric body of the earth and the etheric body of the human being. Today, DNA discoveries lead researchers to find mythological cities through the combined efforts of biologists reading the etheric forces in DNA and comparing them against the etheric record of a culture in outer nature that is aligned with archeological finds. Thus, we can see that what is inside the human being is also played out in the history of humankind, and this history is personal to every growing child.

The fifth-grader hears myths and stories from Ancient India, Ancient Persia, Babylon, Sumeria, Chaldea, Egypt, Greece and more. Manu and the Seven Holy Rishis, Zoroaster, and Gilgamesh are examples of possible literature material. This particular sequence of civilizations reveals the evolution of the historical development of mankind, according to Steiner.

The fifth-grader studies Greek myths, including the creation of the world and the lesser gods, like Zeus and Apollo, and the overthrow of their own parents. So once again, the child experiences more creation stories and sees the central position of humanity in the scheme of the world. The fifth-grade child still has the natural sense of movement and grace that was so much a part of Greek art and life. Greek and Latin are also begun in this grade, so the children can experience the sounds of the languages.

Towards the end of the fifth-grade, Greek history is taught to the children. Alexander the Great is usually introduced in the Main Lesson if the teacher has the time. This is good preparation for Roman history, which comes next.

The fifth-grade child is beginning to have the capacity to orient herself in the flow of time. This particularly comes at age twelve when she becomes aware of herself as a being in time and develops the capacities to understand cause and effect in the world. Fairy tales, legends, the Old Testament, and myths are the *path of descent* of imaginative pictures of the past coming into the modern picture of cause and effect, space and time.

> If you will observe children under eleven-years old, you will see that all their movements still come out of their inner being. If you observe children of over twelve-years old, you will see from the way they step how they are trying to find their balance, how they are inwardly adapting themselves to leverage and balance, to the mechanical nature of the skeletal system. This means that between the eleventh and twelfth year the soul's experience of nature is much more inward. And only now that

> he has taken hold of that remotest part of his humanity, the bone system, does man's adaptation to the outer world become complete. Only now is man a true child of the world, only now must he live with the mechanics and dynamics of the world, only now does he experience what is called causality in life. (GA 307)

In the fifth grade, the telling of Indian, Persian, Egyptian, and Greek mythologies present a series of creation motifs that begin to develop the child's ability to distinguish the flow of historical time sequencing. The literature should give a taste of the different cultures and their relationship to the world and how they experienced it. Greek myths are studied thoroughly because the balance and beauty in Greek art and lifestyle are indicative of the balance inherent in the child's age—"the golden age of childhood." The last glimpses of *childlike imagination* still linger as the new, wakeful consciousness of the world begins to unfold. Some Greeks believed in the gods, while others scorned the gods and turned to empirical logic and philosophy. The fifth-grader is presented with the same philosophical questions.

Five cultural epochs are introduced in the fifth-grade curriculum. The fifth grade has the most complex and wide-ranging selection of materials for the language arts curriculum. The epochs are generally described by Rudolf Steiner as: ancient Indian, ancient Persian, Egyptian/Chaldean/Babylonian, Greco-Roman, Anglo-Germanic, future Russian, and future American. We will look at the literature selections for five of the seven epochs in the fifth-grade curriculum. The other two, future Russian and future American, are experienced in the sixth and seventh grade curriculum and constitute an etheric Imagination of the future.

The fifth-grade teacher has the huge task of selecting only a few pieces of literature to examine in the short period of one year. Essentially, the fifth-grade curriculum covers all of known history and delves into pre-history with ancient India and ancient Persia.

Five Cultural Epochs in Grade Five Literature

Ancient Indian Cultural Epoch 120

Persian Cultural Epoch 134

Egyptian/Chaldean/Babylonian Cultural Epoch 150

Greco-Roman Cultural Epoch.................................. 162

Anglo-German Cultural Epoch 187

Ancient Indian Cultural Epoch

7227–5067 BC
Leo, Old Saturn, Physical Body

Aum mani padme hum! Hail thou jewel in the heart of the lotus!

An aspirant's search for happiness and eternity is looking for what, in the East, is called enlightenment. Enlightenment is defined as the merging of emptiness and wisdom in right action that leads to liberation from the physical and union with wisdom. This wisdom is sought for the sake of all other sentient beings. We can only help others and pull them from the mire if we ourselves have first been removed from the entanglements of suffering, old age, and death. Enlightenment brings to our hearts that which is eternal and can strengthen our resolve to help all others attain freedom from the suffering and illusion of the world. Enlightenment is the only true happiness, and it brings us into the possibility of transforming every moment into an eternal moment that embodies the past and brightens the future. It is only action that can lead to perfect good—to love given in freedom. Otherwise, without enlightenment, we can only add to the suffering of everyone we meet and incur karma instead of freeing ourselves and others from karmic indebtedness.

What seems to drive the search for enlightenment is the longing for union with the other. Through learning from others' lessons in life, we can experience the spectrum of human existence without having to incur personal karma. It follows that all other sentient beings could hold a piece to the puzzle of our personal enlightenment. Essentially, we cannot reach enlightenment alone. Our motivation must be for the sake of all others, and our attainment is solely for the purpose of helping all others free themselves from delusion and negative karma that keeps them from enlightenment. The vow of the Bodhisattva entails a promise that the aspirant will not enter into heaven until she has helped all others enter first, so that none may be left behind. Quan Yin is the embodiment of that vow. That is why Quan Yin is often depicted with the dragon, the embodiment of all animal desires (astral body) that must be purified before enlightenment can be reached and the passage to heaven opened.

The orient is the source of the light of philosophy and mind-training that is epitomized in the philosophical thought of the most ancient writings in the Indo-Aryan tradition, the Upanishads. These ancient teachings have existed for millennia in an oral tradition whose beginning is lost in pre-history. The author of many of the ancient Hindu writings is the mythical Manu, the Noah of Indian tradition, replete with an ark, mates of each animal species, the seeds of all plants, and the Seven Holy Rishis (with the sacred books of wisdom—Upanishads, Gathas, and ancient ragas and dances from the Seven Mystery Centers of Atlantis).

According to the *Manu Smirtri*, Manu ties his ark to Mount Everest and, as the water recedes, descends to the Holy River Ganges and gives birth to the ancient Indian culture. Archeological evidence from the Harappian period of settlement of the Indus and other river valleys throughout northern India demonstrates a highly advanced city-culture prior to the ninth millennium before Christ. Atlantis finished sinking in 10,500 B.C., and the City of Manu was founded at that time at the eastern end of the Tarim Basin, at the confluence of the Tarim and Altai Rivers. From this city, cultural planning migrated into the river valleys of India at an early period. About two millennia later, another cultural infusion again flowed out of the City of Manu into the high mountains of northern Iran: ancient Persia. Later, another infusion, complete with city plans, temple architecture, religious rites, and elaborate priesthoods that answered the people's questions about planting, building, domestication of animals, recording time and history and the other earmarks of civilization, migrated into the fertile crescent of Mesopotamia (Ancient Egypt, Babylon, Chaldea).

Ancient Indian, ancient Persian, Sumerian-Babylonian-Chaldean-Egyptian, Greek-Roman, and Anglo-Germanic periods comprise the cultural epochs, or eras, that Rudolf Steiner characterizes as the modern human's re-enacting of ontogeny recapitulating phylogeny—the evolving development of the individual recapitulating the stages of development that the evolution of humanity as a whole went through at an earlier time. Dr. Steiner's penultimate expression of this profound insight is embodied in the language arts curriculum of the Waldorf school curriculum. Students in a Waldorf school experience these cultures and their writings, customs, and traditions in a particular order that marks the outer development of human consciousness throughout history. The stories, songs, dances, foods, and celebrations from different cultures that the children experience in the curriculum meet the developmental needs of the growing child at the particular age when this exposure will answer a deep need and yearning required by a particular stage in child development. This developmentally based curriculum truly helps the children become world citizens who have a great appreciation of diverse cultures and traditions.

The literature selections for the fifth grade follow the sequential order of the development of modern human consciousness. Ancient Indian lineages carried great wisdom for thousands of years in an unbroken oral tradition. Those who were fully clairvoyant in ancient times, were able to directly perceive the nature of the interaction between physical matter and spirit. Ancient India had the task of thoroughly understanding the nature of the physical body in all of its wonders. That is why Vedic wisdom about the physical body is profound, second only to the Chinese understanding of the human body. India's inspiration originated in the Central Asian City of Manu. Ancient Indian traditions were the legacy of Atlantis and the Seven Sacred Temples of the Holy Rishis that healed people through the forces of individual planets and their powers in minerals, plants, animals, human organs, and physiology. The Yogis of Hindu tradition taught a distillation of that ancient wisdom.

The Ancient Indians understood the physical body and its many gifts (sidhas) that can make humans look supernatural. Stories of yogis with great powers abound throughout the Far East. These traditions promise enhanced powers gained through great austerities. Direct communion with higher beings is found at all levels of Indian religious experience.

In Ancient Indian philosophy, the stream of communication with the divine is clear and steady. The *Upanishads* touch on most of the philosophical questions the mind has ever considered. The *Upanishads* were direct and empowering. Crystal clear clairvoyance of many levels of heaven and hell fill these teachings. There is direct contact with divine forces that transform the body through control of the mind via the breath. Concentration, contemplation, meditation, and communion with higher spiritual beings were mapped out in great detail in these traditions. Ritual practices, spiritual rites, communion through sutrayana, mantrayana, vajrayana, and tantrayana led the aspirant to the enlightenment practices of visualizing, invoking, and embodying higher deities. Deity worship pervades the tradition with early accounts of goddess worship as a primary source of the wisdom tradition. Each god has a consort goddess. The ten thousand Buddhas have the female tantric goddess Vajrayogini as their only consort, the embodiment of the Great Goddess of Wisdom.

The philosophy of ancient India is one of dualism that bridges the chasm between the personal self (Atman) and the self of all creation (Brahma) through renunciation and purification of the soul into a vessel created for the union of the all (Brahma) with the higher self of the aspirant (Atman). The physical body is considered the lowest realm of consciousness that darkens the soul's ascent and confuses the aspirant through desire and pleasure. Renunciation resolves this negative attachment and liberates the efforts toward detachment and the understanding of impermanence. The physical world is the lowest form and should be disdained and avoided. Great austerities, fasting, devotions, and spiritual practices produced communication with the being of Christ, who at that time resided on the Sun as the Solar Word of Life. The Hindus referred to Christ as Vishnu in their trinity of gods: Brahma the Creator—Vishnu the Sustainer—Shiva the Destroyer. They also saw Christ as Vishvukarman.

Vishnu pervades all time, space, and consciousness through a series of ten incarnations, from the Flying Boar of Creation, to the Lion-Headed King, to Rama, Krishna, and Gautama Buddha. Vishnu was the "One-Horned Fish" that pulled Manu through the flood to Mount Everest. Vishnu is the eternal Groom of Creation, sustaining divine love for all things. This is the same Solar Deity that Christians refer to as Christ, the Son of God, who was with God the Father and the Sophia the Mother at creation and has descended from heaven to Earth to embrace all creation in the redemption of humanity. Christ had yet to come to the Earth in the ancient Indian epoch, and therefore could not be fully understood at that time in relationship to the future mission of Christ and the Mystery of His passion and resurrection.

The entire course of history is centered on the three years in which Christ embodied Jesus of Nazareth, called the *Mystery of Golgotha* by Rudolf Steiner. Christ's deed of embracing and redeeming the collective karma of humanity and the Earth has transformed all material substance and is now irradiating the etheric realms of the Earth to birth a new star: the *Earth Star* or *Earth Sun*. Christ's light illuminates our hearts, no matter what religion we practice. This revelation of the mission of the Cosmic Christ in our present time was not known to Ancient Indian clairvoyant consciousness.

To answer questions about consciousness, we need a complete cosmology to picture the growth and development of consciousness over time. What the ancients believed and perceived was thoroughly different than what modern humans experience. We can barely have a dim understanding of the ancients' direct experience with the spiritual hierarchy. If we listen to the wisdom of their philosophy, we will know that spirit is always evolving and must be reinterpreted for modern-day consciousness. The philosophy of the Ancient Indians can point us in the right direction when taken in perspective with our changing organs of perception and the new levels of consciousness that have developed since those ancient times. When Ancient Indians experienced the being we now know as Christ, they thought of the Sustainer God, Vishnu, who has been with the Indian people since the beginning of time and will be with them until the end of time.

Literature Selections for Grade Five Students— Ancient India

"Manu and the Flood"
from The Golden Bough by James George Frazer

The great sage Manu, son of Vivasvat, practiced austere fervor. He stood on one leg with upraised arm, looking down unblinkingly, for 10,000 years. While so engaged on the banks of the Chirini, a fish came to him and asked to be saved from larger fish. Manu took the fish to a jar and, as the fish grew, from thence to a large pond, then to the river Ganga, then to the ocean. Though large, the fish was pleasant and easy to carry. Upon being released into the ocean, the fish told Manu that soon all terrestrial objects would be dissolved in the time of the purification. It told him to build a strong ship with a cable attached and to embark with the seven sages (rishis) and certain seeds, and to then watch for the fish, since the waters could not be crossed without it. Manu embarked as enjoined and thought on the fish. The fish, knowing his desire, came, and Manu fastened the ship's cable to its horn. The fish dragged the ship through roiling waters for many years, at last bringing it to the highest peak of Himavat, which is still known as Naubandhana ("the Binding of the Ship"). The fish then revealed itself as Parjapati Brahma and said Manu shall create all living things and all things moving and fixed. Manu performed a great act of austere fervor to clear his uncertainty and then began calling things into existence.

The Laws of Manu **(1500 BC), translated by G. Buhler**

1. The great sages approached Manu, who was seated with a collected mind and, having duly worshipped him, spoke as follows:

2. "Deign, divine one, to declare to us precisely and in due order the sacred laws of each of the (four chief) castes (varna) and of the intermediate ones.

3. "For thou, O Lord, alone knowest the purport, (i.e.) the rites, and the knowledge of the soul, (taught) in this whole ordinance of the Self-existent (Svayambhu), which is unknowable and unfathomable."

4. He, whose power is measureless, being thus asked by the high-minded great sages, duly honored them, and answered, "Listen!"

5. This (universe) existed in the shape of Darkness, unperceived, destitute of distinctive marks, unattainable by reasoning, unknowable, wholly immersed, as it were, in deep sleep.

6. Then the divine Self-existent (Svayambhu, himself) indiscernible, (but) making (all) this, the great elements and the rest, discernible, appeared with irresistible (creative) power, dispelling the darkness.

7. He who can be perceived by the internal organ (alone), who is subtle, indiscernible, and eternal, who contains all created beings and is inconceivable, shone forth of his own (will).

8. He, desiring to produce beings of many kinds from his own body, first with a thought created the waters, and placed his seed in them.

9. That (seed) became a golden egg, in brilliancy equal to the sun; in that (egg) he himself was born as Brahman, the progenitor of the whole world.

10. The waters are called Narah, (for) the waters are, indeed, the offspring of Nara; as they were his first residence (ayana), he thence is named Narayana.

11. From that (first) cause, which is indiscernible, eternal, and both real and unreal, was produced that male (Purusha), who is famed in this world (under the appellation of) Brahman.

12. The divine one resided in that egg during a whole year, then he himself by his thought (alone) divided it into two halves;

13. And out of those two halves he formed heaven and earth, between them the middle sphere, the eight points of the horizon, and the eternal abode of the waters.

14. From himself (Atmanah) he also drew forth the mind, which is both real and unreal, likewise from the mind egoism, which possesses the function of self-consciousness (and is) lordly;

15. Moreover, the great one, the soul, and all (products) affected by the three qualities, and, in their order, the five organs which perceive the objects of sensation.

16. But, joining minute particles even of those six, which possess measureless power, with particles of himself, he created all beings.

17. Because those six (kinds of) minute particles, which form the (creator's) frame, enter (a-sri) these (creatures), therefore the wise call his frame sarira, (the body.)

18. That the great elements enter, together with their functions and the mind, through its minute parts the framer of all beings, the imperishable one.

19. But from minute body (framing) particles of these seven very powerful Purushas springs this (world), the perishable from the imperishable.

20. Among them each succeeding (element) acquires the quality of the preceding one, and whatever place (in the sequence) each of them occupies, even so many qualities it is declared to possess.

The Upanishads, translated by Shree Purohit Swami

Chhandogyopanishad
That Self which is beyond sin, decay, death, sorrow; which requires no food nor drink; which is all accomplished desire, all fulfilled thought; should be looked for, should be inquired after. He gains access to all worlds, has all his desires fulfilled, who, having known this Self, realizes it fully in himself and all.

Kenopanishad
It is the ear of ears, the mind of minds, the speech of speech, the breath of breaths, the eye of eyes. The wise, transcending these and renouncing this world of experience, rest in eternal immortality.

S'vetasvataropanishad
That which, in the beginning, sent forth the Creator and favored him with the storehouse of all knowledge, the Veda; I, desirous of liberation, betake myself to It, the ever-effulgent light, revealing Its eternal Self through the intellect.

Panchadasi
Setting aside every thing which becomes the object of knowledge in this world, there yet remains a residuum, the real essence of knowledge. The knowledge that this is the Real Self, is true knowledge of the Self.

Yogavasishtha
He continually sees the Real Self, who studies to unify philosophy, and the teacher's explanations, with the facts of his own consciousness.

Literature for Grade Five Teachers and Parents— Ancient India

Tagore is one of the most beautiful writers of modern times. He embodies the spirit of India seen through the lens of modern consciousness. The ancient spirit of renunciation is traded for blissful indulgences in the many mansions of the human condition. His poetry and plays define purity of thought, cleansed through the oblations of human suffering and love of the personal, divine creator present in the subtle nuances of every perception that brings joy or sorrow. Consciousness dialogues with itself to gain more consciousness through wakefulness imbued with gratitude. Life has its most profound moment of bliss when the beholder wonders with awe at the beauty of active creation inherent in human awareness and awakened consciousness. For Tagore, the smallest breath of life holds the vast universe in its nature of inhalation and exhalation. Human striving and victory feed the gods, and then the gods feed us in return. We must simply embrace the divine in every moment with gratitude, and then love has a chance to blossom freely in every thought, feeling, or deed.

Tagore gleaned the wisdom of Ancient India and merged it with a modern experience of the Consciousness Soul. He has embodied the spiritual aspects of the etheric nature developed in Ancient India that were based on harmonizing thinking, feeling, and willing. The Masters of Wisdom speak through Tagore's words, harmonizing the feelings and thoughts of the reader. Tagore is a prefiguring of what individuals will be able to attain in the future. He is a *Forerunner*, whose illuminating use of the *Word* brings life to otherwise dead language. His *Imaginations* have independent life and being that connect us to archetypes. He points us towards the right use of inner perceptions, called by Rudolf Steiner *Imaginations*, which are driven by moral force— *Moral Imaginations*. *Imaginations* are much like the living archetypes of the Greeks. Tagore's images of life are filled with creative force, the type of force that myths are made of.

Gitanjali, Rabindranath Tagore

Thou hast made me endless; such is thy pleasure. This frail vessel thou emptiest again and again, and fills it ever with fresh life. Only let me make my life simple and straight, like a flute of reed for thee to fill with music.

I dive down into the depth of the ocean of forms, hoping to gain the perfect pearl of the formless. No more sailing from harbor to harbor with this, my weather-beaten boat. The days are long passed when my sport was to be tossed on waves. And now I am eager to die into the deathless. Into the audience hall by the fathomless abyss where swells up the music of toneless strings, I shall take this harp of my life. I shall tune it to the notes of forever, and, when it has sobbed out its last utterance, lay down my silent harp at the feet of the silent.

Deliverance is not for me in renunciation. I feel the embrace of freedom in a thousand bonds of delight. Thou ever pourest for me the fresh draught of thy wine of various colors and fragrance, filling this earthen vessel to the brim. My world will light its hundred different lamps with thy flame and place them before the altar of thy temple. No, I will never shut the doors of my senses. The delights of sight and hearing and touch will bear thy delight. Yes, all my illusions will burn into illumination of joy, and all my desires ripen into fruits of love.

In desperate hope I go and search for her in all the corners of my room; I find her not. My house is small, but infinite is thy mansion, my lord, and seeking her I have come to thy door. I stand under the golden canopy of thine evening sky and lift my eager eyes to thy face. I have come to the brink of eternity from which nothing can vanish—no hope, no happiness, no vision of a face seen through tears. Oh, dip my emptied life into that ocean, plunge it into the deepest fullness. Let me for once feel that lost sweet touch in the allness of the universe. The world with eyes bent upon thy feet stands in awe with all its silent stars.

Bibliographical References and Recommending Reading
Grade Five—Ancient India

Arnold, Edwin Sir. *The Light of Asia*. CreateSpace Publishing, 2013.

Avari, Burjor. *India: The Ancient Past: A History of the Indian Sub-Continent*. Routledge, New Edition, 2007.

Buhler, George. *The Laws of Manu*. BiblioBazaar, 2009.

Bulfinch, Thomas. *Bulfinch's Mythology: The Classic Introduction to Myth and Legend*. Penguin Group, Tarcher, USA, 2014.

Colum, Padraic. *Great Myths of the World*. Dover Publications, 2005.

Frazer, James George. *Golden Bough*. Wordsworth Collection, 1998.

Harrer, Dorothy. *Ancient History*. Mercury Press, Spring Valley, New York, 1995.

Jukerju, Dhan Gopal. *Rama the Hero of India*. Dutton & Co. New York, 1937.

Krishnamurti, Jiddu. *The Search*. Doni & Liveright, New York, 1927.

Merry, Eleanor. *The Ascent of Man*. Classics of Anthroposophy, Floris Books, 2008.

Mills, Dorothy. *The Book of the Ancient World*. Putnam, New York, 1951.

Purohit, Shree Swami and W. B. Yeats. *The Ten Principal Upanishads*. Macmillan Publishing, New York, 1937.

Ramachandran, R. *Hinduism in the Context of Manusmriti, Vedas and Bhagavat Gita*. Vista Publishing, 2010.

Savitiri. *Tales from Indian Classics*. South Asia Books, 1996.

Schure, Edouard. *The Great Initiates: A Study of the Secret History of Religions*. HarperCollins, 1980.

Seeger, Elizabeth. *The Ramayana*. Dent & Sons, England 1975.

Steiner, Rudolf. *Ancient Myths and the New Isis Mystery*. Rudolf Steiner Press, New York, 1994.

Tagore, Rabindranath. *Gitanjali*. The Macmillan Company, New York, 1913.

Tagore, Rabindranath. *Stories from Tagore*. CreateSpace Publishing, 2013.

Tagore, Rabindranath. *The Home and the World*. ADS, Inc., 2012.

Tagore, Rabindranath. *Sadhana: the Realisation of Life*. CreateSpace Publishing, 2013.

The Spirit of the Upanishads or The Aphorisms of the Wise. The Yogi Publication Society, Chicago, 1936.

Watson, Jane Werner. *Rama of the Golden Age*. Garuard Publishing, Illinois, 1971.

Ancient Persian Cultural Epoch

5067–2907 BC
Gemini, Old Sun, Etheric Body

Having mingled the spark of the Soul with two in unanimity,

Mind and Breath Divine, He added to them a Third, Pure Love,

the august master binding all.

The Chaldean Oracles

The *Chaldean Oracles* are attributed to the great master Zoroaster, the founder of the culture Rudolf Steiner called Ancient Persia. He was also the author of the *Zend Avesta* and the *Gathas*. The *Chaldean Oracles* are the penultimate expression of Ancient Persian philosophy and creationism, somewhat equivalent to the Hindu *Upanishads*. Their similarity is remarkable and obviously stems from a common source. The *Chaldean Book of Genesis* is clearly the source of the Hebrew *Book of Genesis*.

Zoroaster was a student of Manu during one of Manu's incarnations in the Central Asian Mystery Center referred to as the City of Manu. Zoroaster was also a student of Manu on Atlantis and was carrying on a living tradition that went back to the Sun Mystery Center on Atlantis. Zoroaster embodied the highest qualities of a priest-king and ruled Ancient Persian religious, political, social, scientific, and daily life. Zoroaster was the sole source of revelation for the *Gathas*, the *Zend Avesta*, and the cultural folklore that later became caricaturized as the playing cards, chess, checkers, dice, and other forms of divination of chance. Zoroasterians used these oracles as sources of social, political, and agricultural planning.

Many of our modern fruits, vegetables, grains, and domestic animals were crossbred into the standards we still use today by Zoroaster. Zoroaster was the father of agriculture. He used a golden knife given to him by the Sun-God to plow the earth for fertility. Roses were crossbred with other trees into our modern fruits that have the characteristic five-petalled blossom. Lilies were crossbred with the various grasses of the plains, and our modern grains were born. The domestication of cattle, pigs, sheep, chicken, dogs, and cats was attributed to Zoroaster. Many of our modern strains were created through his breeding programs.

Zoroaster, like Manu, had many conscious incarnations wherein he was repeatedly recognized as the priest-king leader of the Ancient Persian culture. Zoroaster had at least six incarnations as the leader of the Ancient Persians. He worked tirelessly to inspire that culture through his continuous revelations of wisdom. He particularly understood the workings of the etheric formative forces in nature—those forces of growth that design our genetic makeup. He was in direct contact with the Solar Logos, the Christ, who was approaching the Earth from His throne on the Sun. Zoroaster directly perceived Christ in the rays of the Sun as they carried the life forces of the Tree of Life, the pure etheric forces of Sound ether and Life ether. These forces inspired Zoroaster to become one of the creative architects of modern civilization.

Ancient Persians believed in the battle between Light and Dark; Ahura Mazdao (Christ) against Angri Manu (Ahriman). Christ had not yet descended into a physical incarnation, and therefore could be seen approaching the Earth as the renewing life-force of the Sun. Zoroaster taught the message of Christ that was appropriate for his time and place. Zoroaster communed with the entire host of angelic hierarchies, and thus also the redeemer of all hierarchies: Christ. This close communion between Zoroaster and Christ becomes the human bond that helps birth the forces of Christ in the body of Jesus of Nazareth. Zoroaster comes again and again to sustain his people, just as Vishnu does in the Hindu myths. Zoroaster is a human who becomes myth, so that a myth can become human in Christ. Mankind is indebted to few humans more than Zoroaster.

In modern times, we see very little understanding of the ancient teachings of Zoroaster. History and myth become blurred when trying to understand the sources of Ancient Persian inspiration. Zoroaster looms like a demagogue on the level of Prometheus, Hermes, Heracles, Orpheus, Theseus, and Pythagoras. It is hard to fathom that one priest-king, Zoroaster, could lead the Ancient Persian people for thousands of years through the Age of Gemini, just as Manu led the Ancient Indian people through the Age of Leo.

It was said of Zoroaster's book, *The Chaldean Oracles*, that it was "unlawful to disbelieve" it. Truth and clarity prevail in these clairvoyant descriptions of the processes of creation and the constitution of the soul and spirit of the tenth hierarchy, humanity. The clear hindsight of Epimetheus and the powerful foresight of Prometheus are found in these writings, which are the crystallization of the ancient oral tradition that originated with Zoroaster and Manu. These ancient traditions are some of the most accurate descriptions of the heavenly worlds and the paths that lead there.

Zoroaster's description of the polar regions and the "wall of color" that stands as guardian to the spiritual world is one of the deepest secrets of any spiritual tradition. He describes the process of offering the higher thoughts, feelings, and deeds of the day to the hierarchy each night as a path of initiation for the aspirant.

The experience of the "etheric Christ" is spoken of by Rudolf Steiner as the second greatest event of Earth's history. The greatest event was Christ's cosmic deed of His passion and resurrection in the Mystery of Golgotha. Christ conquered death and gained eternal life for conscious human beings as the fulfillment of all previous spiritual revelations found in religions, mythologies, and folk-wisdom. The "Mystery of Golgotha" is the "Turning Point of Time" and the meaning and purpose of human spiritual evolution. Zoroaster was the harbinger of the Christ and his closest companion and spirit-bearer (the original St. Christopher, Christ-bearer) in his incarnation at the time of the Mystery of Golgotha.

Zoroaster incarnated as one of the two Jesus boys: one born in a house in Jerusalem, and the other in a manger in Bethlehem, as the Bible tells us. Zoroaster incarnated as the Jesus of Jerusalem, and was visited by the Persian Magi (Zoroastarians) who were awaiting his return. They had followed the Star of Bethlehem to find the reincarnating Zoroaster because Zoroaster's birth was always clearly indicated in the celestial skies. Who was better prepared to be the playmate of Jesus of Nazareth than the one who had prepared for his coming for millennia? Zoroaster knew Christ as Ahura Mazdao, who he had spoken with through the rays of the Sun. It was Zoroaster who later offered his consciousness (developed over many incarnations to be a highly-developed priest-king initiate of humanity) to the growing adolescent Jesus of Nazereth, who would later become the Christ. No two people have ever been closer than Jesus of Nazareth and Jesus of Jerusalem (Zoroaster). These secrets are amongst the most powerful in history and are linked to the ultimate question: "Who was able to witness the Mystery of Golgotha?"

The Chaldea Oracles reveal the awe-inspiring breadth and depth of the author, who seems more divine than human. They are key to understanding the larger questions of spiritual history and the "Turning Point of Time," as Rudolf Steiner calls the passion and resurrection of Jesus Christ. Time and space are not limiting boundaries for the author of *The Chaldean Oracles*, as he tells us about past, present, and future states of consciousness. Clearly, *The Chaldean Oracles* are proof that the author communed with the everlasting and spoke with authorities, powers, and dominions. Even the appearance of Christ's resurrected body in the etheric realm of the earth is clearly described in pictures of the colored aurora-wall around Eden-Reclaimed, or New Jerusalem at the north pole. The path to redeem thinking, feeling, and willing is described in detail by Zoroaster, who continues to be a prophet, king, priest, and leader of humanity's spiritual development.

Literature Selections for Grade Five Children— Ancient Persia

The Chaldean Oracles by Zoroaster

Keep Silence, Thou Who Art Admitted to the Secret Rites!
   There is above the Celestial Lights an Incorruptible Flame always sparkling; the Spring of Life, the Formation of all Beings, the Original of all things! This Flame produces all things, and nothing dies that is not reborn in It. It makes Itself known by Itself. This Fire cannot be contained in any place, it is without body and without matter. It encompasses the Heavens and there goes out from it little Sparks, which make all the Fires of the Sun, of the Moon, and of the Stars. Behold! What I know of God! All is full of God, and God is in all!
   There is in God an Immense Profundity of Flame! Nevertheless, the Heart should not fear to approach this Adorable Fire, or to be touched by it; it will never be consumed by this sweet Fire, whose mild and Tranquil Heat makes the Binding, the Harmony, and the Duration of the World.
   Between the Fathers the center of Hecate is whirled. The Vivific Intellectual Deity—Hecate, Cybele, or Rhea—receives into Her bosom the Demiurgic power of the First Intellect and is said to pour this forth into the Second Intellect. She is the middle center of the Paternal Intellectual Triad.
   Hecate is the fount and river of the Blessed Intellectual Natures. For having first received the potentialities of all things in Her ineffable bosom, She pours forth upon each perpetual generation. From about the hollows beneath the ribs of Her right side there bursts in mighty fullness a fountain of Primordial Soul, animating to the uttermost light, fire, ether, worlds. In the left side of Hecate there is a Fountain of Virtue, remaining wholly within, not sending forth its virginity. And about the shoulders of the Goddess, vast Nature hangs. In accordance with the Purpose of the Father, I, the Soul, dwell, animating all things with heat.

The Triple Sun is the Light of the Divine Intellect, which is hidden, as it were, in the heart of the Great World Mother as well as in the deeps of the Soul.

Love, therefore, supernally descends from the Intelligibles into mundane natures, calling all things upward to Divine Beauty. Truth proceeds through all things, illuminating them all with Knowledge; and Faith proceeds through the universe, establishing all things united in the Good.

For that Fire, which is First Beyond, shut not His own Power in matter by actions, but by Mind. For the Mind of Mind is the Artificer of the Fiery Cosmos.

The Fire of the Demiurgus is the creator of wholes, that is, He makes the Cosmos manifest as one great unity; all differentiation and particularization being the work of other powers.

By the bond of wondrous Love, who first leapt forth from Intellect, clothing Himself with the Fire with which He is bound, that He might mingle the ever-welling vessels, pouring on to them the Flower of His own Fire.

For from Him leap forth the Amiliktoi and the thunderings and the whirlwind-receiving vortices of the all-gleaming radiance of Father-begotten Hecate; and the Flower of the Fire, and the mighty breath beyond the fiery poles. The Empyrean Realm is surrounded by a Fiery Wall, which, as it were, separates the Seen from the Unseen, the Apparent from the Unapparent, the Manifested from the Unmanifested. This Fiery Wall is called Oceanus, who is the Mysterious Boundary of Limit who separates the Above from the Below. And through Oceanus, the potentialities of all souls are to be made actual as they blossom into the Flower of the Creative Fire and pierce the Mystic Borders of Eternity, at the Pyramid of Creation and the Summit of Everlastingness.

By the Power of the Father is Soul a radiant fire that both remains immortal and is Mistress of Life, and hath, power to fill with plenitude the many wombs of the cosmos. Souls dwell on high in union with the Father living a supernal life according to Divine Providence and transcending the limitations imposed by the laws of Fate; but when Souls descend into manifestation, although these laws are announced to them by the Father, they drink of the waters of forgetfulness, and lose temporarily the memory of their pristine purity and bliss.

Having mingled the spark of the Soul with two in unanimity, Mind and Breath Divine, He added to them a Third, Pure Love, the august master binding all. The blending of these three unities in the Soul give to it, throughout all its trials, an unquenchable thirst for beauty, an irresistible tendency towards goodness, and an inextinguishable yearning for truth.

The eternal orders are the courts and dwelling-places of the Gods, and the paternal order is the all-receiving abode of the Father, which receives and unites all the souls that are born upwards. But the order of the Angels leads up the Soul in a certain manner, appearing about the Soul, that is, shining upon Her from every side and causing Her to be full of pure fire, thereby imparting to Her a stable order and power, through which She is not hurled forth into the disorder of mater, but is united to the light of the Gods; this moreover holds Her in Her native home and makes Her to be unmixed with matter, lightening Her with the warmth of the spirit, and raising Her on high through spiritual life. For the warmth of the spirit is participation in life; and all that hastens to the regions above is lightened, just as that which verges to matter becomes heavy. But the end of such ascents is the enjoyment of divine fruits and the filling of Her up with self-radiant fire, and this is the contemplation of God, since it places Her before the eyes of the Father.

And the Soul being perfected breaks forth into hymns about divine things having before Her the offering to the Father, the ineffable symbols which the Father places in Her in the first going-forth of being. For such are the noetic and invisible hymns of the ascending Soul, which arouse in Her the memory of the harmonious words (logoi), which bear inexpressible images of the divine powers which are in Her.

The root of evil is the body, just as that of virtue is the mind. For virtue blossoms out for Souls from above, but evil forces its way in from worse natures below. But to hurl evil down to earth is to cut it out of ourselves, and enable the Soul to ascend to Her native order.

For we are not mind alone; but reason and opinion and attention and freewill, and, prior to these faculties, an essence both one and manifold.

The Soul, performing when the channels are mingled, can create works of imperishable fire. When the soul is united consciously with this Spiritual Sun then it is at one with the Integral Divine Light from which nothing is hidden, either on earth or in heaven. The Soul is a unity of essence, power, and energy.

Hence, the Way of Return is to be found first within the deeps of the Soul where the seal or word of divinity is concealed, and by the interpretation of which the Soul enkindles the light of divine ideas which makes plain the pathway of the Great Ascent to the Holy Paradise of True Piety where Virtue, Wisdom, and Good Law together dwell. Let the immortal depth of the Soul lead thee, and open all thine eyes earnestly to the Above.

Seek Paradise, and the Choir of Angels leads up the Soul in a certain manner, appearing about the Soul and causing Her to be full of pure fire, thereby imparting to Her stable order and power. Then the Soul breaks forth in hymns about divine things. Alive in power She runs as an Angel in the Angelic regions lightening Her with the warmth of the spirit. Clad in the full armor of the strength of the Sounding Light, arming both mind and soul with three-barbed might, thou must set in thy heart the whole symbol of the Triad, nor wander dispersedly on the fiery ways, but advance with steadfast tread. For truly Thou art fully-armed and arrayed for battle like unto the Goddess. Her shield is the untamed and uninclining power of reason, but the spear is that power which severs matter's hold and liberates the Soul from fatal passions.

Urge thyself towards the center of the Sounding Light, the Choir of Muses, the harmony of exultant light. Call forth the mystery names of the Gods. Then, the souls of those who have speech will clasp God to Herself: having nothing mortal She is wholly intoxicated with God.

Fire-warmed conception has the first rank in sacred worship. In the second place, there is required a conformation of our life with that which is divine, accompanied by all purity, discipline, and order, through which, our concerns being introduced to the Gods, we shall invite Their beneficence and our Souls will become subject to Them; in the third place, contact or communion is necessary, according to which we touch the divine essence with the summit of our Soul and merge into a union with it. Then the mortal who approaches the Fire shall have light from God. Then the converted Soul finds symbols of the Gods in all things—even the smallest—and through these renders everything familiar and allied to the Gods.

But when Thou shalt behold a Sacred Fire without form shining with leaping flashes through the depths of the whole cosmos, Hear the Voice of the Fire.

The Soul, being a brilliant Fire, by the power of the Father remains immortal, and is Mistress of Life, and fills up the many recesses of the bosom of the World.

The Soul does in a manner clasp God to Herself. Having nothing mortal, she is wholly inebriated with God. For she glories in the harmony under which the mortal body subsists.

For the Paternal Self-Begotten Mind, understanding His works sowed in all, the fiery bonds of love, that all things might continue loving for an infinite time. That the connected series of things might intellectually remain in the Light of the Father; that the elements of the World might continue their course in mutual attraction.

For the Goddess brings forth the Vast Sun, and the lucent Moon. She collects it, receiving the Melody of Ether, and of the Sun, and of the Moon, and of whatsoever things are contained in the Air.

Let fiery hope nourish you upon the Angelic plane. The conception of the glowing Fire has the first rank, for the mortal who approaches that Fire shall have Light from God; and unto the persevering mortal the Blessed Immortals are swift.

The Gatha of the Mystery-Marriage by D. J. van Bemmelen

The greatest good, that is known, is that from Zarathustra,
    That was bestowed upon him
As a blessing through Asha, O Ahura Mazda, for an eternal
    and blissful life,

And also for all those who practice and observe his good
  message, words and deeds.
Therefore, shall they strive in thought, word and deed to honor
  him to His satisfaction, through homage to Mazdah,
To maintain the straight path of the Mystery which Ahura has
  founded for the Savior.
To him do Ye give in marriage Pourucista, youngest daughter
  of Zarathustra
In order to put in hand together the renovation of the land
  for the holy Earth Mother Armaiti.
Instruction will thou be given, O bridemaiden, and also ye
  witness
Through the Mystery-teaching, that ye may note,
Receive the knowledge of the living Vohumanah into your
  Soul-Beings.
Each one vies with the other in the rite of Asha for meritorious
  spiritual life.

Zarathustra's Third Gatha **by D. J. van Bemmelen**

And now shall I proclaim to you, who are drawing near,
      the knowledge of the mystery,
With the hymns of Ahura, with the prayers to Vohumanah
      and with the inspired songs to Asha,
Who may be seen in the radiant stars of heaven.
Harken with open ears, see with enlightened eyes
Make your choice between the two, man for man, each for
  himself
Before the last judgement, that it may be favorable for us.
Thus the primeval spirits, who as twins have been
Revealed to the awakened consciousness of sleep,
Are the good and the evil in thought, speech and deed.
Between these two the enlightened have chosen aright
      and the unenlightened have not.
When the two spirits came together in the beginning
      to make life and absence of life,

Then they apportioned to the wicked the most evil existence
    and to the followers of Asha the perfect existence.
May we belong to those, who renew the world and make it to
    progress.
O Ye Sun-spirits, Ahura Mazda, come to us Thy allies with
    Asha
So that the good thought will be united in us with the
    clairvoyance.

Literature for Grade Five Teachers and Parents— Ancient Persia

Commentary on the Persian Cultural Epoch

We can find the mood of soul of *The Chaldean Oracles* reflected in the love poems of the Persians found in the Dabistan and the Demetre. In later times, the teachings of Sufism continued the traditions of Ancient Persia. The Sufi esoteric society merged teachings from India, Persia, Chaldea, and other Mesopotamian cultures with ecstatic practices of tantra to create cults that would later be called Magi, Theurgists, Parsi, Mandeans, Chaldees, and many other names. In the end, Sufism was absorbed as an unconscious esoteric sect deep within Islam. These ancient roots have led Chaldean Christians to believe that they were the first to receive the transmission of Jesus Christ and therefore found a papal seat in Armenia. These traditions were also active sources of clairvoyant revelations that have great value and application, even in modern times. Manicheans have merged Eastern wisdom with Christianity and presented the modern conscious spiritual dilemma as a dualistic battle between good and evil, light and dark, just as Zoroaster did thousands of years before.

    The great Sufi poet Rumi has given modern humans the path of ecstasy and indulgence in the bliss of spiritual light. His words are like moral forces that reveal the stark contrasts of life and the existential challenges of struggling human consciousness. Rumi can take us to places where spiritual beings inhabit our Earth experience as nourishment like the cherished ambrosia of the gods. The *All* is contained in the small, like human sense perception and its reflection of God's creative forces. The divine becomes as close as the scent of a flower or the saltiness of a tear. To identify with the divine, we become the divine. Humans are divine when the gods perceive through us with our eyes wide open.

Daylight by **Rumi**

Of all the things to know, the best preparation and provision on the day of death is the knowledge of spiritual poverty.

If you are wholly perplexed and in straits, have patience, for patience is the key to joy.

Fasting is the first principle of medicine; fast, and behold the strength of the spirit.

If you are irritated by every rub, how will your mirror be polished?

What does it mean to learn the knowledge of God's Unity? To consume yourself in the presence of the One. If you wish to shine like day, burn up the night of self-existence. Dissolve in the Being who is everything. You grabbed hold of "I" and "we," and this dualism is your ruin.

Every prophet and every saint has a way, but all lead to God. All ways are really one.

O God, reveal to the soul that place where speech has no letters, so that the pure soul might go headlong towards the expanse of nonexistence out of which we are fed.

The cause of narrow mindedness is multiplicity: the senses are drawn in many directions. Know that the world of unification lies beyond sense: if you want unity, march in that direction.

Stir a little like the fetus that you may be given the senses to behold the light.

Everyone is a child except the one who's intoxicated with God. No one is an adult except the one who is free from desire.

Those with mirror-like hearts do not depend on fragrance and color: they behold Beauty in the moment. They've cracked open the shell of knowledge and raised the banner of the eye of certainty. Thought is gone in a flash of light.

The body, like a mother, is pregnant with the spirit-child: death is the labor of birth. All the spirits who have passed over are waiting to see how that proud spirit shall be born.

If the heart is restored to health, and purged of sensuality, then The Merciful God is seated on the Throne. After this, He guides the heart directly, since the heart is with Him.

Fiery lust is not diminished by indulging it but inevitably by leaving it ungratified. As long as you are laying logs on the fire, the fire will burn. When you withhold the wood, the fire dies, and God carries the water.

When the mirror of your heart becomes clear and pure, you'll behold images which are outside this world. You will see the image and the image-Maker, both the carpet of the spiritual expanse and the One who spreads it.

What do you really possess, and what have you gained? What pearls have you brought up from the depth of the sea? On the day of death, bodily senses will vanish: do you have the spiritual light to accompany your heart? When dust fills these eyes in the grave, will your grave shine bright?

By a single thought that comes into the mind, in one moment a hundred worlds are overturned.

The faithful one is a fountain of mercy: the pure spirit of the well-doer is the water of life.

The ocean of the body crashes against the ocean of the heart. Between them is a barrier they cannot cross.

My soul is a furnace happy with the fire. Love, too, is a furnace, and ego its fuel.

It is the nature of Reason to see to the End; it is the nature of desire not to.

The beginning of pride and hatred lies in worldly desire.

Bibliographical References and Recommending Reading

Grade Five—Ancient Persia

Aude, Sapre. *The Chaldean Oracles of Zoroaster*. Occult Research Press, New York.

Bemmelen, D.J. van. *Zarathustras' Gathas with Introduction*. Uitgeverij Vrij Geestesleven, The Netherlands, 1968.

Bryson, Bernard. *Gilgamesh*. Holt, Rinehart & Winston, New York.

Heidal, Alexander. *The Babylonian Genesis: The Story of Creation*. University of Chicago Press, 1963.

Mead, G.R.S. *The Chaldean Oracles*. The Theosophical Publishing Society, London, 1908.

Nanavutty, Piloo. *The Gathas of Zarathustra: Hymns in Praise of Wisdom*. Mapin Publishing, 2006.

Rumi, Jalalu'l-Din. *Selected Poems of Rumi*. Dover Thrift Edition, 2011.

Sandars, N.K. *The Epic of Gilgamesh*. Penguin, New Impressions, 1973.

Shea, David. *The Dabistan*. Kessinger Publishing, 2006.

Unknown. *Firdausi, The Epics of Kings: Hero Tales of Ancient Persia*. EbooksLib, 2005.

The Egyptian/Chaldean/ Babylonian Cultural Epoch

2907–747 BC
Taurus, Old Moon, Sentient Soul/Astral Body

For the modern thinker, ancient Persia is very distant in experience. We cannot imagine living in a culture led by a semi-divine being who speaks directly with the forces of nature and can then manipulate them like Zoroaster did. This type of direct communication with higher beings was typical of all cultures on the Earth at that time. The shamanistic priest-king created a divine city plan that reflected a divine nature. The architecture of temples reflected the understanding of the heavens and the higher hierarchies and embodied those active spiritual realms. "As above, so below" was the watchword of the Egyptian mysteries, where the secrets of nature lay hidden behind the veils of Isis, the goddess of nature and wisdom. "I am Isis; no man hath lifted my veil and lived," was the inscription at the Temple of Sais. But one Egyptian did lift the veil of nature and philosophy and wrote the sacred textbooks of Egyptian life; he was known as Hermes. Again, like the incarnations of Zoroaster, there were numerous incarnations of Hermes. He gave out the core of Egyptian priest-lore, philosophy, and divine dogma that ruled Egypt for centuries. The power of the priest-king was tantamount to divinity.

Through the indications of Rudolf Steiner, we know that the being of Hermes Trismegistus used the perfected astral body of Zoroaster. In this manifestation of the spirit of Zoroaster, Hermes developed the astral body to the point of perfection and used the perfected vehicle of Zoroaster (Zarathustra) to understand the stars and the great rhythms of time as they affected mankind. Hermes laid down the spiritual and temporal laws of the land, just as Zoroaster and Manu had done before him. Spiritual powers in this world and the next inspired Hermes.

We can see the perfected astral body of Zoroaster develop more fully through the *star teachings* of Hermes's Egyptian wisdom, which began to wrestle with the impulses of physical, material concerns. A strong need to build the bridge to the starry realms was aided by focused preparations of the physical body for the journey into the afterlife. The normal Egyptian had lost direct contact with the divine, so the Egyptian hierophant had to initiate the prepared candidate for wisdom. In the inner chamber of the pyramid, the candidate was led through the realms of the stars (astral) with the help of twelve hierophants representing the twelve zodiacal forces raying into the body of the candidate lying in a death-trance in the sepulchre (coffin).

The gods and goddesses of the Egyptians found the stars embodied the heavenly virtues for the Egyptians and gave them models to emulate. Hermes was known as both divine and human, just as in Ur, King Gilgamesh was both god and human. Hermes communed with the gods, while Gilgamesh wrestled with and killed gods. The Egyptian Osiris was Father of All and yet was killed by his brother, Seth. Osiris, the Sun God, then became the God of the Underworld, and his son Horus became king of all. Osiris and Isis gave birth to Horus, who then became greater than either parent. Horus, the inspirer of Pharaohs, ruled the land for centuries through the prescribed laws of Hermes, the High Priest of Egypt. Hermes, a human, pronounced the words of the divine gods who spoke through him. Hermes was the bridge to the divine lands beyond the stars and beyond death.

The Sun-Wisdom of Egypt stood in contrast to the Moon-Wisdom of Sumeria, Chaldea, Akkadia, Babylonia, and the other cultures of the Near East. The great hieroglyphs of the Egyptians are still mysteries to be decoded, whereas, the phonetic alphabet of the Akkadians and Hebrews led modern humanity into exploration, trade, and commerce. The picture language of Hermes evolved into the written phonetic language of the Hebrews, who were forbidden from making any pictures of the divine. We can see the great atavistic clairvoyance of the past turning into the clear, materialistic thinking of our age during this epoch. This can be seen in the development of the Hebrew people, who were both independent from Egypt and a key part of Egyptian history.

Moses was an Egyptian who married Deporah, daughter of Jethro, a priest of Babylon. Moses was raised as a prince of Egypt, and he suffered the burdens of a Jewish slave. He had access to the Egyptian temples and priesthood, and yet found the *One God* in a burning bush, from which he made a staff that had magical powers over nature. Moses knew God and witnessed Him carving the Ten Commandments on stone tablets. Moses built the Ark of the Covenant and led the Hebrews with many miracles and wondrous signs. His religion was close and personal, while the religion of Hermes was distant and impersonal. Moses took the next step in human development to bring the divine closer to the soul of humanity.

Moses mastered the etheric body and used the perfected etheric body of Zarathustra that is preserved in the etheric sheath of the earth: New Jerusalem or Shamballa. Hermes mastered the stars—the astral realm of time found in the human astral body. Moses used the perfected etheric body of Zarathustra found in the etheric realm of "spiritual economy," an etheric ring or sheath around earth. These perfected etheric and astral bodies of Zarathustra can be replicated for the use of any person who needs to embody that archetype. Hermes and Moses' use of replicated astral and etheric bodies of Zoroaster are significant steps in the development of humanity as a whole.

Zoroaster was a student of Manu, both on Atlantis and again in the Central Asian Mystery Initiation Center. Under the tutelage of Manu in the Sun Mystery Temple of Atlantis, Zoroaster was shown the seven mysteries and their dominions. The Seven Holy Rishis focused the planetary forces through the Sun Mystery Temple and the surrounding Heavenly City. These plans of a "heavenly city" are used throughout Aryan sun-based religions. The Holy City Four-Square is used as the basis of city planning by the Harappian, Trochaian, Persian, Sumerian, Babylonian, Chaldean, and Anatolian cultures. The city centers around the main Sun Temple and the elaborate system of canals surrounding it. Water flows out in four directions from the Sun Temple and surrounds the magnificent crystalline structure of the city. There are Harappian cities in the Indus Valley that housed over 10,000 inhabitants in multi-story structures, complete with plumbing and lighting throughout. These cities are now being found to be as much as 10,000 years old, with highly developed architectural plans. These plans of the heavenly city of the priest-kings came from the same source: Manu, and the traditions he developed and disseminated after the sinking of Atlantis. Indian, Persian, Sumerian, Egyptian, Chaldean, and Babylonian mythologies are very similar and originate from a time of Edenic peace before the Atlantean Flood. In light of the many cross-migrations that have happened since 10,500 B.C., mythologies tend to agree that spiritual revelation lay in the hands of priest-kings who led their people through the cultural development that their folk-tribe-nation had to offer as an advancement of general cultural evolution.

The individual's needs were secondary to the city-state-kingdom; that is, until Moses led the Hebrews out of slavery into independence in the deserts of Arabia. Was Moses a priest-king? Moses needed his brother Aaron's help to rule the Hebrew tribes. Moses had the staff, and Aaron had the rod. Moses, like Hermes and Zoroaster before him, had a direct revelation of God. The Hebrew people had faith in his faith. Again and again, Moses had to demonstrate signs and wonders to the Hebrew people to keep their faith alive and focused on the One God, but even a direct connection to God didn't earn Moses the reward of entering the land of milk and honey. Moses died before he could receive his physical reward, preparing him for the next incarnation, in which he would complete his task of helping his people see heaven on earth.

Moses laid out the Holy Books (Pentateuch) and the laws for the people to follow. He wrote the doctrine and acted as judge, prophet, and leader. The Sun and Star Wisdom of Egypt's astral-vision was mixed by Moses with the etheric Moon Wisdom of Mesopotamia, and a new type of human was born: an independent thinker inspired by the forces of nature's etheric and astral mysteries. Moses had the power to embody the forces of God and nature and to speak for God to an entire nation. Miracle after miracle strengthened Moses into the penultimate man of faith. Finding mana in the wilderness, striking water from desert rocks, and the trials of forty years in the dessert tempered Moses into a true Son of God—a witness of the divine.

The next two selections show the contrast between Hermes and Moses. Both are similar in nature but focused in different ways to bring forth new gifts to their culture. We could say that the cultural seeds of Manu took root in his student Zoroaster, who planted them anew in the cultural development of Egypt and the Hebrews. Hermes and Moses advanced their cultures in the development of modern human thinking. Hermes received the messages from on high and brought them to the Egyptian people, who were pleased to live their lives accordingly. Moses wrestled with the people of Judah to turn them again and again to the One God. Moses took on a physical task that Hermes did not; Hermes tamed the dragon of the Nile, but Moses parted the Red Sea and brought down the plagues on Egypt to win freedom for his people. Both were conduits to the divine and messengers of the spiritual hierarchies.

Literature Selections for Grade Five Children— Egyptian/Chaldean/ Babylonian

Egyptian Isis Poem (**3000 BC**)

I gave and ordained laws for men, which no one is able to change.
I am she that is called goddess by women.
I divided the earth from the heaven.
I showed the paths of the stars.
I ordered the course of the sun and the moon.
I devised business in the sea.
I made strong the right.
I brought together women and men.
I appointed to women to bring their infants to birth in the tenth month.
I ordained that parents should be loved by children.
I laid punishment upon those disposed without natural affection towards their parents.
I made with my brother Osiris an end to the eating of men.
I revealed mysteries unto men.
I taught men to honor images of the gods.
I made right to be stronger than gold and silver.
I ordained that the true should be thought good.
I am the Queen of rivers and winds and sea.
No one is held in honor without my knowing it.
I am the Queen of war.
I am the Queen of the thunderbolt.
I stir up the sea and I calm it.
I am in the rays of the sun.
I set free those in bonds.
I overcome Fate.

An Ancient Egyptian Inscription

Look to this day,
For it is life,
The very life of life,
In its brief course lie all,
The realities and truths of existence,
The joy of growth,
The splendor of action,
The glory of power;
For yesterday is but a memory,
And tomorrow is only a vision,
But today well-lived,
Makes every yesterday a memory of happiness,
And every tomorrow a vision of hope,
Look well therefore to this day.

The *Poimandres* of Hermes Trismegistus

Once upon a time, when I had begun to think about the things that are, and my thoughts had soared high aloft, while my bodily senses had been put under restraint by sleep, yet not such sleep as that of men weighed down by fullness of food or by bodily weariness, methought there came to me a Being of vast and boundless magnitude, who called me by name, and said to me:

"What do you wish to hear and see, and to learn and come to know by thought?"

"Who are you?" I said.

"I," said he, "am Poimandres, the Mind of the Sovereignty."

"I would fain learn," said I, "the things that are, and understand their nature, and get knowledge of God. These are the things of which I wish to hear."

He answered, "I know what you wish, for indeed I am with you everywhere; keep in mind all that you desire to learn, and I will teach you."

When he had thus spoken, forthwith all things changed in aspect before me, and were opened out in a moment. And I beheld a boundless view; all was changed into light, a mild and joyous light; and I marveled when I saw it. And in a little while, there had come to be in one part a downward-tending darkness, terrible and grim. And thereafter I saw the darkness changing into a watery substance, which was unspeakably tossed about, and gave forth smoke as from fire; and I heard it making an indescribable sound of lamentation; for there was sent forth from it an inarticulate cry. But from the Light there came forth a holy Word, which took its stand upon the watery substance; and methought this Word was the voice of the Light.

And Poimandres spoke for me to hear, and said to me, "Do you understand the meaning of what you have seen?"

"Tell me its meaning," I said, "and I shall know."

"That Light," he said, "is I, even Mind, the first God, who was before the watery substance which appeared out of the darkness; and the Word which came forth from the Light is son of God."

"How so?" said I.

"Learn my meaning," said he, "by looking at what you yourself have in you; for in you too, the word is son, and the mind is father of the word. They are not separate one from the other; for life is the union of word and mind."

Said I, "For this I thank you."

"Now fix your thought upon the Light," he said, "and learn to know it."

And when he had thus spoke, he gazed long upon me, eye to eye, so that I trembled at his aspect. And when I raised my head again, I saw in my mind that the Light consisted of innumerable Powers, and had come to be an ordered world but a world without bounds. This I perceived in thought, seeing it by reason of the words which Poimandres had spoken to me.

And when I was amazed, he spoke again, and said to me, "You have seen in your mind the archetypal form, which is prior to the beginning of things, and is limitless." Thus spoke Poimandres to me.

Ishtar Poem (**2000 BC**)

Praise to the Goddess, most awesome of goddesses
She is clothed with pleasure and love
She is laden with vitality, charm and voluptuousness
The goddess—with her counsel
The fate of everything she holds in her hand
At her glance is created joy
Power, magnificence the protecting deity, and the guardian spirit.

The Chaldean Oracles (**720 BC**)

The Triple Sun is the Light of the Divine Intellect,
Which is hidden, as it were,
In the heart of the Great World Mother
As well as in the deeps of the Soul.

To the Mother of the Gods, **Orphic Hymn** (**600 BC**)

Divinely honored, mother of the deathless gods, nurse of all.
Look in our direction; accomplishing Goddess, thou Lady, be
    with us.
Your fast-running chariot is drawn by bull-killing lions.
You carry the scepter of command,
The famous axis of the sky, thou, many named, majestic.
Your throne is in the center of the world, and therefore,
Yours is the earth, gently granting nourishment to mortals.
From you the race of immortals and mortals poured out.
From you grew mighty rivers and all the oceans.
Once you were called Hestia, now we name you Giver of
    Prosperity.
Because you graciously provide all good things to mortals.
Attend our Mysteries, Lady who loves the drumbeat.
All subduer, Phrygian, Savior, Bedfellow of time.
Celestial, ancient, life-gathering, frenzy loving.
Come in joy, Agreeable one, to our holy celebrations.

Literature for Grade Five Teachers and Parents— Egyptian/Chaldean/ Babylonian

Timaeus, Plato (423-348 BC)

But soul, being interwoven everywhere to the uttermost bounds of the universe, and enfolded round it externally in a circle, and herself revolving within herself, gave rise to the divine beginning of an unceasing and wise life throughout all time. And, indeed, the body of the universe was created visible; but she (the soul) invisible, participating in reason and harmony, and the most excellent of the created things, being made by Him Who is of Intelligible and Eternal Beings the most excellent.

The soul descends either by the will of the Intelligibles or by losing its wings, which allow it to rise to the perception of the Intelligibles. The souls that descend through losing their wings are those that are not yet perfected and cannot therefore sustain the flight to the Intelligibles.

The natural power of a wing is to raise up on high that which is heavy, and bring it to that place where the race of the Gods dwell; and indeed among the parts of the body wings share most in the divine nature. But that which is divine is beautiful, wise and good, and has every similar perfection. It is by such things, then, that the growth of the soul's wings is chiefly nourished and increased, but through the opposites of these, the base and the evil, the wing languishes and is destroyed.

Love therefore is the "fire-laden bond" which connects all things, and gives to the soul the wings by which she may mount to the contemplation of the Beautiful and thereby attain to union with the Good.

Since, therefore, every artist is a lover, and since the highest of all arts and that for which all others exist is the Art of the Perfect Life by which the soul is restored and enabled to ascend to Reality and to God, he that loves the souls of his fellow-men and leads them, by whatever path, by his paintings, his music, his laws, his discourse or his philosophy, along the way that leads to the heights, will be the greatest artist, for he will both himself attain to initiation into the most perfect Mysteries and will confer like a blessing upon those he loves.

The Transformations of Lucius, Apuleius (125-180 AD)

"I am Nature, the universal Mother, mistress of all the elements, primordial child of time, sovereign of all things spiritual, queen of the dead, queen also of the immortals, the single manifestation of all gods and goddesses that are. My nod governs the shining heights of Heaven, the wholesome sea breezes, the lamentable silences of the world below. Though I am worshipped in many aspects, known by countless names, and propitiated with all manner of different rites, yet the whole round earth venerates me."

I fell prostrate at the Goddess's feet, and washed them with my tears as I prayed to her in a voice choked with sobs: "Holiest of the Holy, perpetual comfort of mankind, you whose bountiful grace nourishes the whole world; whose heart turns towards all those in sorrow and tribulation as a mother's to her children; you who take no rest by night, no rest by day, but are always at hand to succor the distressed by land and sea, dispersing the gales that beat upon them. Your hand alone can disentangle the hopelessly knotted skeins of fate, terminate every spell of bad weather, and restrain the stars from harmful conjunction. The gods above adore you, the gods below do homage to you, you set the orb of heaven spinning around the poles, you give light to the sun, you govern the universe, you trample down the powers of Hell. At your voice the stars move, the seasons recur, the spirits of earth rejoice, the elements obey. At your nod the winds blow, clouds drop wholesome rain upon the earth, seeds quicken, buds swell. Birds that fly through the air, beasts that prowl on the mountain, serpents that lurk in the dust, all these tremble in awe of you. I will keep your divine countenance always before my eyes and the secret knowledge of your divinity locked deep in my heart."

Bibliographical References and Recommending Reading

Grade Five—Egyptian/Chaldean/Babylonian

Abd, Ruwaida. *Ishtar*. Xlibris, Amazon Digital Services, Inc., 2012.

Carroll, Mark. *Wisdom of Solomon*. Lulu, Amazon Digital Services, Inc., 2014.

Hermes. *Corpus Hermeticum*. Translated by G. Mead. Amazon Digital Services, Inc., 2010.

Kenney, E. J. *The Golden Ass by Apuleius*. Penguin Classics, New York, 1999.

Orpheus. *The Hymns of Orpheus*. Forgotten Books, 2007.

Plato. *Timaeus*. Translated by Peter Kalkavage. Focus Publishing, ADS Inc., 2012.

Snaith, John G. *Ecclesiasticus or the Wisdom of Jesus, Son of Sirach*. Cambridge Bible Commentaries on the Apocrypha, 1974.

Greco-Roman Cultural Epoch

747 BC–1415 AD
Aries, Greco-Roman, Earth, Intellectual Soul

In the beginning was the Word, and the Word was with God, and the Word was God. The same was in the beginning with God. All things were made by him; and without him was not any thing made that was made. In him was life; and the life was the light of men. And the light shineth in darkness; and the darkness comprehended it not. And the Word was made flesh, and dwelt among us, and we beheld his glory, the glory as of the only begotten of the Father, full of grace and truth.

The Gospel of John

The Greco-Roman Cultural Epoch was inculcated from the north with Indo-Aryan influences that emanated from the Central Asian mystery initiation center of Manu. Around Athens, there were seven mystery centers that each had a relationship to one of the seven planetary temples of Atlantis. Athens became the new Sun Temple, with the six planetary temples surrounding it. Dodona, Eleusis, Samothrace, Delphi, Olympia, Castalia, and the Greek Dramas and Bacchian Rites comprise seven planetary mystery initiation centers that surrounded Athens, which was the center of the Great Goddess mysteries subsumed from the

Minoan culture. The Acropolis, where the triple goddess Pallas-Athena-Nike lived, arose from the divine city plan of Manu.

Greece was the home of the individual who lived for his city (polis) and the gods and goddesses associated with that city. In Greece, the true individual thinker (philosopher) was born. Greek philosophy, art, warfare, politics, and architecture reached a golden age that embodied the Intellectual Soul nature of humanity. Aristotle, Socrates, Plato, and the other philosophers were the pinnacle of the free human beings questing for the true, the beautiful, and the good. A true turning point in history happened in the Greek/Roman world of Israel that would show that humanity was ready to stand independently as free, self-conscious, creative thinkers who can define the cosmos around himself; "Oh man, know thyself, and you will know the gods and the world" was the Greek Mystery temple injunction.

Christ incarnated in Israel, and the birth of the thinking ego was accomplished. The Israelites had been prepared for centuries to develop thinking that could understand nature around them and find their place among the mundane and the divine. Christ was the first harbinger of what would become an everlasting burgeoning of "Christened Thinkers" acting for the good through the Holy Spirit. This is consummated through the central event of evolution, the "Turning Point of Time," the "Mystery of Golgotha"—the life, death, and resurrection of Jesus Christ. This reality makes the Greco-Roman epoch the most important epoch of all.

The unusual thing about this epoch is that only a few people were developed enough at the time to understand what had happened through the cosmic gifts and Earthly sacrifices of Christ. Very few beings in this world, or the spiritual world, could witness the power of these events. These select few knew that the Earth had been redeemed for all time, that evil had been conquered, and that humanity had been saved from the brink of ruin by the Lord of Karma who came to judge and forgive mankind. These realities will only come to be understood in the distant future. At this time, they are still open mysteries that are unfolding. Some select aspirants do understand the Mystery of Christ and His connection to human spiritual development. Christ has conquered death for all humanity with his physical sacrifice, and now the Earth can become a star and humans can grow into angels. Christ's physical body has penetrated the physical earth and redeemed it. Christ's etheric body is resurrected and is available to all who can behold it and receive its grace and blessings in the etheric realm. Christ's etheric body is the Holy Grail and is there to feed and strengthen aspirants who can "take wing" and rise into the etheric realm. This message of the Greco-Roman Epoch is planted in the East (Jerusalem), but blossoms in the West through esoteric Christianity's moral spiritual development.

Just as Zarathustra had perfected his astral and etheric bodies and placed them in the Realm of Spiritual Economy, the etheric ring around the earth, so, too, Jesus of Nazareth perfected all human bodies/vehicles and placed them in this realm of New Jerusalem. These perfected vehicles can now be "tapped into" by humans who raise themselves up to these moral heights to receive these gifts. The nine bodies, or vehicles, that were perfected by Jesus Christ are described by Rudolf Steiner quite thoroughly in his teachings. Steiner names these bodies: physical, etheric, astral, sentient soul, intellectual soul, consciousness soul, spirit self, life spirit, and spirit man. Current humanity is developing the consciousness soul vehicle. This period of development runs from 1415 A.D. for approximately 2,160 years. Prior ages of humanity developed the previous five vehicles. Of course, the forces of Christ descended from the realms of the hierarchies and ensouled the bodies of humanity, both the developed ones and the ones that will be developed in the future. Christ perfected all nine bodies while he was here on Earth because He is much further advanced than humanity. Therefore, when Christ donated all nine of the perfected bodies to the realm of Shamballa, he laid the path for all humans to follow—far into the distant future. Christ redeemed humanity for all time to come and donated the vehicles that can inspire humanity throughout every stage of development.

Since the time of Christ, there have been some humans who have, through superior moral force, raised themselves up to a level where they could receive these gifts of the perfected vehicles of Christ. Only Rudolf Steiner gives details of this inspiration of humanity.

After Christ's death, these vehicles were used by individuals who manifested great gifts for humanity through their use of these perfected vehicles. St. Augustine used the perfected Etheric Body of Christ to manifest his work. St. Francis was an example of one who used the perfected Astral Body of Christ to tame astral forces on earth. The perfected Sentient Soul of Christ was used to inspire Johannes Tauler, and Christ's perfected Intellectual Soul vehicle was used by Meister Eckhart. Rudolf Steiner refers to Novalis as an example of a developed Consciousness Soul who embodies aspect of Christ. It is said that Rudolf Steiner himself was inspired by the perfected Life Spirit vehicle of Christ, and that is why he was able to reveal such great mysteries about Christ. The perfected Spirit Man vehicle of Christ is the collective higher self of humanity as it unfolds in the future. "I will be with you unto the end of times," and, "Not I, but the Christ in me."

Rudolf Steiner said that the resurrection of the Etheric Body of Christ would be the second greatest event of evolution and can be seen two ways: one general, and the other very intimate. The general manifestation of Christ becoming visible in the etheric realm is seen in the aurora borealis as it interacts with the solar wind (Solar Word) and creates the beautiful display of colors as a halo of the Earth. Christ interacts with humanity and warms thinking into spiritual *Imagination*, feelings into moral forces of *Inspiration*, and acts of will into moral deeds fired by *Intuition*. These three forces of *Moral Imagination*, *Moral Inspiration*, and *Moral Intuition* rise up from sleeping people each night and rush to the magnetic North Pole, where they exit the Earth and enter the cosmos to receive our nightly spiritual nourishment. On the way to this threshold door to the spiritual world, we illuminate the spaces around us with the three moral forces that interact with Christ's gifts from the Sun, and together they light up the north with a wall of fiery colors that stands as the guardian to the spiritual world. We also approach this world each time we meditate deeply and free our souls from physical constraints, or when we pass over the threshold of death.

These same forces can be seen in the human aura hovering around the pineal gland as it reacts to the same forces in a microcosmic fashion. A clairvoyant can see this rainbow bridge leaping from the pineal gland (crown chakra) to the pituitary gland (brow chakra). Many Eastern practices offer refined details about this type of manifestation. As time goes on, this "rainbow body" becomes more evident in morally developed individuals and less developed in humans who are selfish and egotistic. This "mark on the brow" has been commented on by many psychics and is referred to as the "mark" of Christ. Steiner called it the "etherization of the blood" that creates the "frontal spinal-column" that is similarly described in the *Chaldean Oracles* and by the prophet Mani. This "relationship" to one's rainbow body is also described as the living relationship to Anthroposophia, the being who inspires each individual person, like a conscious relationship to one's own guardian angel. Both macrocosmically and microcosmically, the Christ illumines our world with visible and invisible light to show the path of spiritual development for all humanity.

The greatest secret of all concerning Christ is the question, "Who was able to witness the death of Christ?" Tradition tells us one story, but Rudolf Steiner's teachings about Christ tell us much more and fill in the gaps that exist in tradition. To find many of these indications, you can read Steiner's *Fifth Gospel*. This gospel is written as a clairvoyant view of the Mystery of Jesus Christ. The Christology of Rudolf Steiner comprises not only a new doctrine, but a new religion. Steiner renewed the Catholic seven sacraments through his newly created Christian Community, but with his Christology, he created a new religious revelation. The secrets of Steiner's Christian cosmology will one day become common knowledge because clairvoyance will be commonplace in the future and the truth of these secrets will be revealed to everyone who has properly advanced in spiritual development. All of the various religious traditions will be clarified when humanity as a whole becomes clairvoyant (clairaudient, clairsentient). Rudolf Steiner was far ahead of his time, and his *Fifth Gospel* demonstrates that reality. Most of the missing pieces and unanswered questions about Jesus Christ are found in Steiner's Christology.

Tradition tells us that of the Apostles of Christ, only the "Beloved Disciple" was able to witness the horror of the crucifixion. Nicodemus was able to witness it in a dream. Joseph of Arimathea was there to catch the blood and water in the grail. The *Three Marys* were there throughout and were totally devoted to Christ's passion. Longinus, the blind centurion, pierced the side of Christ with the spear of destiny, the lance of Longinus. If Longinus was blind, who aimed his spear? And, of all the hierarchies, only the Archangel Michael, who is known as the "countenance of Christ," was able to bear the suffering of witnessing the crucifixion.

After John the Baptist, it was Mary Magdalene, the sister of Martha, who next recognized Christ by anointing his feet with oil. Mary of Jerusalem (Virgin Sophia), Christ's foster Mother, was there throughout. The "other" Mary was Mary of Jerusalem's sister. All others had deserted Jesus. Even the crowd turned away at the darkening of the sky and the quaking of the earth. They cried out in fear, "Perhaps he was the Son of God!" In a certain unknowing way, this reverse clairvoyance was an evil witness. Lucifer and Ahriman could not look upon the event at all. Official history has no physical evidence whatsoever as proof of Christ's crucifixion, except a one-line sentence in a Roman notebook. In essence, whoever was awake enough at the crucifixion to witness it must have been very important beings who are intimately connected to spiritual human evolution.

Rudolf Steiner fills in the missing pieces of this most important of puzzles. Truly amazing revelations detail exactly who witnessed the crucifixion. These witnesses are the great human spirits who have led humanity throughout time. All of the "loose ends of karma" play out on the stage of the crucifixion. The meaning of human development is spelled out in the passion of Jesus Christ and the circle of souls around him. Christ's deed is the fulcrum of evolution, and therefore its nature shows the past, present, and future of humanity. The many incarnations that led to the crucifixion and the many that have ensued since are made meaningful by Steiner's inspirations. To speak of such wisdom is to pull back the veil of the temple and reveal the full presence of the divine. I would highly recommend that anyone interested in a fuller description of some of these details read Steiner's books on Christ. Steiner spoke more about Christ than any other topic in his over 350 volumes of books and lectures. Steiner is the new prophet of esoteric Christianity; he has given a revelation that will stand the test of time. In a few hundred years, he will probably be considered a saint. By then, we will have advanced his work through our own clairvoyance and will know that what he taught was true.

Few understood at the time what had happened on the Golgotha Hill in Jerusalem. It took the apostles forty days to understand Christ's active revelation, even though He was in their presence, creating miracle after miracle. Only the Three Marys and John the Beloved believed Christ's prophecy that he would rise on the third day in glory. Even Mary Magdalene, his closest disciple, mistook him for the gardener. The apostles huddled around Christ's step-mother and the two other Marys for comfort and direction. Lazarus, who was now called John the Beloved (often shown with his head upon Christ's heart), the one Christ commended his mother to on the cross, now became the spiritual leader of the apostles because he and the Three Marys were direct witnesses of the crucifixion. John the Beloved (writer of the Epistles, the Gospel of John, and the Book of Revelations) now accompanied Mary wherever she went. They ended up in Ephesus, where Mary was *assumed* into heaven. John the Beloved was exiled to the Island of Patmos, and at age 105 wrote the *Book of Revelations* after a violent earthquake shook his cave and left a fissure, much like the one that shook Christ's burial cave and received his body into the Earth.

One secret of the crucifixion is that the first Adam and Eve were present and redeemed at the crucifixion by the new Adam and Eve. The Fall from Eden was redeemed, and New Jerusalem was born. All past, present, and future lines of karma were untangled and reunited in the eternal knot of Christ and Sophia's love. Even the hierarchies envy humans that they were able, in freedom, to witness the most loving event in creation: the gift of the life of a God, given freely to lead human development for all time to come.

Dionysius the Aereopogite of Athens knew that the spiritual hierarchy of the Christians and the Aristotlean categories were two descriptions of the same beings. The Athenians had reserved a temple station for the "Unknown God," who sounded a great deal like Jesus Christ. Greeks had been prepared beforehand to worship a mysterious Sun god who would descend to Earth to become a human so that he might help mankind evolve. The Greeks believed in the great flood and the notion that a human could be a god, and a god could become human. Greek heroes were immortalized in the stars to remind humans of the days when gods and humans communed together and had affairs that affected the heavens, Earth, and the underworld.

Christ's participation throughout the hierarchy and in the Holy Trinity is the key to spiritual evolution. The Holy Trinity pervades all aspects of the nine hierarchies, and through the Trinity, the connective tissue of the hierarchy is woven. The Trinity of Father God, Christ Jesus the Son God, and the Holy Spirit creates our local solar mysteries, even though they are far beyond it and cannot be properly conceived of by humans at this time in evolution, with our limited cognitive abilities. The Holy Trinity is beyond time and space and penetrates all aspects of human consciousness and spiritual development. The entire "intent" of human evolution was displayed in the Greco-Roman Epoch.

Literature Selections for Grade Five Children— Greco-Roman

Words of Jesus of Nazareth

You shall know the truth, and the truth shall make you free.
In your patience possess you your soul.
Have salt in yourself, and have peace with one another.
Whatsoever you shall ask in prayer, believing, you shall receive.
Ask, and it shall be given you; seek, and you shall find; knock, and it shall be opened unto you.
A good man out of the good treasure of the heart brings forth good things.
Lay up for yourselves treasures in heaven, for where your treasure is, there will your heart be also.
He that is greatest among you shall be your servant and he that shall humble himself shall be exalted.
The things which are impossible with men are possible with God.
As you would that men should do to you, do you also to them likewise.

You are the light of the world. Let your light so shine before men,
that they may see your good works, and glorify your Father who is in heaven.

Suffer the little children to come unto me, and forbid them not: for of such is the kingdom of God.
Whosoever shall not receive the kingdom of God as a little child, he shall not enter therein.

Thou shalt love the Lord thy God with all thy heart, and with all thy soul,
and with all thy mind, and with all thy strength: and Thou shalt love thy neighbor as thyself.

Love you your enemies, and do good, and lend, hoping for
    nothing in return;
and your reward shall be great, and you shall be the children of
    the highest:
be you therefore merciful, as your Father also is merciful.
Judge not, and you shall not be judged: condemn not, and you
    shall not be condemned:
forgive, and you shall be forgiven: give, and it shall be given
    unto you.

The kingdom of heaven is at hand!
Heal the sick, cleanse the lepers, raise the dead, cast out devils:
    freely you have received, freely give.
Be you therefore wise as serpents, and harmless as doves, for
    there is nothing covered,
that shall not be revealed; nor hid, that shall not be known.

Be you therefore perfect, even as your Father who is in heaven
    is perfect.
If you will be perfect, go and sell what you have, and give to the
    poor,
and you will have treasure in heaven.

Seek you first the kingdom of God, and his righteousness; and
    all things shall be added unto you.
Take therefore no thought for the morrow: for the morrow
    shall take thought for the things of itself.

Blessed are the poor in spirit: for theirs is the kingdom of
    heaven.
Blessed are they that mourn: for they shall be comforted.
Blessed are the meek: for they shall inherit the earth.
Blessed are they which do hunger and thirst after
    righteousness: for they shall be filled.
Blessed are the merciful: for they shall obtain mercy.
Blessed are the pure in heart: for they shall see God.
Blessed are the peacemakers: for they shall be called the
    children of God.
Blessed are they which are persecuted for righteousness' sake:
    for theirs is the kingdom of heaven.

The hour now is, when true worshippers shall worship the
    Father in spirit and in truth:
for the Father seeks such to worship him.
God is a Spirit: and they that worship him must worship him
    in spirit and in truth.

Our Father who art in heaven, hallowed be thy name.
Thy kingdom come, Thy will be done on earth, as it is in heaven.
Give us this day our daily bread.
And forgive us our trespasses, as we forgive our trespassers.
And lead us not into temptation, but deliver us from evil:
For thine is the kingdom, and the power, and the glory, forever.
Amen.

Aristotle (384-322 BC)

A friend to all is a friend to none.

All human actions have one or more of these seven causes: chance, nature, compulsions, habit, reason, passion, desire.

All men by nature desire to know.

All virtue is summed up in dealing justly.

At his best, man is the noblest of all animals; separated from law and justice he is the worst.

Bring your desires down to your present means. Increase them only when your increased means permit.

Character may almost be called the most effective means of persuasion.

Courage is the first of human qualities because it is the quality that guarantees the others.

Education is an ornament in prosperity and a refuge in adversity.

Education is the best provision for old age.

For though we love both the truth and our friends, piety requires us to honor the truth first.

Good habits formed in youth make all the difference.

Happiness depends upon our selves.

Hope is the dream of a waking man.

If one way be better than another, that you may be sure is nature's way.

In all things of nature there is something of the marvelous.

It is the mark of an educated mind to be able to entertain a thought without accepting it.

Love is composed of a single soul inhabiting two bodies.

Nature does nothing in vain.

Pleasure in the job puts perfection in the work.

Quality is not an act, it is a habit.

Suffering becomes beautiful when anyone bears great calamities with cheerfulness, not through insensibility but through greatness of mind.

The aim of art is to represent not the outward appearance of things, but their inward significance.

The aim of the wise is not to secure pleasure, but to avoid pain.

The end of labor is to gain leisure.

The energy of the mind is the essence of life.

Men are naturally apt to be swayed by fear rather than reverence, and to refrain from evil rather because of the punishment that it brings than because of its own foulness.

The gods too are fond of a joke.

The least initial deviation from the truth is multiplied later a thousandfold.

The one exclusive sign of thorough knowledge is the power of teaching.

The secret to humor is surprise.

The soul never thinks without a picture.

The ultimate value of life depends upon awareness and the power of contemplation rather than upon mere survival.

The virtue of justice consists in moderation, as regulated by wisdom.

The worst form of inequality is to try to make unequal things equal.

The young are permanently in a state resembling intoxication.

There is no great genius without a mixture of madness.

Those that know, do. Those that understand, teach.

Those who educate children well are more to be honored than they who produce them; for these only gave them life, those the art of living well.

Thou wilt find rest from vain fancies if thou doest every act in life as though it were thy last.

We are what we repeatedly do. Excellence, then, is not an act, but a habit.

Well begun is half done.

Whosoever is delighted in solitude is either a wild beast or a god.

Wishing to be friends is quick work, but friendship is a slow ripening fruit.

Without friends no one would choose to live, though he had all other goods.

You will never do anything in this world without courage. It is the greatest quality of the mind next to honor.

Select Sentences of Sextus the Pythagorean (406 BC)

Divine Wisdom is true Science.

The erudite, chaste, and wise soul, is the prophet of the truth of God.

A wise intellect is the mirror of God.

The wise man, and the despiser of wealth, resemble God.

God is a light incapable of receiving its contrary, darkness.

You have in yourself something similar to God, and therefore use yourself as the temple of God, on account of that which in you resembles God.

Honor God above all things, that He may rule over you.

The greatest honor which can be paid to God, is to know and imitate Him.

God, indeed, is not in want of anything, but the wise man is in want of God alone.

Endeavor to be great in the estimation of Divinity, but among men avoid envy.

A good intellect is the choir of divinity.

Such as you wish your neighbor to be to you, such also be you to your neighbor.

That which God gives you, no one can take away.

Neither do nor even think of that which you are not willing God should know.

Before you do anything think of God, that his light may precede your energies.

The soul is illuminated by the recollection of deity.

You should not possess more than the use of the body requires.

Possess those things which no one can take from you.

Be not anxious to please the multitude.

Every desire is insatiable, and therefore is always in want.

In all your actions place God before your eyes.

Invoke God as a witness to whatever you do.

He does not know God who does not worship Him.

It is not death, but a bad life, that destroys the soul.

Paradiso, **Dante (1265-1321)**

O supreme light, who dost thy glory assert
High over our imagining, lend again
Memory a little of what to me thou wert.
Vouchsafe unto my tongue such power to attain
That but one sparkle it may leave behind
Of thy magnificence to future men.
I beheld leaves within the unfathomed blaze
Into one volume bound by love, the same
That the universe holds scattered through its maze
Substance and accidents, and their modes, became
As if together fused, all in such wise
That what I speak of is one simple flame,
Love that moves the sun and the other stars.

Literature for Grade Five Teachers and Parents— Greco-Roman

Once Christ had come to the Earth, the need for priest-kings had come to an end. Now each human was their own priest-king and must decide for themselves what was right or wrong. Each person's destiny was now in their own hands, and no city or state needed to tell the individual their role in society or the church. For many years, the church tried to take the place of priest-kings. Priests and popes preached infallibility, indulgences, and inquisitions with crusades and ecumenical councils, heresies and excommunications. Doctrinal splits, reformations, revolts, break-off factions, reorganizations, and many personal revelations later, the "Christian Church" is still no nearer to Christianity than it was two thousand years ago. But throughout the centuries, there have been saints who truly walked with God's virtue and grace. It is such a blessing to become again as little children, to know the goodness of the divine.

Rudolf Steiner tells us that any person using healthy thinking automatically understands that reincarnation (repeated human incarnations) is a natural law of spiritual evolution. Anyone who doesn't understand this is, in fact, ill, and their thinking is flawed. Likewise, anyone with any ability to see into the spiritual world knows that Christ is the leading spirit of the hierarchies and our solar system and that He incarnated only once in a physical human body to redeem the Earth and humanity. To still debate about whether or not Christ's incarnation was the central turning point of time in all of evolution is silly. To not know Christ is seen as an illness by Rudolf Steiner. No healthy conscience rejects Christ, the higher self. The time for debate is over, and we must learn to know the Wisdom of Christ (Sophia) and understand Christ's cosmic nature that is directly connected to the higher self of every human being, no matter what religion they may or may not believe in. After death, there is no chance to "believe" in Christ; it must happen as a *free deed of love* while the soul is incarnated in this Earthly, material condition. Only then does the belief in Christ turn into a spiritually free deed that liberates the soul.

The question in our modern time is quite simple: Is creation redeemable? Is all of creation for nothing? Any healthy mind can see birth, death, and rebirth in nature. Therefore, it must also happen for humans that after death is another life. Christ, the higher spiritual self, is self-evident to the healthy mind looking at the spectrum of human experience.

Rudolf Steiner pointed out that the Egyptians and the Greeks saw a being outside of themselves that they referred to as Theosophia—the Wisdom of God. This being was objective, experienced outside of themselves, and belonged to no one individual, but was the common experience of every philosopher who rose up to meet her in the air between the Earth and the Moon. Later, this being came ever closer to mankind, and the great philosophers of the scholastic period developed what seemed to be a more personal relationship with this being. They called her Philo-Sophia—the Love of Wisdom.

With the advent of Anthroposophy, Rudolf Steiner created a body of work that describes the physical and spiritual nature of the world and the place of mankind as an evolving spiritual being within this world. Since the founding of the first Goetheanum, this being has come ever closer to mankind and is presently found knocking at the heart of each aspirant, interacting with the effects of living with the content of Anthroposophy as this being helps our spirit evolve. This being, named Anthroposophia by Rudolf Steiner, is intimately aware of each spiritual struggle or success that the aspirant experiences. In a way, Anthroposophia is the mid-wife of our higher-self, helping us weather the pangs of spirit-birth into this new land. Anthroposophia is beyond the work of Rudolf Steiner. She awaits the spirit-courage of each individual to forge their own path through the Consciousness Soul to the Spirit Self, that part of ourselves we call the Higher Self. Anthroposophia will evolve in the future to become the fully active *earthly and cosmic nutrition stream* that feeds the soul and spirit of each person as well as the spiritual world—"Give us this day our daily bread." Anthroposophia is the pure Virgin Sophia who awaits the sacred marriage of the soul to the spirit and sleeps not, lest she miss the coming of the groom.

The Consolation of Philosophy
by Theodoric Boethius (480-524 AD)

The love of wisdom is the illumination of the intelligent mind by that pure wisdom, and is a kind of return and recall to it, so that it seems at once the pursuit of wisdom, the pursuit of divinity, and the friendship of that pure mind. This wisdom gives to the whole class of minds the reward of its own divinity and returns it to its proper constitution and purity of nature.

Whoever deeply searches out the truth and will not be deceived by paths untrue, shall turn unto himself his inward gaze, shall bring his wandering thoughts in circle home and teach his heart that what it seeks abroad it holds in its own treasure chest within.

For I have swift and speedy wings with which to mount the lofty skies,
And when thy mind has put them on the earth below it will despise:
It mounts the air sublunary and far behind the clouds it leaves;
It passes through the sphere of fire which from the ether heat receives,
Until it rises to the stars, with Phoebus there to join its ways,
Or Saturn cold accompany as soldier of his shining rays.
Wherever night is spangled bright the orbit of a star it takes,
And when the orbit's path is done the furthest heaven it forsakes.
It treads beneath the ether swift possessing now the holy light,
For here the King of kings holds sway, the reins of all things holding tight,

Unmoving moves the chariot fast, the lord of all things shining bright.
If there the pathway brings you back—the path you lost and seek anew—
Then, "I remember," you will say, "My home, my source, my ending too."

Selected Sayings by Meister Eckhart (1260 AD)

A human being has so many skins inside, covering the depths of the heart.

We know so many things, but we don't know ourselves!

Why, thirty or forty skins or hides, as thick and hard as an ox's or bear's, cover the soul.

Go into your own ground and learn to know yourself there.

A just person is one who is conformed and transformed into justice.

All God wants of man is a peaceful heart.

Do exactly what you would do if you felt most secure.

Every creature is a word of God.

God expects but one thing of you, and that is that you should come out of yourself in so far as you are a created being and let God be God in you.

God is at home; it is we who have gone for a walk.

He who would be serene and pure needs but one thing, detachment.

If God gave the soul his whole creation she would not be filled thereby but only with himself.

If the only prayer you said in your whole life was, "thank you," that would suffice.

Man goes far away or near but God never goes far-off; he is always standing close at hand, and even if he cannot stay within he goes no further than the door.

One person who has mastered life is better than a thousand persons who have mastered only the contents of books, but no one can get anything out of life without God.

Only the hand that erases can write the true thing.

The eye with which I see God is the same eye with which God sees me.

The knower and the known are one.

Simple people imagine that they should see God as if he stood there and they here. This is not so. God and I, we are one in knowledge.

The more we have the less we own.

The outward man is the swinging door; the inner man is the still hinge.

The outward work will never be puny if the inward work is great.

The price of inaction is far greater than the cost of making a mistake.

There exists only the present instant... a Now which always and without end is itself new.

There is no yesterday nor any tomorrow, but only Now, as it was a thousand years ago and as it will be a thousand years hence.

To be full of things is to be empty of God. To be empty of things is to be full of God.

Truly, it is in darkness that one finds the light, so when we are in sorrow, then this light is nearest of all to us.

We are celebrating the feast of the Eternal Birth which God the Father has borne and never ceases to bear in all eternity... But if it takes place not in me, what avails it?

Everything lies in this, that it should take place in me.

What a man takes in by contemplation that he pours out in love.

What we plant in the soil of contemplation, we shall reap in the harvest of action.

When you are thwarted, it is your own attitude that is out of order.

Words derive their power from the original word.

You may call God love, you may call God goodness, but the best name for God is compassion.

True suffering is a mother of all the virtues.

Yea, since God has never given any gift, in order that man might rest in the possession of the gift, but gives every gift that He has given in heaven and on earth, in order that He might be able to give one gift, which is Himself, so with this gift of grace, and with all His gifts He will make us ready for the one gift, which is Himself.

He who has found this way of love, seeketh no other. He who turns on this pivot is in such wise a prisoner that his foot and hand and mouth and eyes and heart, and all his human faculties, belong to God. And, therefore, thou canst overcome thy flesh in no better way, so that it may not shame thee, than by love. This is why it is written, Love is as strong as death, as hard as hell. Death separates the soul from the body, but love separates all things from the soul. She suffers nought to come near her, that is not God nor God-like. Happy is he who is thus imprisoned; the more thou art a prisoner, the more wilt thou be freed. That we may be so imprisoned, and so freed, may He help us, Who Himself is Love.

Johannes Tauler (1300-1361 AD)

If it is true that the Master Jesus (Zoroaster) visited Johannes Tauler and inspired his *Alphabet of Virtues*, then we have a most rare gift in spiritual history. The Friend of God from the Highlands was a hidden figure in history, as often times the Master Jesus's incarnations are obscure and unknown to historians. There is also a legend that the Master Jesus inspired the teacher of Abraham Lincoln and that he taught Jacob Boehme. I have even heard it said that Rudolf Steiner met the Master Jesus a number of times in the Carpathian Mountains and this Master encouraged Steiner to study Fichte and science.

Truly, the taming of the astral body through the perfection of virtue is the path of spiritual development appropriate for our time. Unbridled passions, fear, and psychosis rule the modern soul-scape. Seldom do New Age religions recommend renunciation or austerities as a step in spiritual development. The great ills of jealousy, envy, greed, sloth, gluttony, hatred, and anger are counteracted by the development of the virtues of faith, hope, charity, industry, frugality, love, and patience. In other words, tame the astral body. Spiritual development is now up to the individual, and responsibility is the key; discipline is the foundation, while devotion and dedication are the elements that stoke the fire. There are no excuses for not developing good habits based on the virtues instead of vices.

The Alphabet of Johannes Tauler

Johannes Tauler of Alsace received this Alphabet from the Master Jesus (approximately 1346 A.D.) in order to obtain the power of the Word. Upon receiving it, he retreated for two years in silence within a Dominican monastery. His first sermon following this period left forty people in a dead faint.

The Alphabet contains two secrets. It brings about a purification of the astral body, so that it is possible to eliminate hindrances from it, egotism, self-will, personal ambitions, etc., and the astral body will become clairvoyant through the effect of certain cosmic powers. It is an initiation into the cosmic forces of the planetary system and zodiac. Each letter reveals one secret of a planet or zodiacal sign. Knowledge of how the Logos is incorporated in the zodiac and planets is the result of such a study.

The Alphabet

A pure and godly life begin.
Bad deeds and thoughts avoid, and do the good instead.
Cherish the golden mean; restrain yourself.
Demure in thoughts and actions, practice humility.
Egotism and self-will, let them submit to the will of God.

Firm and with steadfast earnestness remain with God and in God.
Godly things most willingly obey.
Hold not onto the earthly creation.
In your heart strive to practice and meditate on the measure of things, good and divine.
Kourageously and strong, resist the temptation of the flesh and the devil.
Laziness and indifference conquer with force.
Mindful and merciful, exercise love for God and your fellow-man.
Nothing desire, begrudge no one, whatever it be.
Order keep in all things and turn all things to the good.
Punishment from the Creator or from the world of the creatures most willingly accept.
Quicken forgiveness for all who have wronged you.
Reason, soul, and body learn to keep pure.
Stay gentle in soul concerning all things that are truly good.
True and faithful be to all human beings.
Unerringly desist from excess of any kind whatsoever.
Xristos, His Life and His teachings—emulate and meditate upon them without ceasing.
Yearning for heavenly solace, entreat our Lady to aid you.
Zealously tame your nature that in all things divinely created you may attain peace.

Bibliographic References and Recommended Reading

Grade Five—Greco-Roman Epoch

Allen, Paul, M. *Francis of Assisi's Canticle of the Creatures.* Continuum, New York, 1996.

Arnold. *The Living Celestial.* Steiner College Press.

Blakney, Raymond Bernard. *Meister Eckhart: A Modern Translation.* HarperPerennial, New York, 1941.

Bock, Emil. *Old Testament Studies.* Floris Books.

Boethius. *Consolation of Philosophy*. Translated by Joel C. Rellihan. Hackett Co., 2001.

Bryson, B. *Gilgamesh*. Steiner College Press.

Buck. *Mahabarata*. Penguin.

Bulfinch. *Bulfinch's Mythology*. Collier.

Casson. *Daily Life in Egypt*. PaperBook Press.

Colum, Padriac. *About Greek Gods*. MacMillan.

Colum, Padriac. *Golden Fleece*. MacMillan.

Colum, Padriac. *Orpheus: Myths of the World*. Floris Books.

Colum, Padriac. *The Children's Homer*. MacMillan Co., 1946.

Colum, Padriac. *The Tales of Ancient Egypt*. Henry Walck Incorporated, New York, 1968.

Coomaraswamy. *Myths of the Hindus & Buddhists*. Dover.

Fayy, Benen. *The Writings of St. Francis of Assisi*. Franciscan Herald Press, Chicago, 1963.

Firdausi. *Life of the Persian Kings*. Steiner College Press.

Firth, M. *The Golden Verses of Pythagoras and Other Pythagorean Fragments*. The Theosophical Publishing Society, Chicago, 1905.

Green. *Tales of Ancient Egypt*. Langley.

Hamilton. *Mythology*. Signet.

Harrer, Dorothy. *Chapter from Ancient History*. AWSNA Publications.

Hazeltine. *Hero Tales from Many Lands*. Abbington Press.

Heidel. *The Babylonian Genesis*. University of Chicago Press.

Hiebel, Frederick. *The Gospel of Hellas*. Anthroposophic Press, New York, 1949.

Hiebel, Fredrick. *The Gospel of Hellas*. Anthroposophic Press.

Kenney, E. J. *The Golden Ass by Apuleius*. Penguin Classics, NY, 1999.

Kovacs, Charles. *Ancient Mythologies and History*. Resource Books, Scotland, 1991.

Kovacs, Charles. *Greek Mythology and History*. Resource Books, Scotland, 1991.

Longfellow, Henry Wadsworth. *The Song of Hiawatha*. Duell Sloan & Pearce, New York, 1971.

McInerny, Ralph. *Thomas Aquinas: Selected Writings*. Penguin Classics, New York, 1999.

McKeon, Richard. *The Basic Works of Aristotle*. Modern Library Classics, 2011.

Merry, Eleanor. *The Ascent of Man*. New Knowledge Books, England.

Mills, Dorothy. *The Book of the Ancient Greeks*. Putnam, New York, 1951.

Mills, Dorothy. *The Book of the Ancient World*. Putnam, New York, 1954.

Mukerji, Dhan Gopal. *Rama the Hero of India*. Dutton & Co., New York, 1937

Norton, Charles Eliot. *Divine Comedy*. Norton's Translation. Amazon Digital Services, 2011.

Sanders. *Epic of Gilgamesh*. Penguin.

Saviti. *Tales from Indian Classics*. Children's Book Trust.

Schaff, Philip. *The Complete Works of St. Augustine*. Amazon Digital Services, 2011.

Schure, Eduarde. *The Great Initiates*. Anthroposophic Press.

Seeger, Elizabeth. *Fire Sons of Pandu*. Scott.

Seeger, Elizabeth. *The Ramayana*. Dent & Sons, England, 1975.

Shrady, Maria. *Johannes Tauler: Sermons*. Paulist Press, 1985.

Steiner, Rudolf. *Ancient Myths*. Anthroposophic Press.

Steiner, Rudolf. *Egyptian Myths & Mysteries*. Anthroposophic Press.

Steiner, Rudolf. *Gospel of St. Matthew*. Anthroposophic Press.

Steiner, Rudolf. *Wonders of the World, Ordeals of the Soul, Revelations of the Spirit*. Anthroposophic Press.

Steiner, Rudolf. *World History in Light of Anthroposophy*. Anthroposophic Press.

Tappan. *The Story of the Greek People*. Houghton Mifflin, 1936.

Von Bemmelin, D. *Zarathustra*. Anthroposophic Press.

Watson, Jane Werner. *Rama of the Golden Age*. Garnard Pub., Champaign, Illinois, 1971.

Anglo-Germanic Cultural Epoch

1415–3573 AD
Pisces, Anglo-Germanic, Jupiter,
Consciousness Soul/Spirit Self

Look, how the floor of heaven is thick inlaid with patines of bright gold! There's not the smallest orb which thou beholdest but in its motion like an angel sings. Still choiring the young eyed cherubim—such harmony is in immortal souls. But whilst this muddy vesture of decay doth grossly close it in—we cannot hear it.

Shakespeare, *The Merchant of Venice*

Starting in 1415 A.D., a new epoch began. Rudolf Steiner calls it the Consciousness Soul Epoch, or the Anglo-Germanic Epoch. It, like the others, will continue for approximately 2,160 years, or the twelfth part of the Platonic Great Year of 25,920 years. This new epoch will unfold the forces of the Consciousness Soul, as the previous one from 747 BC to 1415 AD developed the forces of the Intellectual Soul, and the one prior to it developed the Sentient Soul/Astral Body. The refined elements of the Consciousness Soul will merge with the spiritual content of each person's Spirit Self as time goes on. Our purified Astral Body of desires helps form refined characteristics that the Consciousness Soul needs to exist in the world of spirit, where the Spirit Self lives.

The Comte de Saint Germain is one of the great initiates who has perfected his Consciousness Soul in advance of humanity, as an example to emulate. In one of his incarnations in Europe, he was the deposed Prince Racogzy, who traveled from court to court performing wonders and seeming miracles. He had a knack for fixing any problem in the kingdom, especially big ones. In Scandinavia, he taught them to tan reindeer hides more effectively, and in France he was a healer, crystologist, and Grand Master Mason. He seemed to be all things to all people and was rumored to have lived to age 105 without aging. He was a master musician, artist, poet, and playwright, and was often credited with healing. One story has him writing two independent documents with both hands simultaneously. According to legend, no prison could hold him, and he possessed the Philosopher's Stone and the Elixir of Life. Certainly, he is a shining example of the spiritual master who perennially makes his presence known.

St. Germain's alchemical poem, *Philosophical Sonnet*, embodies the entire corpus of alchemy in a short, transcendental *Imagination*. This *Imagination* is a perfect example of what we should contemplate and meditate. This poem can also be studied along with the only other extant writing of Saint Germain's: *The Most Holy Trinosophia*, a masonic initiation.

Wisdom-thinkers can now be their own priest/king/prophet/messiah by consciously and freely loving others. No church or priest as intermediary is necessary. Our bodies are our temples, resplendent with Wisdom's creative Word. We stand at the altar of our heart, witness to the divine. We need not study old revelations; we simply receive new ones. Prophets need not prophesize the future; the future is upon us now with apocalyptic force, and the machinations of the "war of all against all" can be seen on many sides. Our threefold nature of thinking, feeling, and willing is splitting apart as the destructive forces of the threshold of death surround and overtake us. Souls that are awake are forging the courage to consciously reassemble our threefold nature, crowning it with new *Imagination* in our heads by thinking sense-free, fiery higher-thoughts; new *Inspiration* that fills our listening souls with harmonic wisdom; and new *Intuition* in the moral heart of spirit-deeds that freely love.

At this point in spiritual evolution, any striving soul can come to the abyss of modern materialistic thinking and build the bridge to the land of imaginative archetypes that enliven souls who witness the spirit. Great thinkers have suffered long to find insight and wisdom on every common path or highway. But when their wisdom is housed together as a pillared temple of beautiful wisdom (Temple of Sophia), we can witness the higher self that is the beauty found in the mirror of nature and the human being.

Every striving human can find Wisdom as close as their own breath, heartbeat, or thought. Anthroposophia is our spiritual mirror that shows us that we are the "fairest in the land." *Wisdom* illuminates *beauty* and births *good* deeds. Every percept is filled with *beauty, wisdom (truth),* and the forces of *goodness*. We no longer need to enjoy nature as a Sentient Soul, nor understand nature as an Intellectual Soul; we need to commune with nature as the Consciousness Soul who goes beyond nature and artistically finds moral application for the terrific forces hidden in the beauty of nature. Humans must rule nature for good, not ill. That is the challenge of the Consciousness Soul Epoch: to understand the forces of birth and death and use them for the good to further spiritual development. The forces of eugenics (birth-mysteries and the past) unlock genetics, while the forces of mechanical occultism unlock the forces of physical immortality (death-mysteries and the future).

Physical, material forces will try to lure mankind into believing that they are bound by matter instead of the moral insight that humans are *consciousness* that cannot be limited by genetics or death because humans are immortal spirits. This simple wisdom has been lost to many modern thinkers because they have severed their connection to the spiritual world—the place they came from before birth and will return to after death. This materialistic blindness is a tragic illness that keeps the spirit world in dark shadows for many people who do not know the face of Wisdom (Sophia) or the Love of Christ.

Throughout the apocalyptic challenges of modern times, many people have found truth and distilled wisdom into simple words. Each of the writers quoted below has found their way through the darkness of Kali Yuga to the New Age of the Archangel Michael (started in 1879). Wisdom lives and breathes everywhere you look, and people are awakening to their divine nature and are becoming more loving, kind, and helpful to others. Life is a balancing act of personal awareness that is determined by where you focus your consciousness: either apocalypse or New Jerusalem.

Literature Selections for Grade Five Children—Anglo-Germanic

***Philosophical Sonnet* by the Comte Saint Germain (1712-1784)**

Curious scrutator of all nature,
I have known of the great whole, the principle and the end,
I have seen gold thick in the depths of the double mercury;
I have seized its substance, and surprised its changing.
I explain by that art, the soul with the womb of a Mother,
Make its home, take it away, and as a kernel
Placed against a grain of wheat, under the humid pollen;
The one plant and the other vine-stock, are the bread and
    wine,
Nothing was, God willing, nothing became something,
I doubted it, I sought that on which the universe rests,
Nothing preserves the equilibrium and serves to sustain,
Then with the weight of praise and of blame,
I weighed the eternal, it called my soul,
I died, I adored, I knew nothing more.

The Cherubinic Wanderer, **Angelus Silesius (1624-1677 AD)**

Could but your soul oh man, become a silent night,
God would be born in you and set all things aright.

Why are you lost in thought? The Woman in the Sun,
Who stands upon the Moon, must first your soul become.

Say what you will, the bride is the most cherished child,
Whom one finds in God's womb and in His arms enshrined.

The world my ocean is, the captain is God's Spirit,
My body is the ship, toward home the soul is steered.

The lightning of God's Son quickly transparent renders
The hearts which are to God entirely surrendered.

I am the temple of God and of my heart the shrine;
The Sacred Mystery, if pure and undefiled.

I am a mighty realm, my heart is the high throne,
The soul reigns as its Queen, the King is God's own Son.

Quite without measure is the Highest, as we know,
And yet a human heart can wholly Him enclose.

Your heart receiveth God with all His Kingdom holds,
When you but turn toward Him and like a rose unfold.

The most delightful news that my soul can receive:
To be eternally bride at the wedding feast.

The voice of God is heard: Listen within and seek;
Were you but always silent, He'd never cease to speak.

Seeds of Wisdom

When God thought of mother, He must have laughed with satisfaction, and framed it quickly—so rich, so deep, so divine, so full of soul, power, and beauty, was the conception. Nothing can compare in beauty, and wonder, and admirableness, and divinity itself, to the silent work in obscure dwellings of faithful women bringing their children to honor and virtue and piety.
Beecher

No man is poor who has had a godly mother.
Abraham Lincoln

Whatever you cannot understand, you cannot possess.
Anonymous

Learn to stand in awe of thyself.
Democritus

The Beauty of the world and the orderly arrangement of everything celestial makes us confess that there is an excellent and eternal nature, which ought to be worshipped and admired by all mankind.
Cicero

A grateful mind is not only the greatest of virtues, but the parent of all the other virtues.
Cicero

Nature is the art of God.
Sir Thomas Browne

Taking the first footstep with a good thought, the second with a good word, and the third with a good deed, I entered Paradise.
Zoroaster

The truly generous is the truly wise; He who loves not others, lives unblessed.
Hume

Glory makes us live forever in posterity; love, for an instant in the infinite.
Weiss

Virtue, truth, and kindness; like love, never fail.
Anonymous

Shakespeare (1564-1616 AD)

The heavens themselves, the planets, and this center observe degree, priority, and place, insisture, course, proportion, season, form, office, and custom, in all line of order; and therefore is the glorious planet Sol in noble eminence enthron'd and spher'd amidst the others, whose medicinable eye corrects the ill aspects of planets evil and posts, like the commandment of a king, sans check, to good and bad. But when the planets in evil mixture to disorder wander, what plagues and what portents, what mutiny, what raging of the sea, shaking of earth, commotion in the winds! Frights, changes, horrors divert and crack,

rend and deracinate the unity and married calm of states quite from their fixture! O, when degree is shak'd, which is the ladder to all high designs, then enterprise is sick! Take but degree away, untune that string, and hark what discord follows!
Troilus and Cressida

This above all: to thine own self be true: and it must follow, as the night the day, thou can'st not then be false to any man.
Hamlet

He who the sword of Heaven will bear should be as holy as severe, pattern in himself to know, grace to stand, and virtue go.
Measure for Measure

We are such stuff as dreams are made of; and our little life is rounded with a sleep.
Midsummer Night's Dream

A Sleep of Prisoners, **Christopher Fry (1907)**

The human heart can go to the lengths of God.
Dark and cold we may be, but this
Is no winter now. The frozen misery
Of centuries breaks, cracks, begins to move;
The thunder is the thunder of the floes,
The thaw, the flood, the upstart Spring.
Thank God our time is now when wrong
Comes up to face us everywhere,
Never to leave us 'til we take
The longest stride of soul men ever took.
Affairs are now soul size.
The enterprise
Is exploration into God.
Where are you making for? It takes
So many thousand years to wake,
But will you wake for pity's sake?

Literature Selections for Grade Five Teachers and Parents

Rudolf Steiner is a forerunner of the Consciousness Soul Epoch, and he leads humanity into the future manifestation of the spirit revealed through his Anthroposophy and the being of Anthroposophia. No other thinker has taken the truth so far in all of its many applications. Others have beautiful pieces of the whole, but Rudolf Steiner has a complete and comprehensive cosmology of correspondences that can be verified and applied in all areas of human life. Dr. Steiner was our first comprehensive, clairvoyant, spiritual researcher whose developed morality could match the needs of his time. It is only due to Dr. Steiner's "good karma" that he was able to give so much to humanity in such a short life. Fortunately, his followers were smart enough to write down most of what he taught. There are other great beings like Steiner, but few who have the substance of Aristotle and the divine connection of Thomas Aquinas.

Rudolf Steiner's work stands on its own, even against the "help" of those who think they are representatives of Steiner. His renewal of the Mysteries is an open secret for all those who work long and hard in earnest effort. The scope of what Steiner taught was great enough for the next hundred years, for it will take that long and much more before humans have tamed their astral bodies sufficiently to comprehend the higher thoughts Rudolf Steiner has brought to humanity. The wisdom of his Christology makes him the greatest prophet of the evolving spirit of humanity. No other theologian has tied up the loose ends of the story of the historical Jesus becoming the Christ as well as Steiner. The comprehensive nature of Steiner's Christology necessitated him authoring a new gospel of Christ. This new gospel, *The Fifth Gospel*, holds secrets underpinning the foundations of Earth evolution and the gifts of Christ in relationship to human spiritual development. Steiner has built the bridge over the abyss of unknowing for aspirants to enter the spiritual world, and he has given the wisdom to help faith take wing to soar to those heavenly realms.

Dr. Steiner created many hundreds of medicines to relieve human suffering with special effectiveness in eliminating cancer with the plant mistletoe. Many of his medicines have three parts which incorporate a mineral, a plant, and an artistic (human) component. Dr. Steiner gave a new pedagogy for our children, agriculture for our nutrition, and religious renewal and Anthroposophy for our spirits. He renewed architecture, painting, education, religion, movement, speech, economics, politics, and many other fields of knowledge. Steiner is so vast that only now do we have a few commentators on Anthroposophy who can encompass the scope of Steiner's teachings.

With any Steiner material, we can rest assured that we are in the best of hands and that the material is perfectly suited for modern times in the West. We are not creating a cult of the personality when we study Steiner's thoughts and then apply the principles that are workable; we are simply being spiritual scientists who are testing theories that either work or do not work.

Steiner will keep any thinker busy discovering whether his predictions in their specific field of knowledge have come to pass. Provable spiritual science is hard to argue with. Steiner was a major inventor in numerous fields. His inventions and discoveries are too many to name and effect such diverse fields of applications as architecture, astronomy, physics, medicine, education, philosophy, literature, agriculture, history, psychology, economics, banking, sociology, organizational growth, Eurythmy, massage therapy, nutrition, homeopathic medicine, bio-dynamic gardening, religion, counseling, and astrophysics, among others. The only limit to Steiner's Anthroposophy seemed to be in the questions his followers did not ask him.

What Steiner has to say about the great mystery of the Holy Grail is profound. In many places and from many perspectives, Steiner discusses the Holy Grail as it appears in history, religion, occult physiology, and the human physical constitution throughout evolution. There is no end to the wisdom that Dr. Steiner can share with us about the Grail, for he has himself lived the life of the grail warrior and has the holiness of Parzival and the wisdom and pain of Amfortas.

Pedagogical Remarks, by Dr. Rudolf Steiner (1865-1925)

The teacher of the present day should have a comprehensive view of the laws of the universe as a background to all he undertakes in his school work.

Man is not merely a spectator of the world: he is rather the world's stage upon which great cosmic events continuously play themselves out.

Art has something in its nature which does not only stir a man once but gives him fresh joy repeatedly. Hence it is, that what we have to do in education is intimately bound up with the artistic element.

All comprehension is really a question of relating one thing to another: the only way we can comprehend things in the world is by relating them to each other.

The teacher must understand also the times in which he lives, for he has to understand the children who, out of these very times, are entrusted to him for their education.

Pedagogy must not be a science; it must be an art, but the feelings in which we must live in order to practice that great art of life, the art of education, are only kindled by contemplation of the great universe and its relationships with man.

It will be our task to find teaching methods that all the time engage the whole human being.

We must realize that what can be developed at a certain age can no longer be developed at a later stage, except in exceptional cases. The forces at work during that period die away.

Imbue thyself with the power of imagination, have courage for the truth, sharpen thy feeling for responsibility of soul.

Adapted from: *The Natural History of the Intellect—*
Ralph Waldo Emerson (1803-1882)

Thinking

Thought is identical, the oceanic one which flows hither and thither and sees that all are its offspring, and coins itself indifferently into house or inhabitant, into planet, man, fish, oak, or grain of sand. Nature is saturated with deity. The particle is saturated with the elixir of the universe. The thinker radiates as suns and revolves as planets. The spiritual determines the practical.

As the world is made of thickened light and arrested electricity, so ideas are the parents of men and things. They are the First Good. For a matter of this kind cannot be expressed by words, like other things to be learnt, but by a long intercourse with the subject, and living with it, a light is kindled on a sudden, as if from a leaping fire, and being engendered in the soul, feeds itself upon itself. The truth takes flesh in forms that can express and execute it, and thus, in history, an idea overhangs like the moon, and rules the tide which rises simultaneously in all the souls of a generation. Now this light, this glory, like the corona which the astronomers have found around the sun, is real, and is the contribution of the mind; it is its announcement of the truth that is in nature.

There are times, and these are the memorable hours of life, when that vault is full of light, when a man finds the world in his own mind, when he sees that outward nature and art and history have their beginnings here—have their origin in his thought. The mind is eternal and abides.

Emotion is the first stage, thence thought, and thence action ... emotion, cognition, will.

Now that surprise and delight which each child finds in his Being, and which animates and exaggerates to him every fact in turn, it is not easy to define or classify: it is both cognition and emotion, and it leads directly to will. It is certain light or glory which invests and magnifies all objects which he beholds, and powerfully affects his will. See how in earnest the child is with his toys, and how imaginative!

Whoever attempts to carry out the rule of right and love and freedom must take his life in his hand.

Every law of matter is only a pictorial representation of a law of mind. The reason why Imagination finds types everywhere in nature is because chemistry or astronomy or zoology all only externalize the laws of the mind.

And as mind, our mind, or mind like ours, reappears to us in our study of nature—nature being everywhere formed after a method which we can well understand, and all the parts, to the most remote allied and explicable—therefore our own organization is a perpetual key, and a well-ordered mind brings to the study of every new fact or class of acts a certain divination of that which he shall find. The doctrine of Identity is the last generalization. To the child all appears different; but later he classifies things which resemble outwardly or inwardly one another. Gradually he finds these resemblances and makes new classification and at last sees what vast identity exists throughout: that every form is parallel with every other; that the laws of each class of beings correspond to the laws of another, and of every other; the laws of the body correspond to those of the mind. But this is a late process. Men are in their thoughts and cannot order them, cannot detach them. Later the man of genius detaches them, compares them, sees their likeness or unlikeness, ranks them, sees that these are above him and others are outgrown, are below him, comes to generalize, as we say, or see that many of his experiences are all examples of one law: he lays up that law in his memory and drops the thousand facts.

Having well accepted this law of identity pervading the universe, we next perceive that whilst every creature represents and obeys it, there is diversity more or less of power; there is high and low; that the lowest only means incipient form, and over it is a higher class in which its rudiments are opened, raised to higher powers; that there is development from less to more, from lower to superior function, and that steadily ascending to man. Ascension of state is the next law—in the least egg to complete maturity; and in the next higher animal to maturity also; up to man, and in man from the child to the adult; from the savage to the Greek, and from the slave to the freeman; from the unwise to the wise and virtuous.

Matter, which, it appears, is impregnated with thought and heaven is really of God and not of the devil. All is resolved into unity again.

Nature through all of her works makes one silent demand of man; it is thus: Be master. "I will finish the house," she says; "Be you the tenant; not a piece of furniture, but the lord and user of all. Be thou the mighty benefactor. Don't be scared by size: only fools are. What are millions of leagues, what are dreary durations to thee? Suns and atoms, tis all the same. An atom is all. One atom is like another, and a sun is nothing but a larger lump of the same atoms. Every breath of air is a carrier of the soul of the world. And when once thy mind knows the law of so much as thine own body, thou hast nothing to learn from galaxies of stars. Tis not diameters, but ideas and insights that make depth and vastness. Ponderable and imponderable agents that work through wild space are only extensions of thy hands and feet."

But there is a metre which determines the constructive power of men—this, namely, the question whether the mind possesses the control of its thoughts, or they of it.

The most manifest sign of wisdom is a continual cheerfulness. Life is incessant birthing. When we have arrived at the question, the answer is already near.

The act of perception instantly throws man on the party of the Eternal.

All thought is perception of truth. All truths are related, and the mind perceives this order and consent of parts throughout nature. All truth is practical, leads and impels to its embodiment or incarnation in facts and institutions. Then the best part of it is—not the fruits or facts, not the profit—but the mind's part herein. Tis a lesson we daily learn in conversing with men that it is not so important what the topic or interest is about which we deal as is the angle of vision under which the object is seen: that means, that it be seen in wide relations, see with what belongs to it near and far, and the larger the mind the more truth. One man astonishes by the grandeur of his scope, another confines by the narrowness of his.

A master can formulate his thought. Our thoughts at first possess us. Later, if we have good heads, we come to possess them. The masters are exact minds, severe with themselves, and can formulate something.

And in every man we require a bit of night, of chaos.

Every soul has a bias or polarity of its own, and each new. Everyone is a magnet with a new north; that every mind is different, and the more it is unfolded, the more pronounced is that difference.

And the height of culture, the highest behavior consists in the identification of the ego with the Universe, so that when a man says, I hope, I find, I think—he might as properly say, the human race thinks, or finds, or hopes; he states a fact which commands the understanding and assents of all the company; and meantime, he shall be able continually to keep sight of his biographical ego.

Imagination

The Soul of the World is the right phrase: soul and world: it holds the two yet is one in the duplex energy. It pours itself through the universe and is finding ever expression in creating and compelling men to utter in their articulate fashion of speech and arts its million particulars of the one fact of Being.

There is no choice of words for him who clearly sees the truth.

Imagination is a spontaneous act; a perception and affirming of a real relation between a thought and some material fact. Whenever this resemblance is real, not playful, and is deep, or pointing at the causal identity, it is the act of Imagination. The very design of Imagination, this gift celestial, is to domesticate us in another nature.

The ideal of existence is the company of a Muse who doesn't wish to wander, whose visits are in secret, who divulges things not to be made popular. Soon as the wings grow which bring the gazing eyes, even these favorites flutter too near earth. No faculty leads to the invisible world so readily as imagination.

Genius certifies its possession of a thought by translating it into a fact or form which perfectly represents it. Imagination transfigures, so that only the cosmical relations of the object are seen. Personal beauty, when best, has this transcendency. Under calm and precise outline, we are surprised by the hint of the immeasurable and divine.

Cleave to truth, and to God, against the name of God.

Inspiration

Sit down to write with weak eyes, and your genius, when it wakes, will make them strong. Wisdom is like electricity. There is no permanent wise man, but men capable of wisdom, who, being put into certain company, or other favorable conditions, become wise for a short time, as glass rubbed acquire power for a while. Every man is entitled to be measured or characterized by his best influence. Every loafer knows the way to the rum shop, but every angel does not know the way to his nectar: why can we never learn our proper economy? Every youth and maid should know the road to prophecy, as surely as the cook-maid to the baker's shop.

Inspiration is very coy and capricious. We must lose many days to gain one, and, in order to win infallible verdicts from the inner mind, we must indulge and humor it in every way, and not too exactly harness and task it. We know vastly more than we can digest.

Happy beyond the common lot if he learn the secret, that besides the energy of his conscious intellect, his intellect is capable of new energy by abandonment to a higher influence; or, besides his privacy of power as an individual man, there is a great Public Power on which he can draw—by only letting himself go—by a certain abandonment to it—shall I say, by unlocking at all risks his human doors, and suffering the inundation of the ethereal tides to roll and circulate through him. This ecstasy the old philosophers called an inebriation, and said, that Intellect by its relation to what is prior to Intellect is a god.

Nothing can be done except by inspiration. The man's insight and power are local; he can see and do this, but it helps him not beyond; he is fain to make that ulterior step by mechanical means. "Neither by sea nor by land shall thou find the way to the Hyperboreans," said Pindar. We poorly strive by dint of time and hoarding grain on grain to substitute labor for the afflatus of Inspiration. Genius has not only thoughts, but the copula that joins them is also a thought. There's a sound healthy universe; the sky has not lost its azure because our eyes are sick. Everything we hear for the first time was expected by the mind: the newest discovery was expected.

Genius—Intuition

In domestic labor or in task work for bread, the hearing of poetry or some intellectual suggestion brings instant penitence: the thoughts revert to the Muse, and under that high invitation, we think we will throw off our chore, and attempt once more this purer, loftier service. But if we obey this suggestion, the beaming goddess presently hides her face in clouds again. We have not learned the law of mind, cannot control and bring at will or domesticate the high states of contemplation and continuous thought,—neither by idle wishing nor by rule of three, nor rule of thumb.

Our philosophy is to wait. We have retreated in patience, transferring our oft-shattered hope how often to a larger and remoter good. We meant well, but were continually forced to postpone our best action, and that which was life to do, could only be smuggled into odd moments of the months and year. But we learn to say at last, Dear God, the life of man is not by man—it is consentaneous and far-related: it came with the sun and nature; it is crescive and vegetative, and it is with us as it is with the sun and the grass. We obey the beautiful necessity. The powers that man wants will be supplied, as man is supplied, and the philosophy of waiting is sustained by all the oracles of the universe.

The truth is that every man is furnished, if he will heed it, with wisdom necessary to steer his own boat if he will not look away from his own to see how his neighbor steers his.

Use your powers, and put them to the best use. Tis the used key which is bright. Those faculties will be sharp, which are employed—imagination, reasoning, numbering, or fighting. What inspiration in every assertion of the will!

All teaching that shows the omnipotence of the will is spiritual—good effect.

The primary rule for conduct of the intellect is to have control of the thoughts without losing their natural attitudes and action. They are oracles: you shall not poke and drill and force but follow them. We believe that certain persons add to the common vision a certain degree of control over these states of mind; that the true scholar is one who has the power to stand beside his thoughts, or to hold off his thoughts at arm's length and give them perspective, to form the many in one.

Wisdom is not found in the hands of those who live at their ease. Life is so affirmative, that we cannot hear of personal vigor of any kind, great power of performance, without sympathy and fresh resolutions.

No hope is so bright but is the beginning of its own fulfillment. Believe in the beneficent unweariable power of Destiny. Belief consists in accepting the affirmations of the soul; unbelief in denying them.

The means of ennobling everything sensuous, and to animate also the deadest facts through uniting them to the idea, Goethe said, is the finest privilege of our supersensuous origin. Man, how much soever the earth draws him, with its thousand and myriad appearances, lifts yet a searching, longing look to the heaven which vaults over him in immeasurable spaces, whilst he feels deeply in himself that he is a citizen of that spiritual kingdom, our belief in which we must not repel or surrender. In this longing lies the secret of the eternal striving after an unknown aim. It is also the lever of our searching and thinking—soft bond between poetry and reality.

Genius is not personal, it is human, the Apotheosis of Man. It lies close to Being. The superiority of the man is in the simplicity of his thought, that he has no obstruction, but looks straight at the pure fact with no colored opinion, so that compared with him, other people appear to be walking in fog. The genius has the gentleness and simple manners and direct speech of childhood, far from the assumptions of public favorites. It does not cost him to see better than they, and he has might by his mere reality and gentleness.

Talent costs exertion: does something. Genius is. He cannot help his power and never needs to see to the proper recognition of his dignity. The greatest men impress by their presence, by their being. High genius is always moral: probity is its ground.

The surprises which genius has for us are in the homeliness of the fact, and the large scope or fruitfulness of the thought. Any path, every path, leads through Nature.

Society is made up of men of talents. That which sleeps in them is Genius, and the use of metaphysics is in every way to lay bare this fact, and if possible awake this slumberer, and subordinate these too proud and busy hands to the good.

The eye of genius looks through to the causal thought. Whilst the world of men give undivided heed to fact, Genius has been startled by perceiving the fact to be a mask, and detecting eyes that peer through it to meet its own. It knows that facts are not ultimates.

Intellect never again seems as before: for the state of Being, which is always divinely new—ever flowing from its ineffable fountain—is a condition of each experience. Thus Genius, like good generals, carries his base with him.

Commentary on the Consciousness Soul Cultural Epoch

Rudolf Steiner indicated that there are only a few paths of initiation left to westerners at this time in history. One of them entails being a Waldorf class teacher for eight years (grades 1–8) with the same class of students. Another path of initiation is to embody the meaning and rhythms of the *Foundation Stone Meditation* as given at the refounding of the Anthroposophical Society during the Christmas Foundation Meeting of 1924. The entire spiritual content of the first Goetheanum was encapsulated in the *Foundation Stone Meditation*. Though Steiner was very sad that westerners would not have the physical first Goetheanum to enter and study, he was confident that laying the dodecahedron of the *Foundation Stone Meditation* in our hearts would allow us to create our own temple of wisdom. All mysteries have been revealed, and the Master appears when the student is ready. Our higher self, our guardian angel, and the being of Anthroposophia stand ready to teach us through every percept or thought. We do not need an Eastern master, or yogi, or a New Age channeler to show us the way. Steiner said we should simply read his ideas and check them against reality. He asked that no "blind faith" ever be given towards the ideas of Anthroposophy without first directly applying the content of those ideas to real life. Anthroposophy is supposed to relate to everything that matters in real life; it is to enliven our understanding of life in all its many facets.

Steiner's mantric poem, the *Foundation Stone Meditation*, is one of the great prayers to the Hierarchies and the Holy Trinity. It addresses the Christian hierarchical hosts in the traditional rankings with their corresponding duties and rulerships. An entirely new religion of the Hierarchies is possible through Steiner's revelations of their functions and associations. The Hierarchy donated the constitution of the human being and is found active in all that is created in and around humanity. To fully understand the donations and gifts of the Hierarchies is tantamount to divining the entire overview of the meaning of human development: past-present-future. There is no end to the applications of this knowledge in relationship to the development of consciousness. Time, space, and consciousness are explained as aspects of ourselves connected to the workings of higher Hierarchies. Our true place in the cosmos becomes clear and the meaning of life is found anew in every moment of hierarchical manifestation. Great cycles of time unfold before the inner eye and the Archangelic rulerships of each 360-year period play out according to an ancient pattern that has meaning, purpose, and direction. Faith is no longer "blind" but, in fact, becomes a meaningful function of spiritual scientific investigation that produces answers that affect all aspects of life.

The Foundation Stone Meditation, **by Rudolf Steiner**

Soul of Man!
Thou livest in the Limbs
Which bear thee through the World of Space
Into the ocean-being of the Spirit.
Practice Spirit-Recollection
In depths of soul,
Where in the wielding World-Creator-Life
Thine own I comes to being
Within the I of God.
Then in the All-World-Being of Man
Thou will truly live.

For the Father-Spirit of the Heights holds sway
In Depths of Worlds begetting Life.
Seraphim, Cherubim, Thrones
Let this Ring out from the Heights
And in the Depths be echoed,
Speaking: From the Divine Springeth Mankind.
The Spirits hear it
In East and West and North and South:
May human beings hear it!
Soul of Man
Thou livest in the beat of Heart and Lung
Which leads thee through the Rhythmic tides of Time
Into the feeling of thine own Soul-Being.
Practice Spirit-Mindfulness
In balance of the soul,
Where the surging
Deeds of the World's Becoming
Do thine own I unite
Unto the I of the World.

Then 'mid the weaving of the soul of man
Thou will truly feel.
For the Christ-Will in the encircling Rounds hold sway

In the Rhythms of the Worlds, blessing the soul
Kyriotetes, Dynamis, Exsusiai!
Let this be fired from east and through the West be formed,
Speaking: In Christ Death Becomes Life.

The Spirits hear it
In East and West and North and South:
May human beings hear it!

Soul of Man!
Thou lives in the Resting Head
Which from the ground of the Eternal
Opens to thee the Thoughts of Worlds.

Practice Spirit-Vision
In quietness of Thought,
Where the eternal aims of gods
World-Being's Light
On thine own I bestow
For thy free Willing.
Then from the ground of the Spirit in Man
Thou will truly think.
For the Spirit's Universal Thoughts hold sway
In the Being of all worlds, craving for Light.
Archai, Archangeloi, Angeloi
Let this be prayed in the Depths
And from the Heights be answered,
Speaking: In the Cosmic Spirit-thoughts the Soul awakens.

The Spirits hear it
In East and West and North and South:
May human beings hear it!

At the turning-point of Time
The Spirit-Light of the World
Entered the stream of earthly Being.
Darkness of Night
Had held its sway;
Day radiant Light

Poured into the souls of men:
Light that gives warmth
To simple Shepherd's Hearts,
Light that enlightens
The wise Heads of Kings.
O Light Divine;
O Sun of Christ!
Warm Thou our Hearts,
Enlighten Thou our Heads,
That good may become
What from our Hearts we would found
And from our Heads direct
With single purpose.

Commentary on *The Kalevala*

Rudolf Steiner pointed out that during the epoch of the Consciousness Soul, the individual should read and learn to understand the content and images of the Finnish National Epic, The *Kalevala*. This epic, like the Icelandic *Prose Edda* and *Elder Edda*, was not written down until a very late period in history and had remained as an oral tradition late into the modern age. In both national epics, many individual stories have been compiled from numerous oral traditions to create a somewhat cohesive whole. The *Kalevala* is obviously three or four story lines woven together. First is the story of creation told from a simple perspective highlighting the central place of the Goddess Ilmatar, who seems to have existed before creation. She is the Water-Mother of the undefined "waters" that exist in many myths and legends as the primal source of creative matter. She is amorphous and undefined. She births a son, the magic wonder-worker Vainamoinen, who eventually sings all things into creation. He is the sole God of creation, who later in the story has many human characteristics, not the least of which is passion and desire for a mate. As a matter of fact, this desire for a beloved mate is the central theme of the whole story.

After Vainamoinen has brought about creation, a peculiar event happens early in the story. A young, prideful human named Joukahainen meets Vaimamoinen and inexplicably challenges the Father of Creation to a duel in singing magic forces into being. Of course, the boastful Joukahainen is sung into a puddle of mud until he finally submits to the stronger and more skillful magician. This battle is much like the story of Lucifer and his prideful battle with the Archangel Michael. In the end, "pride cometh before the fall," and Joukahainen is humbled and relegated to the lower realms, but not before he offers the Old Singer his beautiful sister, Aino, as a gift of capitulation. This is where pride is beaten and compassion arises. Vainamoinen forgives Joukahainen of his prideful boasting and accepts his offer of love and involvement in the processes of creation that he put into motion. Vainamoinen is rejected by his sister, Aino, and she hides in the sea until she is caught by Vainamoinen while he is fishing. He is still unable to hold her, and she escapes again, never to return. Vainamoinen is crushed by the rejection and now longs for true love, the fulfillment of his creation.

His desire for a lovely wife now becomes the driving force of the rest of the story. Vainamoinen sets his eye on one of the beautiful rainbow-maiden daughters of Old Louhi, the Witch of the Northland. He travels to the North and tries to bargain with Old Louhi for one of her daughters. The maidens reject Vainamoinen because he is too old. Old Louhi wants Vainamoinen to forge the ultimate prize for her: the Sampo, which is a magic mill that can grind out gold, salt, and meal. This prize can only be forged by a master blacksmith who can weld together the forces hidden in the tips of white swan feathers, the milk of greatest virtue, a single grain of barley, and the virgin wool of a lambkin.

Vainamoinen knows that he is not capable of forging the Sampo, so he leaves the Northland dejected and returns to his home with a plan. Vainamoinen knows that his brother, Ilmarinen, can forge the Sampo, but then Ilmarinen may want the rainbow-maiden. Vainamoinen tricks Ilmarinen into a fir tree that he has enchanted with the light of sun and moon and stars, and then sends it flying in a whirlwind to Old Louhi in the Northland. Ilmarinen successfully forges the Sampo but is refused the rainbow-maiden because he will not agree to stay in the Northland with her. Dejected, Ilmarinen returns to his home without a bride.

The next character to appear is Lemminkainen, who is a great human hero who wins the heart of his beloved but agrees to not engage in war as long as his wife does not wander into town to dance with the young men. She breaks her promise, so Lemminkainen goes off to war with Old Louhi and her people in the Northland. He subsequently kills Old Louhi's husband and starts a war with the people of the North. He must run and hide to avoid death.

Ilmarinen returns to the North and eventually accomplishes the forging of the Sampo for Old Louhi and wins one of the rainbow-maidens. He brings her back to his home, where she is killed by the mysterious character Kullervo. Ilmarinen is so sad at the death of his wife that he tries to forge a gold and silver wife, but she is too cold for him or Vainamoinen. Subsequently, another rainbow-maiden is forcefully taken by Vainamoinen, but on the trip home, she kills herself rather than wed the old man.

Finally, all three heroes—Vainamoinen, Ilmarinen, and Lemminkainen—join together to war on Old Louhi and the North people, but not until Vainamoinen almost dies (going to Tuonela) and Lemminkainen dies and is brought back from Tuonela (the Land of Death) by the efforts of his mother. Once the three heroes have stolen the Sampo and are escaping from Old Louhi, Lemminkainen starts to sing and awakens the North people from the slumber Vainamoinen has sung them into with his fish-bone harp. Old Louhi descends on the thieves, breaks the Sampo during the fight, and steals back the lid and handle before the majority of the Sampo falls into the ocean. Vainaminen rakes small pieces of the Sampo from the sea, but he is not able to reunite the pieces.

Old Louhi then steals the sun and moon and the heroes have a hard time winning it back. In the end, Vainamoinen leaves the story after pronouncing a death sentence on a newborn boy child, who is the prophesized New Creator.

Rudolf Steiner tells us that this newborn boy is a pre-image of Jesus Christ, the new spiritual king. Steiner indicates that modern humanity should study and learn the lessons of the *Kalevala* because they are the same lessons we must learn during the Consciousness Soul Epoch.

The story of Cupid and Psyche (Beauty and the Beast) is a psychological and topographical map of the soul that "falls in love." Like the Kalevala, it is centered around developing a proper relationship between two people. In Cupid and Psyche, it seems that the challenge of "marriage to the mysterious" has many contact points with modern-day relationships. This story, usually taken from *The Golden Ass* by Apuleias, is a psychological treasure-house of archetypes that seem to have arisen ubiquitously in many stories and in many lands. It is an archetypal myth created deep in the human psyche, usually through dreams, just as fairy tales of different nations contain similar archetypes that worked through dreams to create a commonly shared group of morality stories. These living archetypes arise while humans struggle between vices and virtues—a type of morality training. Fairy tales often tell the story of an internal battle to find love and know good from evil. The story is always the same, but the characters change.

In the *Kalevala*, we have one of the last oral traditions to be written down. The freshness of the images and the fantastic nature of the characters, who are both human and divine, draw the reader into a world of imaginations that are close to home and yet removed from time and space, as fairy tales always are: "Once upon a time, in a land far away." Therefore, to interpret the *Kalevala*, we must use *Imagination* to find the messages appropriate for modern humans.

Laplanders were one of the last folk-souls who lost their atavistic clairvoyance, and therefore have the latest connection to the spiritual world and its interactions with humans. The imaginative stories of the *Kalevala* are also physically true, as well as figuratively and archetypally true. The challenge to seek the perfect bride in a "Rainbow-Maiden of the North," a daughter of Old Louhi, Mistress of the Northland, is somewhat literal. To forge the Sampo and win a perfect consort is the modern injunction to seek the Holy Grail, or to alchemically marry the soul to the spirit in the "mysterious conjunction" of the the queen to the king. This heavenly marriage can only arise after the hero (feeling) goes north (thinking) and demonstrates the ability to forge the Sampo (willing), the magical mill that produces three substances, meal (thinking), gold (feeling), and salt (willing) while it spins and rocks the lid of glowing colors (ego).

In nature, we see the loving interaction of the breath of the Sun's solar wind light up the Earth's aurora borealis (and australis) in a rainbow-bridge reaching into heaven with colors that are fueled by carbon, hydrogen, oxygen, and nitrogen gases streaming up from the earth at the poles, meeting the plasma of the solar winds, and bending to the Earth through magnetic fields (Van Allen Belts). I like to call the aurora the *Night-Rainbow* or the *Rainbow Bridge* between the physical and spiritual worlds, where the gods and humans meet under the branches of the World Tree.

There are many myths, legends, and stories about the spiritual nature of the northern lights. Steiner tells us that the Archangel Michael (Archangel of the Sun—the Face of Christ) is active in this "Wall of Color" that surrounds the ultimate peak (Mt. Meru) of the Earth. This circumpolar land of the gods, which apparently does not move and is the center of our world, fits all of the descriptions for Shamballa, New Jerusalem descending, Mount Meru, or any other description of the bridge between worlds. Steiner also tells us that the Archangel Michael is one side of a coin that has Sophia on the other side. Together, Michael and Sophia stand at this auroral portal (threshold) to the spiritual realms at the top of the world. Each night, every human soul excarnates through this doorway into the spiritual world as they sleep. All newborn souls hover about this polar region before incarnating into a new life. This threshold is the door to the spiritual world that we must cross to sleep or die. The spiritual world is where souls sojourn between lives, and where our dreams are born and our souls are renewed during sleep.

The Polar Mysteries are often depicted as a rainbow bridge to the stars, the Milky Way, or the World Tree that reaches into the heavens. The Greeks thought the polar lands were the Gardens of the Hesperides, where the apples of immortality grew under the watchful eyes of Atlas. The Chinese believed that the

Jade Emperor and his Queen lived in the North, where they grew the peaches of immortality. Many polar myths abound because the ancients saw this land as the land of the gods—the world above humans where the ancient gods still rule. In Greek mythology, the new gods are always throwing the old gods down from the mountain and taking their place.

In Norse mythology, there were nine worlds, and they existed among the branches and roots of the World Tree, Yggdrasil. At the base of Yggdrasil, the three Nornies measured out the fates of gods and men. The Aesir gods rode down from Asgard across the rainbow-bridge (Bifrost) to meet humans in their world, Midgard. When the old Norse gods died in the battle of Ragnarok, only a few old gods and some children of the old gods lived on and crossed a new rainbow bridge into a new heaven.

In his wonderful book *Aurora*, Harald Falck-Ytter shares some brilliant insights that may help us understand the nature of the aurora and its connection to the *Kalevala* and modern human consciousness. He points out the threefold nature of light as it manifests in lightning, the rainbow, and the aurora. He believes that lightning is much like human willpower: arising from the hidden depths, like Vulcan the lightning-smith of Zeus, with incredible strength and mystery. Rainbows are like the human heart, adding feeling to the spirit that temporarily incarnates in the physical, an illusion of living color that turns the Sun's rays into the colors of creation. The aurora, which is like human thinking, is centered in the far north in a dome filled with lights. The aurora arises from the depths as gases rush to the stars, illuminated by the breath of the Sun. The aurora is a new Pentecost, with its rushing sound of winds (the whistling of the aurora) and tongues of fire upon the heads of the blessed. The aurora is the sense-free thinking of humans enkindling fire, shining as an offering of light—a new, fledgling star in the first stages of illumination.

There is great wealth of wisdom in this analogy of Faulk-Ytter's and many hierarchical truths come to bare and validate these timely ideas. We need to know our creative place in the universe and the methods of illumination and enlightenment. The aurora is an image of the appearance of Christ active in the etheric life-force of the earth. The dynamic interaction of Sun and Earth is reflected in the mission and passion of Christ's redemption of humanity and the Earth. Christ does for the soul and spirit of humanity what the Sun does for the Earth and the planets in our solar system. The Earth stands midway between the inner and outer planets, just as humanity stands midway in its evolution from past to future. What is happening to the Earth is the same thing that is happening to humanity. Human evolution creates the evolution of the Earth, not the reverse. Lightning, rainbows, and the auroral lights reflect some of the light created in humans. We know that thinking, feeling, and willing light up different parts of the brain with different intensity and combinations. These light-patterns are not unlike heat lightning and auroral displays. Who can deny the deep feelings and sensations that arise when witnessing a rainbow or the northern lights?

The *Chaldean Oracles* speak of the Amiliktoi, the wall of color in the north that surrounds the waters of the Earth and can hold the "flower of fire" that arises from the higher intellect. These descriptions are similar to the ideas found in the *Kalevala*. Also, Mani describes meeting a being who is much like the descriptions of the rainbow-maidens. These different stories are pointing at the same thing, which is an imperative for our Consciousness Soul Epoch: the need to find Sophia, the female being of Wisdom, and to hold her close as a wife until the light of the north (sense-free thinking or Imagination) is found in the process. The forging of the Sampo is the development of the prerequisite skill of mastering thinking, feeling, and willing and having spiritual substance arise from these three to illuminate and rotate the "lid of colors," which can "grind out" the gifts of thinking/meal (food for thought—*Imagination*), feeling/gold (purified virtues—*Inspiration*), and willing/salt (taming desires—*Intuition*). These refined elements of thinking, feeling, and willing become the food we feed the gods (ionized carbon—physical, oxygen—etheric, nitrogen—astral, and hydrogen—ego) as we transform them into *Imagination*, *Inspiration*, and *Intuition*. Each night as we sleep, this process of regeneration and nourishment happens as we feed the gods and they, in turn, feed us with cosmic Light, Sound, and Life ethers that bathe our seven chakras with the nourishment we need. Steiner calls this the "earthly and cosmic nutrition stream" or the "frontal spinal column" that bathes the pineal gland with rarified carbon substances to coagulate calcium carbonate crystals in the pineal gland, which directly enhances the development of human consciousness.

This awakening process can also be imagined as the growing relationship of the human soul to the spirit of Wisdom, called Sophia, or Anthroposophia by Rudolf Steiner. Mani calls Her the Blessed One and says that She goes ahead of us to prepare the way for our spiritual development. She is intimately connected with the marriage of soul to spirit. She prepares the Virgin Soul for the wedding to Christ, our spirit nature (Spirit Self, Life Spirit, Spirit Man). As humans evolve, we meet and interact more and more with Sophia. She is the primal spirit-consort of the Buddhists, called Vajrayogini. Vajrayogini is a fiery being who dances in the flames of transcendental wisdom and is happy to sacrifice her body and blood to purify all sentient beings. She carries a cross over her left shoulder and conquers pride with compassion. She dances on the Sun and the Moon simultaneously, with rainbows leaping from her heart while lightning and thunder is all about her, creating a magical rainbow emanation from her head, where the northern mountain of the world is raised as a temple from her crown chakra, shining like colorful ribbons blowing in the wind. Vajrayogini sounds like a description of the northern lights.

The similarity of traditional religions is clearly seen to the observant eye. Everywhere you study, you will come to the same archetypes in different clothes. What we find in the universe, we find in the human temple of the body. What we find in Earth evolution, we find in human evolution. Everywhere we look, we are peering into a mirror that reflects the same natural wisdom. All we need to do is realize that our percepts reveal living beings that demonstrate the connectivity of the entire world that is mirrored in the human body. The human being is the hieroglyph of the universe, a riddle that is always evolving. The image of God, or the universe, is only limited by the image of what a human being truly is and will become.

In one version of creation, God imagines projecting Himself into Sophia, thus actualizing in finite forms the infinite richness of his creative potential. Sophia translates the Divine Word into forms and colors that are God Himself, who becomes knowable through Her. The mirror of God and creation groans in pain. Sophia is the promised Beloved of Man, the supreme mediating and "magical" entity. She casts Her look, deep as a mirror reflecting the starry sky, a mirror whose function is to transform our image, and that of Nature, into a body of eternal substance: the body of Paradise Regained. Everything in the manifest world is born through this divine mirror that makes possible the birth of fire and light, sound and life. Our hearts are this mirror, and they reflect everything in Nature. We see our self looking back from the mirror: God or the devil, depending on our purity and morality. Sophia is the divine mirror and the bridesmaid who is preparing our Virgin Soul to reflect the image of our Spirit Groom, our own Christened-Self. This gnostic tradition of Sophia echoes the heroes' quest in the *Kalevala* for the rainbow-maiden and the seemingly insatiable need to reflect their greatness in the mirror of the beloved.

Studying the *Kalevala* can bring revelations for our Consciousness Soul Epoch. The *Kalevala* tells of the soul struggle of the human being who is challenged with becoming either angelic or animalistic. Should we steal the "perfect wife" or win her through trials and challenges that require magic skills? Does descending to Hell (Tuonela), winning the war, or forging the Sampo truly win the longed-for rainbow-maiden of the North? What is the way to find her and win her love with dignity and compassion? Does the great singing magic of Vainamoinen, with its spells, win the maiden? Or the strength and boldness of Lemminkainen? Or does the skill and magic of the cosmic-smithy Ilmarinen win the heavenly maiden? Perhaps we have to merge all three great heroes into one and smooth our rough edges before we are presentable to the wondrous land of the North, where our beloved awaits our arrival to forge the magic Sampo.

The Consciousness Soul transforms the Astral Body of personal lower desires into a vessel of purified higher desires

(Sampo/Fountain of Virtue/Holy Grail) called the Spirit Self, which directs our spiritual evolution. When the *Virtuous Fountain of Colors* lights up the night of the soul, the watchfires of the North show that the rainbow warriors are gathering for the spirit feast and the wedding of soul to spirit. The colorful plumes of *Imagination* and *Inspiration* that arise in the heavens about this Island of the Blessed are calling us. Will we answer?

Rudolf Steiner's Curriculum Recommendations for Grade Five

Karl Stockmeyer's Waldorf Literature and History indications for Grade Five

History: First historical concepts; civilizations of the Oriental people up to the Greeks.

In history too, give a survey covering the entire historical background, beginning with oriental history, to be followed by Greek history and reaching the later Christian development. You are then quite free to introduce content of real inner spirituality—without teaching anthroposophical dogma.

Similarly, the development of oriental history is built up in a very beautiful way: in the Indian history we witness a fashioning of the physical body, in the Persian of the etheric body, and in the Egypto-Chaldaic of the astral body, but of course you cannot give it in this form. Show how people living in the astral element have developed astronomy, how the Jews expressed the ego-principle in the Jehovah-principle and how the Greeks were the first people to develop a real conception of nature. Earlier conceptions of nature were merely part of a whole world outlook. You can give a survey which will stand the test of time and which will show how historical events really unfold in the manner described. (Karl Stockmeyer)

Bibliographical References and Recommended Reading
Grade Five—Anglo-Germanic

Adams, George. *Verses and Meditations by Rudolf Steiner.* Rudolf Steiner Press, London, 1972.

Russell, George William. *The Candle of Vision.* University Press, New York.

Crawford, John Martin. *The Kalevala: The Epic Poem of Finland.* John B. Alden, New York, 1888.

Fry, Christopher. *Christopher Fry Plays: A Sleep of Prisoners.* Oxford University Press, 1970.

Hall, Manly P. *The Most Holy Trinosophia of the Comte De St. Germain.* The Philosophical Research Society, Inc., Los Angeles, 1983.

Shakespeare, William. *The Complete Works of Shakespeare.* Latus ePublishing, 2011.

Shrady, Maria. *Angelus Silesius: The Cherubinic Wanderer.* Paulist Press, New York, 1986.

Grade Six

Venus Incarnation of the Earth
Stage Six of Seven of the Eternal Curriculum
Planetary Influence is Jupiter
The Mystery of the Word Transformed by Number

The Sixth Cultural Epoch

3573-5733 AD Aquarius, Venus, Life Spirit, Future Russian

And there appeared a great wonder in heaven; a woman clothed with the sun, and the moon under her feet, and upon her head a crown of twelve stars: And she being with child cried, travailing in birth, and pained to be delivered. And there appeared another wonder in heaven; and behold a great red dragon, having seven heads and ten horns, and seven crowns upon his heads. And his tail drew the third part of the stars of heaven, and did cast them to the earth: and the dragon stood before the woman which was ready to be delivered, for to devour her child as soon as it was born. And she brought forth a man child, who was to rule all nations with a rod of iron: and her child was caught up unto God, and to his throne. And the woman fled into the wilderness, where she hath a place prepared of God, that they should feed her there a thousand two hundred and threescore days.

The Book of Revelation 12

The sixth-grader is developing the forces to understand the Greco-Roman Cultural Epoch when they struggle with the events of the death of Jesus Christ, just as the modern thinker must understand the central place of Christianity in the Fifth Post-Atlantean Epoch. The question arises: "Is this myth or history?" We must look to the future to find the New Earth, which will be called the Venus Incarnation of the Earth; where the collective good of every community member creates the living environment—not unlike the Christian monastic life of the Middle Ages.

History has now entered an age when nothing is certain due to the speed of hyper-materialism that destroys community values and leaves the individual feeling homeless, hopeless, and fearful of the future. Some people choose to cluster together in belief-communities to find quieter lifestyles away from the maddening throngs. Our beliefs are separated from thinking in the modern, rational world-view of science. Roman law still rules everywhere we look. We are held responsible for knowing every law because we are held accountable for them. We must comply with the cold logic all around us, or retreat to our sheltered communities.

The sixth-grade student in a Waldorf school studies monastic orders of the Middle Ages and learns about the development of Christianity and its early history. The student delves deeply into the life of a monk in a monastery and tries to imagine what it was like to be part of a living community trying to do the work of the divine, both in the soul and in the world. Perhaps this Christian monastic life of community was an idea far ahead of its time. The Venus Incarnation of the Earth might look much like monastic life. Novalis immortalized these monastic communities of the early church in his *Christianity or Europe*. He insinuates that Christian monasticism was one of the highest expressions of human spiritual development.

Rudolf Steiner spoke only a little about the future cultural epochs that he named the Future Russian Epoch (6th) and the Future American Epoch (7th). He warned us that the Russia and America of these periods will not resemble the Russia and

America that we know now. Great changes will come to each nation before the proper preparation will have occurred to engender the characteristics necessary to develop the inner force that will evolve into the predominant cultural advancement. Each cultural epoch has their own distinctive gift to give in the process of cultural evolution. The Russians of Rudolf Steiner's day were experiencing cruel repression and a lack of tolerance for freedom of any type. This repression of the soul and spirit of the Russian people created strong forces of longing and desire for freedom of worship and freedom in the social sphere. Certain soul forces were held back from forming, and yet great strength and endurance developed in those who kept the faith and hoped a better day would come soon. Historically, the longing for the rightful Russian king (Demetrius) to return developed in Russia, as well as the longing for the spiritual Grail-City of Kietesch to return. Many hopes and dreams developed in Russians that created a profound spiritual longing in an entire folk-soul. This longing developed great capacities for long-suffering and a natural inwardness of soul akin to the "Grail Mood." This mood of soul will exist for centuries before it has its fulfillment in the coming Russian Epoch, when Sophia, the being of Wisdom, will become visible to the aspirant, and Christ's counsel will be as close as our own hearts.

When we speak about the Consciousness Soul Epoch, we need to remember that the modern aspirant is merging aspects of the Consciousness Soul with newly birthed aspects of the Spirit Self. Together, these aspects of the soul and spirit transform the desires and passions of the Astral Body, and an independent Spirit Self is born into the spirit world of sense-free *Imaginations*. The Spirit Self is just a child in the early stages of development. The Consciousness Soul is also a newly developing faculty that distills the higher aspects of the Intellectual Soul and Sentient Soul. The Consciousness Soul is singular and focused on individual development, and is often not very social in its early stages. The aspirant is encouraged to develop individual organs of perception in the Consciousness Soul that become new sense organs in the spiritual world—supersensible organs for spiritual perception. Each higher stage of soul development becomes more singular and personal until a refined part of the Consciousness Soul is developed called the Spiritual Soul, which is comprised of eternal elements derived from wakeful consciousness. The soul burns off the dross of sentience and lower mental development for immediate, personal gains in self-discipline and spiritual advancement. As the aspirant crosses the threshold of the spiritual world, she stands alone, facing the truth of karma and destiny balanced against moral experience and spiritual love. It is a path that the aspirant takes alone, and the gains and losses are personal and inward.

The Consciousness Soul Epoch is inherently anti-social, and communities find it hard to create harmony and cooperation in modern life. In a way, we are asking souls to find the power of Christian love of the other, though there may be no community to express it in. We walk the path across the threshold alone with the moral strength we have created by our good deeds. Many fall short of having the moral fiber to remember what they experience in the spiritual world each night and between incarnations. Egotism is outrunning ego-development. Selfishness is finding social expression everywhere, and selflessness hardly has an avenue for expression of social love and community building. Ego strength is needed in our epoch, but often the modern world breeds only aberrations of the ego through sex, violence, and mental instability. True human freedom is now possible, and therefore the extremes of human behavior can manifest for good and evil. We can now begin to see the spectrum of human expression from angelic to animalistic. Each aspirant must take control of their spiritual evolution and either develop higher thinking, feeling, and willing, or be pulled into the degradations of those forces: neurosis, psychosis, aberrations of sex, and violence.

Theosophists define the three human *spirit bodies* with the Eastern terms Manas, Buddhi, and Atman. Manas comes from the word *Manu*: the thinking individual. When a soul raises their thinking into the realms where spiritual wings are necessary to ascend to the archetypes, the soul has reached "Manasic Thinking." Steiner called this realm the Spirit Self or the realm of *Imagination*, where angels abide. He calls the realm above that Life Spirit, or the Buddhi plane, where Christ makes the Christened higher ego available for each individual. This realm is where refined feelings are turning into *Inspiration* that weds the higher aspects of the Virgin Soul to the Spirit Groom—the Christened Self. The elements of the Consciousness Soul that can *make it across the rainbow bridge* to the Spirit Self unite with the forces of Christ that hold the essence of the reincarnating individual human spirit. Thus, Theosophists say it is the Buddhi-Manas that reincarnates from one life to the next.

The element of the spirit that is beyond the personal, reincarnating ego is the universal realm of non-personal archetypes that feed the higher nature of each individual spirit, called Atman or Spirit Man (Spirit Human). These archetypes unite all manifestation into "One Thing" that mirrors the Father Ground of Being. The personal Spirit Man adds each distinctiveness to the whole. This is the realm where the seed archetype of each spirit holds a timeless record of the development of that individual spirit. It is also where the archetypal seeds that were imagined even before creation came into being are held. All personal and collective karma resides there.

The spirit-land is described by Rudolf Steiner in great detail in his book, *Theosophy*. In *Theosophy*, Steiner tells us that the spirit-land is being created by our every thought, feeling, and action in our present world. In the Future Sixth Incarnation of the Earth, called Venus, the environment will be the result of the love that was shared between people in the previous Incarnation of the Earth. In the Sixth Cultural Epoch, the Future Russian Epoch, society will be centered in local communities of agreement that clearly state their beliefs, goals, intentions, and the methods they will use to attain them in relationship to a conscious global community. These Christian Communities will be fired by the fuel of moral longing for the incarnation of new spiritual, cultural, and religious archetypes. This longing will be prepared by years of repression and the repression of freedom through social, political, religion, and political means. The Future Russian soul will choose to live in conscious communities that unite spiritual ideas with cultural ideals.

The sixth-grade Waldorf student is taught Greek and Roman history up to the Middle Ages. They cover Greek city-states, the gods and goddesses, Roman history through the kings of Rome, the birth and death of Jesus of Nazareth, the founding of Christianity, and the developing Christian church through feudalism and monastic orders. The sixth-grade student deeply studies one or another Christian monastic order, like the Cistercians, Franciscans, Benedictines, Jesuits, or some other order of the Roman Catholic Church. The rules of the order hold the group together in a *conscious community* focused on spiritual goals that perfect the belief culture of the community and the monks involved. As Novalis insinuated in his essay *Christianity or Europe*, the church of the Middle Ages was a picture of an ideal community centered on the truth of Christ. In a way, we have lost the simplicity of life that refines morality like a Franciscan monastery focused on harmlessness and service to all sentient life. A certain naive simplicity of group consciousness seemed to have produced a condition that mimicked a future state of development. This is the logic that places the sixth-grade language arts and history curriculum in correspondence with the Future Russian Cultural Epoch.

When we speak about the seven stages of incarnation, it is important to remember that the fifth stage of development holds the key aspect of development that will go on into the future as the dominant effect of progressive development. The fifth stage holds the key to new cultural archetypes and motifs. The fifth-grade student is in the "golden age of childhood" and is presented the miniature recapitulation of all Post-Atlantean Epochs up to the present (Indian, Persia, Egypto-Chaldean, Greco-Roman, Anglo-Germanic). The sixth-grade student proceeds into the future (just as puberty empowers their physical bodies with the ability of propagating the future) beyond where humanity has already gone. The sixth and seventh epochs have yet to happen, let alone the Future Jupiter, Venus, and Vulcan Incarnations of the Earth. Therefore, sixth-graders already have challenges in their lives that may go beyond the teacher's experience.

The sixth, seventh, and eighth grades are full of unimaginable potential for student growth. The students should develop beyond their teacher's ability to lead. The limits of the teacher now begin to show, and the challenges the students bring for the future begin to present themselves. The taming of the astral nature is important, and music, Gregorian chanting, singing in parts, instrumental music, and choral singing are great tools to harmonize astral influences. The same was true with European humanity in the Middle Ages. The individual found a personal path through music, and the monastic life and found a spiritual *unity* in the efforts of fellow believers. This type of social order is what the sixth-grade child needs. The astrality of sex is mitigated by the monk's vows of chastity, the wildness of soul is mitigated by the vow of obedience, and the materialism of the desire body is mitigated by the vow of poverty.

The teachings of the troubadours and the chivalric orders of romance are another solution to sixth-grade astrality. The path of renunciation and the quest of the Holy Grail are realities in the sixth-grader's soul. Finding the similarities of the Holy Grail legends with the holy chalice in the Eucharist of the church was an easy transition for many Europeans. Roman villas became monasteries, which often became feudal keeps, and later became fortified cities of commerce and trade. The original monastic communities were the greatest seats of learning and culture. The Roman roads became the network of the Roman Catholic Church, and Roman law ruled everywhere until Roman Catholic Canon Law came to power. The use of logic and the capacity to understand law are two characteristics that sixth-graders need to develop to become members of a conscious community.

The spiritual wedding depicted in *The Alchemical Wedding of Christian Rosenkreutz* by Johann Valentin Andreas is a good parable that embodies the nature of the Jupiter Incarnation of the Earth. In the grand picture of the future, such wonders occur that cause the Moon to reunite with the Earth some six thousand years from now. Major alchemical transformations will take place in our solar system that will cause scientists to throw out their mistaken theories. The Sun, Earth, and planets transform in manners that can hardly be imagined. In the Age of Discovery, such shocking news of voyages to the west, like North and South America or the wonders India and China, plagued the simple monk and drew some adventurous monks out of the protected monastic communities to explore the greater world around them. The ideal would be to have the best of both spiritual communities and great explorations.

The language arts curriculum for sixth-grade is so vast that it can only be sampled. Augustine's *City of God*, Campanella's *City of the Sun*, Dante's *Paradisio*, and the many works of the scholastics are good examples of the archetype of New Jerusalem, the celestial City of Heaven descending to Earth. These were the archetypes of the Middle Ages that drove the many monastic orders to found conscious communities to do the work of the spirit.

Literature Selections for Grade Six Children

The Book of Revelation 21-22, **King James Version**

And I saw a new heaven and a new earth: for the first heaven and the first earth were passed away; and there was no more sea. And I John saw the holy city, New Jerusalem, coming down from God out of heaven, prepared as a bride adorned for her husband. And I heard a great voice out of heaven saying, Behold, the tabernacle of God is with men, and he will dwell with them, and they shall be his people, and God himself shall be with them, and be their God. And God shall wipe away all tears from their eyes; and there shall be no more death, neither sorrow, nor crying, neither shall there be any more pain: for the former things are passed away. And he that sat upon the throne said, Behold, I make all things new. And he said unto me, Write: for these words are true and faithful. And he said unto me, It is done.

I am Alpha and Omega, the beginning and the end. I will give unto him that is athirst of the fountain of the water of life freely. He that overcometh shall inherit all things; and I will be his God, and he shall be my son. But the fearful, and unbelieving, and the abominable, and murderers, and whoremongers, and sorcerers, and idolaters, and all liars, shall have their part in the lake which burneth with fire and brimstone: which is the second death. And there came unto me one of the seven angels which had the seven vials full of the seven last plagues, and talked with me, saying, Come hither, I will shew thee the bride, the Lamb's wife. And he carried me away in the spirit to a great and high mountain, and shewed me that great city, the holy Jerusalem, descending out of heaven from God, having the glory of God: and her light was like unto a stone most precious, even like a jasper stone, clear as crystal; and had a wall great and high, and had twelve gates, and at the gates twelve angels, and names written thereon, which are the names of the twelve tribes of the children of Israel: on the east three gates;

on the north three gates; on the south three gates; and on the west three gates.

And the wall of the city had twelve foundations, and in them the names of the twelve apostles of the Lamb. And he that talked with me had a golden reed to measure the city, and the gates thereof, and the wall thereof. And the city lieth foursquare, and the length is as large as the breadth: and he measured the city with the reed, twelve thousand furlongs. The length and the breadth and the height of it are equal. And he measured the wall thereof, an hundred and forty and four cubits, according to the measure of a man, that is, of the angel. And the building of the wall of it was of jasper: and the city was pure gold, like unto clear glass. And the foundations of the wall of the city were garnished with all manner of precious stones. The first foundation was jasper; the second, sapphire; the third, a chalcedony; the fourth, an emerald; the fifth, sardonyx; the sixth, sardius; the seventh, chrysolyte; the eighth, beryl; the ninth, a topaz; the tenth, a chrysoprasus; the eleventh, a jacinth; the twelfth, an amethyst. And the twelve gates were twelve pearls: every several gate was of one pearl: and the street of the city was pure gold, as it were transparent glass. And I saw no temple therein: for the Lord God Almighty and the Lamb are the temple of it. And the city had no need of the sun, neither of the moon, to shine in it: for the glory of God did lighten it, and the Lamb is the light thereof. And the nations of them which are saved shall walk in the light of it: and the kings of the earth do bring their glory and honour into it. And the gates of it shall not be shut at all by day: for there shall be no night there. And they shall bring the glory and honour of the nations into it. And there shall in no wise enter into it any thing that defileth, neither whatsoever worketh abomination, or maketh a lie: but they which are written in the Lamb's book of life.

And he shewed me a pure river of water of life, clear as crystal, proceeding out of the throne of God and of the Lamb. In the midst of the street of it, and on either side of the river, was there the tree of life, which bare twelve manner of fruits, and yielded her fruit every month: and the leaves of the tree were for the healing of the nations. And there shall be no more curse: but the throne of God and of the Lamb shall be in it; and his servants shall serve him: And they shall see his face; and his name shall be in their foreheads. And there shall be no night there; and they need no candle, neither light of the sun; for the Lord God giveth them light: and they shall reign for ever and ever.

City of God, St. Augustine (354-430)

Being, then, for the present established in this hope, let us do what the Psalmist further indicates, and become in our measure angels or messengers of God, declaring His will, and praising His glory and His grace. For when he had said, "To place my hope in God," he goes on, "that I may declare all Thy praises in the gates of the daughter of Zion." This is the most glorious city of God; this is the city which knows and worships one God: she is celebrated by the holy angels, who invite us to their society, and desire us to become fellow-citizens with them in this city; for they do not wish us to worship them as our gods, but to join them in worshipping their God and ours; nor to sacrifice to them, but, together with them, to become a sacrifice to God. Accordingly, whoever will lay aside malignant obstinacy, and consider these things, shall be assured that all these blessed and immortal spirits, who do not envy us, but rather love us, and desire us to be as blessed as themselves, look on us with greater pleasure, and give us greater assistance, when we join them in worshipping one God, Father, Son, and Holy Ghost, than if we were to offer to themselves sacrifice and worship.

The City of the Sun by Tommaso Campanella (1568-1639)

A Dialogue between a Grandmaster and a Genoese Sea-Captain

G.M. Prithee, now, tell me what happened to you during that voyage?

Capt. I have already told you how I wandered over the whole earth. In the course of my journeying, I came to Taprobane, and was compelled to go ashore at a place, where through fear of the inhabitants I remained in a wood.

When I stepped out of this I found myself on a large plain immediately under the equator.

G.M. And what befell you here?

Capt. I came upon a large crowd of men and armed women, many of whom did not understand our language, and they conducted me forthwith to the City of the Sun.

G.M. Tell me after what plan this city is built and how it is governed.

Capt. The greater part of the city is built upon a high hill, which rises from an extensive plain, but several of its circles extend for some distance beyond the base of the hill, which is of such a size that the diameter of the city is upward of two miles, so that its circumference becomes about seven. On account of the humped shape of the mountain, however, the diameter of the city is really more than if it were built on a plain.

It is divided into seven rings or huge circles named from the seven planets, and the way from one to the other of these is by four streets and through four gates, that look toward the four points of the compass.

G.M. Tell on, I pray you! Tell on! I am dying to hear more.

Capt. The temple is built in the form of a circle; it is not girt with walls, but stands upon thick columns, beautifully grouped. A very large dome, built with great care in the center or pole, contains another small vault as it were rising out of it, and in this is a spiracle, which is right over the altar. There is but one altar in the middle of the temple, and this is hedged round by columns. The temple itself is on a space of more than 350 paces. Without it, arches measuring about eight paces extend from the heads of the columns outward, whence other columns rise about three paces from the thick, strong, and erect wall. Between these and the former columns there are galleries for walking, with beautiful pavements, and in the recess of the wall, which is adorned with numerous large doors, there are immovable seats, placed as it were between the inside columns, supporting the temple. Portable chairs are not wanting, many and well adorned. Nothing is seen over the altar but a large globe, upon which the heavenly bodies are painted, and another globe upon which there is a representation of the earth. Furthermore, in the vault of the dome there can be discerned representations of all the stars of heaven from the first to the sixth magnitude, with their proper names and power to influence terrestrial things marked in three little verses for each. There are the poles and greater and lesser circles according to the right latitude of the place, but these are not perfect because there is no wall below. They seem, too, to be made in their relation to the globes on the altar. The pavement of the temple is bright with precious stones. Its seven golden lamps hang always burning, and these bear the names of the seven planets.

At the top of the building several small and beautiful cells surround the small dome, and behind the level space above the bands or arches of the exterior and interior columns there are many cells, both small and large, where the priests and religious officers dwell to the number of forty-nine.

A revolving flag projects from the smaller dome, and this shows in what quarter the wind is. The flag is marked with figures up to thirty-six, and the priests know what sort of year the different kinds of winds bring and what will be the changes of weather on land and sea. Furthermore, under the flag a book is always kept written with letters of gold.

G.M. I pray you, worthy hero, explain to me their whole system of government; for I am anxious to hear it.

Capt. The great ruler among them is a priest whom they call by the name Hoh, though we should call him Metaphysic. He is head over all, in temporal and spiritual matters, and all business and lawsuits are settled by him, as the supreme authority. Three princes of equal power—viz., Pon, Sin, and Mor—assist him, and these in our tongue we should call Power, Wisdom, and Love. To Power belongs the care of all matters relating to war and peace. He attends to the military arts, and, next to Hoh, he is ruler in every affair of a warlike nature. He governs the military magistrates and the soldiers, and has the management of the munitions, the fortifications, the storming of places, the implements of war, the armories, the smiths and workmen connected with matters of this sort.

But Wisdom is the ruler of the liberal arts, of mechanics, of all sciences with their magistrates and doctors, and of the discipline of the schools. As many doctors as there are, are under his control. There is one doctor who is called Astrologus; a second, Cosmographus; a third, Arithmeticus; a fourth, Geometra; a fifth, Historiographus; a sixth, Poeta; a seventh, Logicus; an eighth, Rhetor; a ninth, Grammaticus; a tenth, Medicus; an eleventh, Physiologus; a twelfth, Politicus; a thirteenth, Moralis. They have but one book, which they call Wisdom, and in it all the sciences are written with conciseness and marvelous fluency of expression. This they read to the people after the custom of the Pythagoreans. It is Wisdom who causes the exterior and interior, the higher and lower walls of the city to be adorned with the finest pictures, and to have all the sciences painted upon them in an admirable manner. On the walls of the temple and on the dome, which is let down when the priest gives an address, lest the sounds of his voice, being scattered, should fly away from his audience, there are pictures of stars in their different magnitudes, with the powers and motions of each, expressed separately in three little verses.

Christianopolis—An Ideal State of the Seventh Century
by Johann Valentin Andreae (1641)

While wandering as a stranger on the earth, suffering much in patience from tyranny, sophistry, and hypocrisy, seeking a man, and not finding what I so anxiously sought, I decided to launch out once more upon the Academic Sea though the latter had very often been hurtful to me. And so, ascending the good ship *Phantasy*, I left the port together with many others and exposed my life and person to the thousand dangers that go with desire for knowledge. For a short space of time conditions favored our voyage; then adverse storms of envy and calumny stirred up the Ethiopian Sea against us and removed all hope of calm weather. The efforts of the skipper and the oarsmen were exerted to the limit, our own stubborn love of life would not give up, and even the vessel resisted the rocks; but the force of the sea always proved stronger. Finally, when all hope was lost and we, rather of necessity than on account of bravery of soul, had prepared to die, the ship collapsed and we sank. Some were swallowed up by the sea, some were scattered to great distances, while some who could swim or who found planks to float upon, were carried to different islands scattered throughout this sea. Very few escaped death, and I alone, without a single comrade, was at length driven to a very minute islet, a mere piece of turf, as it seemed.

Everything here pleased me, except I did not please myself. The island, moreover, small though it had appeared, had a great abundance of all things, and there was not a foot of soil to be seen which was not under cultivation or in some way put to use for mankind. The form is that of a triangle, whose perimeter is about 30 miles. This island is rich in grain and pasture fields, watered with rivers and brooks, adorned with woods and vineyards, full of animals, just as if it were a whole world in miniature. One might think that here the heavens and the earth had been married and were living together in ever-lasting peace.

While I was drying my undershirt, the only garment I had saved, in the rays of the morning sun, an inhabitant of the island, some one of the many watchmen of the place, came upon me suddenly. He inquired into my mischance with all kindness, and while sympathizing with my misfortune, bade me trust him and accompany him to the city, where, with their usual consideration toward strangers and exiles, the citizens would supply my needs; and he added: "Happy are you whose lot it has been, after so severe a shipwreck, to be thrown on land at this place." And I answered only, "Thank God! Glory to God!"

Meantime the sight and the beauty of the city as we approached it surprised me greatly, for all the rest of the world does not hold anything like it or to be compared with it. So, turning to my guide I said: "What happiness has established her abode here?" And he answered: "The one that in this world is generally very unhappy. For when the world raged against the good and drove them out of her boundaries, religion, an exile, gathering about her the comrades whom she regarded the most faithful, after crossing the sea and examining various places, finally chose this land in which to establish her followers. Later she built a city which we call Christianopolis, and desired that it should be the home, or, if you prefer, the stronghold of honesty and excellence. The generosity of this our republic to all in want, you are about to experience. So, if you desire to traverse the city (but you must do it with dispassionate eyes, guarded tongue, and decent behavior) the opportunity will not be denied you; nay, the city lies open to you in its individual parts."

The Way of Light by John Amos Comenius (1668)

We need a sacred society, devoted to the common welfare of all and we may hope that an Art of Arts, a Science of Sciences, a Wisdom of Wisdom, a Light of Light shall at length be possessed. The inventions of previous ages, navigation and printing, have opened a way for the spread of light. We may expect that we stand on the threshold of yet greater advances. The 'universal books' will make it possible for all to learn and to join in the advance. The book of *Pansophia* will be completed. The schools of universal wisdom will be founded. And the prophets of universal wisdom in all countries must be accessible to one another.

There should be a College, or a sacred society, devoted to the common welfare of mankind, and held together by some laws and rules. A great need for the spread of light is that there should be a universal language which all can understand. The learned men of the new order will devote themselves to this problem. So will the light of the Gospel, as well as the light of learning, be spread throughout the world. Whether this or another name is more pleasing, we preferred that of Pansophia because it was our intention to stimulate all people to know everything, to be wise, to fill their spirit with the truth of all things, and not with the fog of opinions. Why however, should the Temple of Pansophia be erected according to the ideas, measurements and laws of the highest Master-Builder Himself? Because we follow the prototype of the whole, according to measure, number, position and purpose of its parts in the way that was indicated by the wisdom of the Godhead Himself.

If we wish to erect the Temple of Wisdom, we shall have to remind ourselves that the Temple to be built is considered great, majestic and praiseworthy throughout all lands, because our God is above all Gods. The foundation of the Temple thus will be the countenance of God. This means through all things visible the invisible One on His throne of the world with His all-might, wisdom, and goodness shall be recognized and beheld by the spirit of man. Thus, the walls of the Temple change into that truth which becomes evident through the certainty of the senses. The wainscoting is made by the conclusions of our reasoning, and the gold comes from the harmony between what has been understood and what has been revealed.

In the temple of Wisdom beauty itself shall be the adornment, the beautiful way of representation. Its contents shall be pure, holy, and devoted to the highest purposes alone. We wish for a school of universal wisdom, a pansophic or school of all-embracing wisdom,—that is, a workshop into which we are admitted in order to attain skill for everything necessary for life—both the present and the future life—and to be able to do this fully.

Christianity or Europe, **Novalis (1772-1801)**

Automatically man rises toward heaven when no other ties bind him; the higher organs emerge automatically out of the general, uniform mixture and complete dissolution of all human faculties and powers, as the original seed of human formation. The spirit of God hovers over the water and above the watery waves a heavenly island is the first thing to become visible—the home of a new human race, the river valley of eternal life.

    As yet, everything is mere intimation, disconnected, and in the rough, but to the historical eye it betrays universal individuality, a new history; a new humanity; a youthful, startled church, in sweetest embrace with a loving god and sensing in her thousand members the approach of the birth of a new Messiah. Who is not in an expectant mood, like the sweetly blushing bride? The new-born child will be the image of his father, a new golden age with dark eyes of infinite depth; it will be a time of prophesy, of miracles, of healing, a comforting and life-kindling flame; a great age of reconciliation, a savior who like an indigenous, real guardian spirit cannot be seen but is accepted on faith, and under innumerable forms is visible to the believers, consumed as bread and wine, embraced as a lover, breathed as air, perceived as word and song, and is received with heavenly bliss, as death is received, with the greatest pains of love, within the dying body.

    This brother is the pulse of the new era; he who has felt it no longer doubts its arrival, but, glad that he is contemporary, steps out from the mass and joins the new group of disciples. He has made a new veil for the holy one, which pliantly betrays her heavenly form and still conceals her more demurely than another. The veil is to the virgin what the spirit is to the body, her indispensable organ, the folds of which are the letters of her sweet gospel; the eternal weaving and folding is a coded music, for speech is too clumsy and harsh for the virgin, only in song does she open her lips. To me it is nothing but the solemn summons to a new first assembly, the powerful wing-strokes of a passing angel-herald. These are the first pains; let everyone prepare for the birth.

    I plunge myself as deeply as possible into the stream of human knowing in order to forget the dream world of fate and destiny, so long as I am submerged in those holy currents. There alone blossom the hopes that I forsake here otherwise—the reversals of this world become steps forward over there—

the sword that wounds us here, there becomes an enlivening wand of magic; and the ash of earthly roses is the motherland of heavenly ones. Is not our evening star the morning star of the antipodes?

O! If the oracles are still at hand, then they speak from the tree of knowledge; thus they sound in us; thus we read them in the sibyline book of nature. My fantasy rises as my hope is completely sunken and nothing remains but a marker that shows its absence, then my imagination will rise high enough to elevate me to a place where I can find what is lost down here. Early in life, I've learned to feel how precarious is my existence, and perhaps this feeling is the first living experience of the future world. Thus must I work from force of will—thus must I learn to transport myself into an intentional state of mind with the effort and enthusiasm of a beginner.

Whoever flees pain no longer wants to love. The lover must feel this gap eternally and keep the wound open always. God grant me to feel eternally this indescribable pain of love—the melancholic remembrance—this courageous longing—the strong resolution and the firm and fast belief. Without my love I am absolutely nothing—With her, everything.

The universe breaks down into an infinite number of worlds, each in turn contained by larger ones. In the end, all minds are one mind. One mind like one world gradually leads to all worlds, but everything has its own time and its own manner. Only the universe as person can understand the relations of our world. Even conscience, this power which generates the universe and meaning, this germ of all personality, appears to me to be like the spirit of the world poem, like the accident of the eternal, romantic confluence of the endlessly changeable totality of life.

Conscience appears in every serious completion, in every embodied truth. Every inclination and skill which reflection turns into a world-image becomes a phenomenon, a transmutation of conscience. Indeed, all development leads to what can only be called freedom, regardless of the fact that thereby not simply a mere concept but the creative basis of all existence is to be designated. This freedom is mastery. The master exercises unfettered power in a purposeful, definite, and deliberate manner. The objects of his art are his and subject to his pleasure, and they do not shackle or cramp him. And precisely this all-embracing freedom, austery, or sovereignty is the essence, the drive of conscience. In him is revealed the holy peculiarity, the immediate creativity of personality, and every act of the master is at the same time a proclamation of the lofty, simple, uncomplicated world—God's word.

Manichaean Psalmbook
Put in Me a Holy Heart

Put in me a holy heart, my God: let an upright Spirit be new within Me!
The holy heart is Christ: if he rises in us, we also shall rise in him.
Christ has risen, the dead shall rise with him.
If we believe in him, we shall pass beyond death and come to life.
The sons of faith, they shall see faith: lo, come let us put oil in our lamps.
Let us gather in and become warm milk; this hope which has come from on high.
The creature of the Darkness is this body which we wear:
the soul which is in it is the First Man.
The First Man who was victorious in the Land of the Darkness,
He also today will be victorious in the body of death.
The Living Spirit that gave help to the First Man,
he also today is the Paraclete-Spirit.
One is the Mind that is to come, that reveals, gathering in,
choosing his holy Church.
Purify me, my God, purify me within, without; purify the body, the soul and the spirit.
Let the body be holy for me; the knowledge of Spirit and Mind.

Jesus has risen: he has risen in three days, the Cross of Light that rises in three powers. The Sun and the Moon and the

Perfect Man—these three powers are the Church of the macrocosm. Jesus, the Maiden of Light, and the Mind which is in their midst—these three powers are the Church of the macrocosm. The Kingdom of the heavens, behold it is within us, behold, it is outside us; if we believe in it we shall live in it forever. Glory, victory to every man that has heard these things and believed in them and fulfilled them in joy. Victory to the soul of the blessed Mary.

Literature Selections for Grade Six Teachers and Parents

Mani as a Leader of Spiritual Evolution

Rudolf Steiner tells us that Mani (216–274 AD) was a forerunner of the Consciousness Soul Epoch. Mani epitomized the spiritual awareness and consciousness that modern seekers need to develop. He synthesized Buddhism, Christianity, Zoroasterism, and other religions into a religion of his own that incorporated sacred music and art. Mani had a revelation of Christ that was advanced for his time and is an example for us to emulate in our time. Mani understood the essential teachings of Zoroaster and the *Chaldean Oracles,* and he was fully aware also of the active revelation of Christ, the Solar Logos. He is one of the greatest leaders of mankind, and his teachings are very appropriate to study along with the teachings of Dr. Rudolf Steiner. In a way, the dualism of Mani prepares us for what is to come in the future evolution of consciousness. We are at an apocalyptic moment in human history that embodies the duality of the War in Heaven as it descends to the Earth. We see the strong polarities of good and evil everywhere. Spirit-courage is needed to combat the three soul forces that have been distorted by the Guardian of the Threshold into forms that confront our cold materialistic thinking, deaden feelings, and aberrant, undisciplined will forces. In this age of the Archangel Michael (the Face of Christ), only a strong Sun-oriented heart dedicated to Christ with the support and loving comfort of the Holy Sophia can meet the need to have a direct, personal experience of the active spiritual revelation of our times.

The veil between the physical and spiritual has been rent, and the spiritual seeker now sees Natura face-to-face, as a being of beauty filled with wisdom and encompassing everything in Her womb of worlds. Mani knew this revelation and gave us a religion that unifies all religions in an active revelation of Christ. Each age must relive the direct connection to the active spiritual beings who hold this universe together and engender a relationship that is aligned with humanity's rightful position as the tenth hierarchy of consciousness (Spirits of freedom and love). Mani is the forerunner who, through many lives, has led the great Masters of Wisdom through prior ages of cultural development. His religion was all but wiped out due to the jealousy of men, which is a good sign that it had what was necessary to inspire the next epoch of consciousness.

Body, Soul and Spirit—Kephalais by Mani

Again, Mani speaks to his disciples: Three images occur in the Elect person. The first is the spiritual image, which is the New Man, which the Light-Mind shall form in him. It enters into him and dwells in him. The second image is the remnant and remainder of the New Man, which is the psychic image that is bound in the flesh like the Old Man. The other one is the corporeal image that is added to them all. Then shall a Virgin of Light come and reveal the spiritual image that is there, which is the New Man. That virgin acts as a guide. She goes on before, and is extended to the heights above, and received into the spiritual image. And she sculpts it and adorns it with the New Man within. It is sealed with all the limbs of this Virgin of Light who is present and dwells in the New Man. So, this is how this living limb shall be purified and live: the one that comes in to the body of the righteous one from without, through the administration of food of various kinds. The Living Soul shall be cleansed entirely every day and traverse these three images. Thus, it shall divest itself of the body which is not its own, in the corporeal image. It shall also divest itself of the soul qualities that are not its own, these that are mixed with it in the psychic, anger and desire and foolishness and envy and strife; these are other wicked teachings that are not its own. However, in the spiritual image it shall itself live and be joined with long-sufferingness, the perfection of faith and love that reigns over them all. It is the Virgin of Light who robes the New Man and who shall be called "the Hour of Life." She is the first, but also the last.

The Cosmic Context: The Redeemer Speaks by **Mani**

Thou art the buried treasure, the chief of my wealth, the pearl which is the beauty of all the gods. And I am the righteousness sown in thy limbs, and in the stature of thy soul—the gladness of thy Mind. Thou art my Beloved, the Love in my limbs; and the heroic Mind, the essence of my limbs. From the holiness of my limbs didst thou descend in the beginning into the dark places, and didst become their Light. Through thee a diadem was bound on all our foes. It became apparent and held sway during the hours of tyranny. For thy sake was there battle and tremor in all the heavens and the bridges of the earths. For thy sake ran and sped all the Dark Powers. For thy sake were bound the Princes and all the Dark Powers. For thy sake, the diadem was taken away. For thy sake shone forth the Apostles and became apparent, who reveal the Light above, and uncover the root of Darkness. For thy sake, the Gods went forth and became apparent. They struck down Death, and Darkness they slew. Thou art the exalted Trophy, the sign of Light that puts Darkness to flight. And I am come forth to save thee from the Sinner, to make thee whole from pain, and to bring gladness to thy heart. All thou hast desire of me I shall bestow upon thee. I shall make new thy place within the lofty kingdom. I shall set open before thee the gates in all the heavens, and shall make smooth thy path, free from terror and vexation. I shall take thee with might, and enfold thee with love, and lead thee to thy home, the blessed abode. Forever shall I show to thee the noble Father; I shall lead thee in, into his presence, in pure raiment. I shall show to thee the Mother of the beings of Light. Forever shalt thou rejoice in happiness. I shall reveal to thee the holy brethren who are filled with happiness. Forever shalt thou dwell joyful among them all, beside all the Jewels and the venerable Gods. Fear and death shall never overtake thee more, nor ravage, distress and wretchedness. Rest shall be thine in the place of salvation, in the company of all the Gods and those who dwell in quietness.

Creation of the Physical Earth **by Mani**

The Living Spirit set in place the Seven Spheres. And he bound and fettered two dragons, and bound them on high to that which is the lowest heaven, and in order to make them turn the firmament at command, he placed in charge of them two Angels, a male and a female.

Furthermore, he led up to the Border and summit of Light those Elements, and made and arranged out of Wind and Light, Water and Fire which had been separated from the mixture (of Darkness) the two Light Vehicles, namely that of the Sun from Fire and Light, with five walls of Ether, Wind, Light, Water and Fire, and twelve doors and five mansions and three thrones and five soul-gathering Angels—all which are within one fiery wall. And he made and arranged that Vehicle of the Moon-god from Wind and Water, with five walls of Ether, Wind, Light, Fire and Water, and fourteen doors and five mansions and three thrones and five soul-gathering angels—all which are within the watery wall. And these he enveloped.

Furthermore, he clothed the Sun-god with three coverings, the Wind, Water and Fire which were formed from that same separation; and the separated Dark portion sank down to the Dark Earth. And in order to create above it the mystery of the great Future Paradise, he levelled those five caverns of death and made them wholly flat. Then, in a manner corresponding to the heavens, he collected above the Dark Earth and deposited, each one covering the other, the Four Deposits, namely the Destructive (Wind or Spirit), the Dark-by-nature, the Fiery and the Watery. And he constructed one Wall, which runs from the Light Earth eastward, southward and westward, joining it back to the Earth of Light (in the north).

Rudolf Steiner's Curriculum Recommendations for Grade Six

Karl Stockmeyer's Waldorf Literature and History indications for Grade Six:

History: Historical accounts of the Greeks and Romans, and the effects of Greek and Roman history up to the beginning of the fifteenth century.

Geography: Consider the Earth regions and try to find the link between climatic conditions and astronomical conditions. Study minerals as part of the entire geographic picture.

Bibliographical References and Recommended Reading—Grade Six

Andreae, Johann Valentin. *Christianopolis*. 1619.

Campanella, Tommaso. *The City of the Sun*. The ProjectGutenberg Ebook, David Widger, 2013.

Coleridge, Samuel Taylor. *The Rime of the Ancient Mariner*. Dover, New York, 1970.

Coolidge, Olivia. *Tales of the Crusades*. Houghton Mifflin, Boston, 1970.

Dods, Marcus. *The City of God*. Saint Augustine of Hippo. Hendrickson Publishers, 2008.

Green, Roger Lancelyn. *King Arthur and His Knights of the Round Table*. Puffin Books, 1977.

Held, Felix Emil. *Christianopolis: An Ideal State of the Seventh Century by Johann Valentin Andreae*. Oxford University Press, New York, 1916.

Hiebel, Frederick. *Novalis: German Poet-European Thinker-Christian Mystic*. The University of North Carolina Press, Chapel Hill, 1954.

Hope, M. J. *Novalis (Friedrich Von Hardenberg) His Life, Thoughts, and Works*. Edited and Translated by M. J. Hope. A. C. McClurg & Co., 1891.

Klimkeit, Hans-Joachim. *Gnosis on the Silk Road: Gnostic Tests from Central Asia*.

Lang, Andrew. *King Arthur Tales of the Round Table*. Schocken Books, New York, 1902.

More, Thomas Sir. *Utopia*. Dover, 1997.

Neeb, Martin Jacob. *Christianity or Europe. A Translation*. Concordia College, Texas, 1937.

Novalis. *Die Christenheit Ober Europa*. Phillip Reclam Jun Verlag, 1998.

O'Brien, Wm. Arctander. *Novalis Signs of Revolution*. Duke University Press, London, 1995.

Plato. *The Republic*. 380 BC. Dover Thrift Editions, 2000.

Prefferkorn, Kristin. *Novalis: A Romantic's Theory of Language and Poetry*. Yalte Press, 1988.

Tappan, Eva March. *When Knights Were Bold*. Houghton Mifflin, New York, 1939.

Thomas, John. *Leonardo Da Vinci*. Criterion Books, New York, 1957.

Wyatt, Isabel. *Tales the Harper Sang*. The Lanthorn Press, New York, 1978.

Yuanming, Tao. *Loving the Land of Peach Blossoms—of Tao Yuanming*. TaoWeniioxXi, 2005.

Grade Seven

Vulcan Incarnation of the Earth
Stage Seven of Seven of the Eternal Curriculum
Planetary Influence is Saturn
The Mystery of Bliss Transformed by the Abyss

The Seventh Cultural Epoch

5733-7893 AD Capricorn, Vulcan, Spirit Man

Behold, he cometh with clouds, and every eye shall see him, and they also which pierced him: and all kindreds of the earth shall wail because of him.

I was in the Spirit on the Lord's day, and heard behind me a great voice, as of a trumpet, saying, I am Alpha and Omega, the beginning and the ending, saith the Lord, which is, and which was, and which is to come, the Almighty.

Revelations 7–10

In the seventh grade, every student ideally becomes an individualized renaissance person with balanced skills in the sciences and the arts; or at least, that is what we are aiming for. Who can live up to the bravery and courage of the explorers and the wit, wisdom, and skill of the Renaissance geniuses who have shown us the way to human brilliance? Are we as gifted and talented as these geniuses from Renaissance history? Each of the characters we teach in our lessons are representative individuals who distinguished themselves through hard work and creative expression. They are the Vulcan souls of our future who show us the way to proceed. They are the vanguard that leads to selfless pursuits for the greater good of humanity. The true calling of the saint or humanitarian is to be willing to lay down their life for others; true selflessness for the greater good—a gift that is seldom seen but will become more common in the future.

From the first grade to seventh grade in a Waldorf school, we witness the development of humanity from the ancient past into the far future through the curriculum and its direct link to the physical and spiritual development of the students. Understanding Steiner's cosmology also provides us with a comprehensive overview of the development of humanity in relationship to the spiritual hierarchies that are intimately associated with the process.

When Rudolf Steiner speaks of the future state of consciousness referred to as the American Cultural Epoch, we can be sure that it will have little resemblance to what we know as America today. Thousands of years of evolution will bring the future to us in forms we will hardly recognize. It is on the continent of North America that this new cultural center will develop, but surely from entirely different cultural archetypes than we see now. America's current tendency to overreact to stimuli rushing at us from beyond the threshold of death fractures the human willpower into aberrations of sex and violence in our modern culture. These modern forces of decay that come from the old Roman forms of legalism and hedonistic self-gratification have torn American moral fabric into tattered shreds. These forces will die off, and out of the fire, a new breed of Americans will arise that take up the lessons learned from the Russian Cultural Epoch that will precede it. During the Russian Epoch, a personal relationship develops with AnthropoSophia, who prepares humanity for the coming of the Kingdom Four-Square, the Heavenly New Jerusalem, Shamballa, which descends from the pure realms of the etheric. It is this period of development that will particularly reunite humanity with the source of its origin and will develop the Spirit Man/Atman nature of humanity.

Throughout the Fifth Cultural Epoch (Anglo-Germanic), the Consciousness Soul and Spirit Self components of the human being worked together to birth a new type of individual that could act in both the physical and spiritual worlds. In the Sixth Cultural Epoch, the Life Spirit nature of the human being will develop the union of the Spirit Self/Manas (Sophia) and the Life Spirit/Buddhi (Christ). This alchemical wedding of Self to Higher Self is the redemption of the etheric body of the individual. The stronger the spiritual habit-life and moral development of the individual, the stronger and more powerful the union of Self (soul) to Higher Self (spirit) becomes. This union can be seen as the soul of Sophia (Wisdom) merging with the spirit of Christ (Love) until, in the Seventh Epoch, a true a-sexual individual arises that has the best of both polarities merged at a higher level. This is the goal of the Seventh Epoch: resolution of duality at a higher level through a divine "marriage." Individualized parthenogenesis evolves into the resolution of duality as a united group of awakened individuals. A prefiguring of this resolution of duality is found in the archetypal artists, architects, explorers, and inventors of the Renaissance Age. These Renaissance individuals explore the entire world with courage and refined human intelligence. This is the goal of the seventh-grade student who becomes the Renaissance person and explores the limits of the world, both outside and inside.

Through all the seemingly miraculous stories they experience, the seventh-grader becomes the discoverer of the Fountain of Youth and finds the legendary Golden Streets of Eldorado filled with the endless riches and eternal life that actually dwell within their own soul. These are the rewards of returning to the origin—Eden regained. A "garden that feeds all needs" is a clear image of the wedding in New Jerusalem. Exploration into the self is exploration into the world, and the realms of the divine. Explorers ultimately found their personal higher self in the outward conquering of natural wonders. The soul explores the spirit realm with the same enthusiasm as that with which the explorers of the Age of Discovery hoped to find the Golden City of the Sun. Explorers longed for the grand reunion awaiting their return, like the prodigal son. The seventh-grade explorer is poised between ancient past and hopeful future, ready to incarnate and stand as an awakened person in modern times.

The eighth-grade curriculum will revisit the eras of Lemuria and Atlantis through scientific study and bring the student into modern times as a person of their own age. The High School curriculum repeats many of the themes of the first through eighth grades but adds little new content that affects the student's introduction to the historic forces that have shaped human development. We want to plant the seeds of things beyond our reach into the eighth-grade curriculum to instill the desire to continue learning and searching to discover the unknown. There is much that is yet to be understood, and we want the student to leave the eighth grade with as many questions as answers. The eighth-grader is beautiful to behold, with the silliness of childhood behind them and the infinite potential of their spirit before them. They have the vision to see the future without the burdens of the past. They stand as forerunners for some future state of consciousness, and their skills and habits learned from exploring the Waldorf language arts and history curricula give them a perspective that is global, inclusive, and united in a comprehensive cosmology of the developing human spirit.

Novalis—Forerunner of Humanity
Georg Friedrich Phillip von Hardenberg (1772-1801)

The sources of Anthroposophy are three; Novalis, the work of creating Anthroposophy, and the being of Anthroposophia. Your relationship to Sophia (Anthroposophia) is your own, and it will show itself in your life work. Reading Rudolf Steiner's Anthroposophy is very difficult and not for everybody, but Novalis is easily approachable. Novalis is the new ground of spirituality through conscious design, using no religious doctrine, just the beings behind all things ordinary and divine. Novalis's language of the "blue flower" is the conscious disenchantment of matter back into free spirit. Novalis could accomplish the greatest task with the least effort, like a rose petal that falls and inspires the poet of a nation.

Only Novalis burns images into your everlasting imagination and fires the soul to enlightened seeing and the art of impassioned living. This is tantamount to living unhindered by separateness and fear, belonging to the whole, and knowing that each thought could birth a world in some nearby future. Novalis's *Fragments and Pollen* holds the secrets to a hyper-connected science where metals transmute into other metals by mental design, lead becomes gold, and the alchemical marriage of soul to spirit may happen by reciting a poem or a passage in a fairy tale where you are a poor beggar and then later become a king. Life's dramas are universities of learning where the mundane reveals cosmic secrets that free or bind the romantic soul to hear the calling of the archetypes, connecting all our thoughts by virtuous embodiment of noble principles and ideals.

Even Goethe tried to match Novalis's longsuffering and blissful melancholy, and fell short. Novalis was living art, the canvas of the archetypal human who suffers for himself and humanity. He embodies the original Adam's innocence, sin, and redemption—the one who led us into this world of maya and delusion, where suffering, old age, and ignorance reign supreme. But now he has led us back to the source: the New Eden, floating above the Earth in the far north, surrounded by a wall of fiery color. Through countless lives—including Elijah, Elias, Phineas, John the Baptist, Raphael Sanzio, and the poet Novalis—this individuality has witnessed the fall and return of the prodigal son. Novalis has taken wing and risen to new heights of human expression. His gift of spiritual seeing was perfected and tested when Christ came before him to be baptized. John the Baptist was the first Adam recognizing the Second Adam, who had come to redeem the fall from paradise. As John said, "I must decrease so that he may increase." John was fully aware of the mission of the messiah and his place beside him.

We have mentioned Novalis before as one of the sources of inspiration for Rudolf Steiner, but he is also the quintessential example of what humanity should be developing in the evolutionary stream of time. Novalis is, essentially, the primal human who has gained wisdom through many incarnations trying to understand his relationship with the spirit. Steiner indicated that Novalis was previously Raphael Sanzio, John the Baptist, and the original Adam. Whether we subscribe to Steiner's ideas about Novalis's prior incarnations or not, the importance of Novalis is unquestionable. Novalis was the father of the German Romantic Movement, and his idea of the "blue flower" became the symbol of that movement. Novalis's influence on modern thinking is profound, and he leads humanity into many new paths of inspiration and revelation throughout human history. What Novalis has to give us comes from the wisdom he has gleaned over the centuries. Truly, Novalis has mastered language as a vehicle of the spirit.

Literature Selections for Grade Seven Children

Notes for a Romantic Encyclopaedia, **Novalis**
Translated by David Wood

What stimulus is to the soul, beauty is to the spirit.

Love proceeds like philosophy—it is and will be—each and everything to everyone.

Therefore, love is the ego—the ideal of every endeavor.

The highest wonder is a virtuous deed—an act of free determination.

A person with prefect presence of mind is a seer.

The present moment—or the perpetual solidification process of earthly time has an unusual life-flame. Time also creates everything, just as it destroys, binds and separates everything.

The highest and the purest is the most common and the most understandable.

Everything perfected does not express itself alone—it also expresses an entire (co)related world. Thus, the veil of the eternal Virgin floats around perfection of every kind—dissolving under the slightest touch into a magic fragrance, to become the celestial chariot of the seer. It is not antiquities alone that we behold—it is at once heaven, the telescope—and the fixed star—and therefore a genuine revelation of a higher world.

The theory of thought corresponds to meteorology.

The blossom is the symbol for the mystery of our spirit.

I think I am best able to express my state of soul in fairy tales.

God is a mixed concept—he has arisen from the union of all our soul faculties by means of a moral revelation, a moral centering miracle.

Is sleep—a mating with oneself?

Therefore imagination, which fashions figurative words, especially deserves the predicate "genius."

Natural genius belongs to experimenting, that is to say, that wondrous ability to capture the sense of Nature—and to act in her spirit. The true observer is an artist—he divines the significant, and knows how to sensitively select the most crucial elements from out of the strangest, most fleeting mixture of appearances.

In time, history must become a fairy tale—it shall be once again, as it was in the beginning.

That will be a Golden Age, when all words become—figurative words—myths—and all figures become—linguistic figures—hieroglyphs; when we learn to speak and write figures and learn to perfectly sculpt and make music with words. Both arts belong together, are indivisibly connected and will become simultaneously perfected.

The magical sciences arise through the application of the moral senses to the other senses—through moralization of the universe and the other sciences.

It seems to me that a grammatical mysticism lies at the basis of everything—which could quite easily call forth the first sense of wonder with regard to language and writing. The propensity for the miraculous and mysterious is nothing more than a striving—toward non-physical—spiritual stimuli. Mysteries are a means of nourishment—inciting potencies. Explanations are digested mysteries.

A true fairy tale must be at once a prophetic representation—an ideal representation—and an absolutely necessary representation. The true poet of the fairy tale is a seer of the future.

Our alphabet is an art of musical writing, and over and above this, one from an individual instrument: the human organ of speech.

The artist belongs to the work, and not the work to the artist.

Our spirit is a substance of associations—it results from harmony—from the simultaneity of the diverse, which also preserves it.

Human beings are in relation to the moral sense, what air and light are in relation to the ear and eye.

Sensual intoxication is to love, what sleep is to life.

Magic—star-like force. Through magic man will become powerful like the stars—on the whole, he is intimately related to the stars.

I can only understand—compare the world—if I myself have a fully developed world in my mind.

Woman is the highest visible means of nutrition, and forms the transition from the body to the soul.

Metaphysics and astronomy are one and the same science. The sun is to astronomy, what God is to metaphysics. Freedom and immortality are like light and heat. God, freedom and immortality will one day form the basis of spiritual physics—just as the sun, light and heat form the basis of earthly physics.

Soul and body make contact with one another in the will—chemically—or galvanically—or electrically—or like fire. The soul eats the body and digests it instantaneously—the body conceives the soul and gives birth to it instantaneously.

Couldn't every sculptural formation, from crystals up until man, be explained in an acoustic manner by means of arrested motion?

Electricity is perhaps immature fire—just as the northern lights are immature electricity.

Oxygen—basis of the mineral kingdom.
Hydrogen—basis of the metal kingdom.
Carbon—vegetable basis.
Nitrogen—animal basis.

Water is a wet flame.

The developing human being should attempt, in accordance with his powers, to overcome everything that he still finds difficult, in order to be able to rise above it and face it with greater facility—and ability. He then begins to cherish it. For we are fond of whatever has cost us pain.

They are fortunate people, who perceive God everywhere—find God everywhere—these people are truly religious. Religion is morality of the highest dignity.

Consciousness is nothing more than a sensation of the (algebraic) sense of comparison—sense of relation. Consciousness is the substance of the senses—consequently its sensations are also substances. Where there is a sense, there is also no consciousness.

Dreams instruct us in a remarkable manner concerning the ease with which our soul penetrates—and instantly transforms itself, into every object.

Laughter is a cramp. Hence the cause of laughter must originate from a sudden discharge of built-up attention—by means of a contrast. Similarity to an electric spark. Laughter is a cure for hypochondria. Everything that excites our attention but leaves us unsatisfied is comical. Yet only the sudden releasing of our attention is the true laughter-creating operation. Weeping is a sthenic crisis. Whatever moves our heart, is the opposite of the comical. It begins with a release—and suddenly increases in tension. Whatever is emotionally moving or penetrating, quickly enters into us before we have time to grasp it. It is an over-saturation—a softening—dissolving—melting. The comical is a process of secretion, the emotional, a process of absorption—the former becomes volatile—hence the coldness of the comical. Weeping shapes the arterial system—laughter, the venous system.

Sleep is a mixed state of the body and the soul. The body and soul are chemically united in sleep. The soul is evenly distributed throughout the body in sleep—the human being is neutralized. Waking is a divided—polarized state. While awake the soul is point-like—localized. Sleep is a digestion of the soul; the body digests the soul—withdrawal of the soul-stimulus. Waking is the state in which the soul experiences stimulation—the body relishes the soul. The bindings of the system are loose in sleep—taut in waking.

Every illness is a musical problem—the cure is a musical solution.

Cramp and inflammation ought to be constantly uniting and alternating within the human body—in distinct proportions. The determinations of these proportions create the individual temperaments and constitutions.

The longer a person remains a child, the older he will live to be.

Nature alters itself by leaps. Synthetic operations are leaps—intuitions—resolutions.

Wisdom is harmony.

All effects are nothing else than the effects of one single force—of the World-Soul—which only manifests itself under certain conditions, relations and circumstances—it is everywhere and nowhere.

Wisdom is moral science and art.

Words are acoustic configurations of thoughts. The human voice is, as it were, the principle and ideal of instrumental music. What really makes the sound, the body or the air? Isn't the elastic fluid the vowel, and the body the consonant—the air, the sun—and the bodies the planets—the former, the first voice—the latter, the second. Every person has his own individual rhythm. Rhythmical sense is genius.

Philosophy is really homesickness—the desire to be everywhere at home.

Philosophy is the science of the universal sense of divination.

Fichte's demand of simultaneous thinking, acting and observing is the ideal of philosophizing—I begin to realize this ideal—by attempting to carry it out.

Every science is perhaps only a variation of philosophy. Philosophy is the substance of science as it were—that is sought everywhere—present everywhere, and yet never appears to the seeker. Nonetheless, it should also appear in concrete form, like the philosopher's stone, and this is the greatest problem.

The spiritual world is indeed already revealed to us—it is always manifest. If we suddenly became as elastic as was necessary, we would see ourselves in its midst.

Our thinking is really nothing more than a galvanization. It is a contact of the terrestrial spirit—and the spiritual atmosphere—with a heavenly, extraterrestrial spirit. Therefore, all thinking is itself already a communal activity in a higher sense.

Should man be the unity for Nature—the universal? i.e. the differential of the infinitely large Nature, and the integral of the infinitely small Nature—the universal homogenizing principle—the measure of all things—their reciprocal principle of realization—and their organ of contact?

We are not an ego at all—however, we can and will become an ego. We are seeds of an ego. We should transform everything into a "you"—into a second ego—only in this manner do we raise ourselves to the Great Ego—that is both One and All.

Novalis on Conscience, from Heinrich Von Ofterdingen

"Then," said Henry, "when will there be no more terror or pain, want or evil in the universe?"

"When there is but one power, the power of conscience; when nature becomes chaste and pure. There is but one cause of evil,— common frailty,— and this frailty is nothing but a weak moral susceptibility, and a deficiency in the attraction of freedom."

"Explain to me the nature of Conscience."

"I were God, could I do so; for when we comprehend it. Conscience exists. Can you explain to me the essence of poetry?"

"A personality cannot be distinctly defined."

"How much less then the secret of the highest indivisibility. Can music be explained to the deaf?"

"If so, would the sense itself be part of the new world opened by it? Does one understand facts only when one has them?"

Even Conscience, that sense and world-creating power, that germ of all Personality, appears to me like the spirit of the world-poem, like the event of the eternal, romantic confluence of the infinitely mutable common life.

"Dear pilgrim," Sylvester replied, "the Conscience appears in every serious perfection, in every fashioned truth. Every inclination and ability transformed by reflection into a universal type becomes a phenomenon, a phase of Conscience. All formation tends to that which can only be called Freedom; though by that is not meant an idea, but the creative ground of all being. To speak accurately, this all-embracing freedom, this mastership of dominion, is the essence, the impulse of Conscience. In it is revealed the sacred peculiarity, the immediate creation of Personality, and every action of the master, is at once the announcement of the lofty, simple, evident world—God's word."

"Conscience is the innate mediator of every man. It takes the place of God upon earth, and is therefore to many the highest and the final. But how far was the former science, called virtue or morality, from the pure shape of this lofty, comprehensive, personal thought! Conscience is the peculiar essence of man fully glorified, the divine archetypal man."

"Yes; and you have often as beautifully shown, before now, the connection between virtue and religion. Everything, which experience and earthly activity embrace, forms the province of Conscience, which unites this world with higher worlds. With a loftier sense religion appears, and what formerly seemed an incomprehensible necessity of our inmost nature, a universal law without any definite intent, now becomes a wonderful, domestic, infinitely varied, and satisfying world, an inconceivably interior communion of all the spiritual with God, and a perceptible, hallowing presence of the only One, or of his Will, of his Love in our deepest self."

Literature Selection for Grade Seven Teachers and Parents

Steiner was asked by Fredrick Rittlemeyer and other priests to renew the Christian seven sacraments and give a new start to a type of Christianity that could grow into a Community of Christians that know Christ. Thus, the Christian Community was founded by Steiner in the last years of his life. He gave great attention to every detail of the church, and especially the liturgy that he wrote for each of the seven sacraments.

Steiner's theological ideas are impressed into every carefully chosen word in every service throughout the Christian Community. Steiner's Christology is the most comprehensive available. Steiner indicated that the aspirant of Christian esotericism needs to understand what Buddha has taught about compassion before a true understanding of what Christ taught about love can be understood. Buddhist thought is a primal foundation of wisdom upon which the modern spiritual revelation of Christ can arise and be understood.

The Christian Community *Creed* is a clear statement of Steiner's Christology. It is one of the most comprehensive prayers in the Christian Community liturgy. Through the exactness of each word and its implications, Steiner explains his "renewed" Christian doctrine.

The Creed by Dr. Rudolf Steiner

An Almighty Being of God, spiritual-physical, is the Foundation of existence, is to this divine Being as the Son, born in eternity. In Jesus, the Christ entered as man into the earthly world. The Birth of Jesus upon earth is a working of the Holy Spirit, Who, that He might spiritually heal the sickness of sin upon the bodily nature of mankind, prepared the Son of Mary to be the vehicle of the Christ. The Christ Jesus suffered under Pontius Pilate the death of the Cross and was lowered into the grave of the earth. In death He became the Helper of the souls of the dead who had lost their divine nature. Then He overcame death, after three days. Since that time He is the Lord of the heavenly forces upon earth and lives as the Fulfiller of the deeds of the Father, the Ground of the World. He will in time unite for the advancement of the World with those whom through their bearing He can wrest from the death of matter.

Through Him can the Healing Spirit work. Communities whose members feel the Christ within them may feel themselves united in a Church which all humans belong who are aware of the health-bringing powers of the Christ. They may hope for the overcoming of the sickness of sin, for the continuance of man's being and for the preservation of their life destined for eternity.

Rudolf Steiner's Curriculum Recommendations for Grade Seven

Karl Stockmeyer's Waldorf Literature and History indications for Grade Seven

History: The fifteenth century until the beginning of the seventeenth century is the most important period of time for the seventh grade. Story material may be drawn from stories about different tribes.

Geography: View of the whole earth—spiritual relationships of civilization in connection with economic relationships; also study trade, industry, and transportation.

Bibliographical References and Recommended Reading—Grade Seven

Asimov, Isaac. *Breakthroughs in Science.* Houghton Mifflin.

Beazley. *Henry the Navigator.* Franklin.

Bixby. *The World of Galileo and Newton.* American Heritage.

Brooks and Walworth. *The World Awakes.* Lippincott.

Clark. *Leonardo da Vinci.* Viking/Penguin.

Clark. *Secret of the Andes.* Puffin.

Coleridge, Samuel Taylor. *The Rime of the Ancient Mariner.* Dover, NY, 1970.

Coolidge, Olivia. *Tales of the Crusades.* Houghton Mifflin, Boston, 1970.

Dreyer. *A Picture of Life in the 16th Century.* Adam & Charles Black.

Green, Roger Lancelyn. *King Arthur & His Knights of the Round Table.* Puffin Books, 1977.

Grimm. *The Life of Michel Angelo.* Little.

Hale. *The Age of Exploration.* Time.

Hale. *The Renaissance.* Time.

Lang, Andrew. *King Arthur: Tales of the Round Table.* Schocken Books, NY, 1902.

Merejcovski, Dmitri. *The Romance of Leonardo da Vinci.* The Heritage Reprints, New York.

Miller, John C. *The First Frontier Life in Colonial America.* Laurel, New York, 1966.

Mills. *Renaissance and Reformation.* Putnam.

Pater. *The Renaissance.* University of California Press.

Penrose. *Travel and Discovery in the Renaissance.* Harvard University Press.

Simon. *The Reformation.* Time.

Spinka. *Jan Hus, A Biography.* Princeton University Press.

Steiner, Rudolf. *Art History Lectures.* Anthroposophic Press.

Steiner, Rudolf. *Background to the Gospel of St. Mark.* Anthroposophic Press.

Steiner, Rudolf. *Occult Science—An Outline.* Anthroposophic Press.

Steiner, Rudolf. *The Karma of Materialism.* Anthroposophic Press.

Steiner, Rudolf. *The Mission of the Archangel Michael.* Anthroposophic Press.

Steiner, Rudolf. *The Spiritual Guidance of Man and Humanity.* Anthroposophic Press.

Steiner, Rudolf. *World History in the Light of Anthroposophy.* Anthroposophic Press.

Sutcliff, Rosemary. *Beowolf.* Dutton & Co., New York, 1962.

Tappan, Eva March. *When Knights Were Bold.* Houghton Mifflin, New York, 1939.

Thomas, John. *Leonardo Da Vinci.* Criterion Books, New York, 1957.

Vasari. *The Lives of the Artists.* Penguin.

Williams. *Joan of Arc.* American Heritage.

Wyatt, Isabell. *Tales the Harper Sang.* The Lanthorne Press, New York, 1978.

Zweig. *Conqueror of the Seas: The Story of Magellan.* Viking.

Grade Eight

Summary of Prior Seven Grades
Zodiacal Influence

Man is not merely a spectator of the world: he is rather the world's stage upon which great cosmic events continuously play themselves out."

Rudolf Steiner (GA 302)

In a Waldorf school, eighth grade is an opportunity to learn about the distant past in scientific terms as students study Atlantis and Lemuria as historical fact. There is a good deal of modern evidence now that can be found to substantiate what Steiner has told us about those ancient cultures. A good researcher will have plenty of evidence to present to the students so that they may independently study and arrive at a scientific conclusion based upon the facts. Once Atlantis and Lemuria have been studied, you can teach Chinese geography and Taoism as a remnant of the Atlantean culture and its religious orientation. As the students learn about European history, we teach American history with a focus on revolutions that have created our modern world.

The eighth-grade graduate stands as a free thinker in the modern world, with the memories and experiences of the many cultures studied over the past eight years. The eighth-grader is now a "world citizen" who can appreciate every culture for its gifts that have added to our collective human development. They also have a "picture" of the goals of future human development that can lead them through the changing tides of time.

The Waldorf curriculum goes from the kindergartener's subjective, timeless connection to their surrounding environment, to the eighth-grade graduate's objective understanding of their environment in modern times. Truly, we can see in the Waldorf curriculum (K-8) that ontogeny does recapitulate phylogeny. From age seven to fourteen, the student develops the characteristics of the etheric body as it is the focal point of human development at that stage. After age fourteen, the astral body becomes the new focal point of development for the next seven years. The etheric body is built up through images, symbols, and parables, as the Waldorf curriculum presents world literature and cultural anthropology as a living image of the Eternal Curriculum.

> *The task of education conceived in the spiritual sense is to bring the Soul-Spirit into harmony with the Life-Body. They must come into harmony with one another. They must be attuned to one another; for when the child is born into the physical world, they do not as yet fit one another. The task of the educator, and of the teacher too is the mutual attunement of these two members."*
>
> Steiner (GA 293)

Literature Selections for Grade Eight Children

Adventure, **Anonymous**

Sometimes I feel that my head is as high as the mountains,
Sometimes my legs are as firm and as strong as the trees;
Courage expands in my heart to surmount every trial
All the wide world is a clay I can mold as I please.
Fiery strength tingles out to my toes and my fingers,
Winds from far countries are stirring and lifting my hair.
Still there are waiting great journeys and gallant adventures,
Waiting for me and the sword of my life to be there.

The Way of Life **by Lao Tzu (Saying 66)**

How could the rivers and the seas
Become like kings to valleys?
Because of skill in lowliness
They have become the valley's lords.
So then to be above the folk,
You speak as if you were beneath;
And if you wish to be out front,
The act as if you were behind.
The Wise Man so is up above
But is no burden to the folk;
His station is ahead of them
To see they do not come to harm.
The World will gladly help along
The Wise Man and will bear no grudge
Since he contends not for his own
The World will not contend with him.

Ultima Thule **by Longfellow**

With favoring winds, o'er sunlit seas,
We sailed for the Hesperides,
The land where golden apples grow;
But that, ah! That was long ago.
How far, since then, the ocean streams
Have swept us from that land of dreams,
That land of fiction and of truth,
The lost Atlantis of your youth!
Whither, ah, whither? Are not these
The tempest-haunted Hebrides,
Where sea-gulls scream, and breakers roar,
And wreck and sea-weed line the shore?
Ultima Thule! Utmost Isle!
Here in they harbors for a while
We lower our sails; a while we rest
From the unending, endless quest.

Yogavasishtah Upanishad

Abandon all latent desire for the multitude of enjoyments pressing round. Nay give up even the desire for life as represented in the body. And finally rise above all sense of being and non-being. Find thus full Bliss in absolute Spiritual Knowing.

Anonymous

He has had a dip in the holy waters of all sacred rivers; he has given the whole earth in pious gift; he has offered a thousand sacrifices; he has satisfied all the gods in heaven; he has lifted his ancestors out of the circle of birth and death; he deserves worship of all the three worlds—the person whose mind has, even for a moment, tasted of peace.

Literature Selections for Grade Eight Teachers and Parents

Imagination by A. E. (George William Russell, 1867-1935)

By imagination what exists in latency or essence is out-realized and is given a form in thought, and we can contemplate with full consciousness that which hitherto had been unrevealed, or only intuitionally surmised. In imagination, there is a revelation of the self to the self, and a definite change in being, as there is in a vapor when a spark ignites it and it becomes an inflammation in the air. Here images appear in consciousness which we may refer definitely to an internal creator, with power to use or remold pre-existing forms, and endow them with life, motion and voice.

The immortal in us has memory of all its wisdom. There is an ancestral wisdom in man and we can if we wish drink that old wine of heaven. This memory of the spirit is the real basis of imagination, and when it speaks to us we feel truly inspired and a mightier creature than ourselves speaks through us.

To find sentences which seemed noble and full of melody sounding in my brain as if another and greater than I had spoken them. I am convinced that all poetry is, as Emerson said, first written in the heavens, that is, it is conceived by a self deeper than appears in normal life, and when it speaks to us or tells us its ancient story we taste of eternity and drink the Soma juice, the elixir of immortality.

The Many-Colored Land (**Inspiration**), A. E.

The highest ecstasy and vision are conditioned by law and attainable by all, and this might be argued as of more importance even than the message of the seers. I attribute to that unwavering meditation and fiery concentration of will a growing luminousness in my brain as if I had unsealed in the body a fountain of interior light. The luminous quality gradually became normal in me, and at times in meditation there broke in on me an almost intolerable luster of light, pure and shining faces, dazzling processions of figures, most ancient, places and peoples, and landscapes lovely as the lost Eden. These appeared at first to have no more relation to myself than images from a street without one sees reflected in a glass; but at times meditation prolonged itself into spheres which were radiant with actuality.

There came through meditation a more powerful orientation of my being as if to a hidden sun, and my thoughts turned more and more to the spiritual life of Earth. All the needles of being pointed to it. I felt instinctively that all I saw in vision was part of the life of Earth which is a court where there are many starry palaces. There the Planetary Spirit was King, and that Spirit manifesting through the substance of Earth, the Mighty Mother, was, I felt, the being I groped after as God. The love I had for nature as garment of that deity grew deeper.

I was bare of all but desire for the Eternal. I was once more the child close to the Mother. She rewarded me by lifting for me a little the veil which hides her true face. To those high souls who know their kinship the veil is lifted, her face is revealed, and her face is like a bride's. In those moments of vision I understood instinctively the high mood they must keep who would walk with the highest; and who with that divine face glimmering before him could do aught but adore!

It is always lawful to speak of that higher wisdom which relates our spiritual being to that multitudinous unity which is God and Nature and Man.

Like these were my first visions of super-nature, not spiritual nor of any high import, not in any way so high as those transcendental moments of awe, when almost without vision the Divine Darkness seemed to breathe within the spirit. But I was curious about these forms, and often lured away by them from the highest meditation; for I was dazzled like a child who escapes from a dark alley in one of our cities of great sorrow where its life has been spent, and who comes for the first time upon some rich garden beyond the city where the air is weighted with scent of lilac or rose, and the eyes are made gay with color. Such a beauty begins to glow on us as we journey towards Deity, even as earth grows brighter as we journey from the gloomy pole to lands of the sun; and I would cry out to our humanity, sinking deeper into the Iron Age, that the Golden World is all about us and that beauty is open to all, and none are shut out from it who will turn to it and seek for it.

Intuition, A. E.

Intuition is that sense of a divinity ever present in act or thought my words do not communicate. The ecstatic, half-articulate, with broken words, can make us feel the kingdom of heaven is within him.

Yet Earth seemed to me bathed in an æther of Deity. I felt at times as one raised from the dead, made virginal and pure, who renews exquisite intimacies with the divine companions, with Earth, Water, Air and Fire. To breathe was to inhale magical elixirs. To touch Earth was to feel the influx of power as with one who had touched the mantle of the Lord. Thought, from whatever it set out, forever led to the heavenly city. But these feelings are incommunicable. We have no words to express a thousand distinctions clear to the spiritual sense.

I believe of nature that it is a manifestation of Deity, and that, because we are partakers in the divine nature, all we see has affinity with us; and though now we are as children who look upon letters before they have learned to read, to the illuminated spirit its own being is clearly manifested in the universe even as I recognize my thought in the words I write. Everything in nature has intellectual significance, and relation as utterance to the Thought out of which the universe was born, and we, whose minds were made in its image, who are the microcosm of the macrocosm, have in ourselves the key to unlock the meaning of that utterance. Because of these affinities the spirit swiftly by intuition can interpret nature to itself.

> I tried to light the candle on my forehead to peer into every darkness in the belief that the external universe of nature had no more exquisite architecture than the internal universe of being, and that the light could only reveal some lordlier chambers of the soul, and whatever speech the inhabitant used must be fitting for its own sphere, so I became a pupil of the spirit and tried as a child to learn the alphabet at the knees of the gods.

Rudolf Steiner's Curriculum Recommendations—Grade Eight

Karl Stockmeyer's Waldorf Literature and History indications for Grade Eight

History: Seventeenth century until the present time, biographically and episodically. Knowledge of nations.

> In the eighth class one tries to bring history up to present times, giving great consideration to cultural history. Most of what forms the content of history today will be merely mentioned in passing. Much of what is still found in our history books is of little value for the education of the child and even Charlemagne and similar historical figures should be treated without too much detail."
>
> "In almost every class you will have to begin from the beginning. You must simply limit your teaching as you find it necessary. If, for instance, you are obliged to begin at the beginning in the eighth-grade, then you must only take a little, but try nevertheless to give a complete picture of the whole of evolution of humanity, only in an abbreviated form. In the eighth-grade you would have to go through the whole world history as we understand it. (9.25.19)

Geography: The whole earth—industries and transport facilities together with spiritual relationships of the different countries (9.6.19). Geological strata; origin of the Alps, the mountain cross; rising and submerging of the continents, the Atlantean catastrophe (9.23.19).

> Let us start from the concept of rhythm. We can show that the British Isles have ascended and descended four times. Then we come to the concept of old Atlantis by way of geology. Then we can pass on to trying to call up in the children a picture of how different it was when this region was above and that one below. We start with the fact that the British Isles have ascended and descended four times—then can be established simply by the strata. We try in this way to show the connection between these things, but we must not shrink from speaking to the children about the land of Atlantis. We must not pass this by. We can establish a link also in connection with history. Only you will have then to discard the usual geology. For the Atlantic catastrophe must be placed in the 7th to 8th millennium" (9.25.19).

Bibliographical References and Recommended Reading List for Grade Eight

Admas, Randolph. *The Gateway to American History*. Ungar Publishing, New York, 1960.

Andrews, Shirley. *Lemuria & Atlantis*. Llewellyn Publications, 2004.

Andrist, Ralph. *George Washington*. Newsweek, New York.

Baravalle. *Introduction to Astronomy*. Waldorf Monographs.

Bennell. *Shakespears's Flowering of Spirit*. Steiner Press.

Churchward, James. *The Lost Continent of Mu*. Adventures Unlimited Press, 2007.

Donnelly, Ignatius. *Atlantis: The Antidiluvian World*. Dover Publications, 2011.

Fleming, Thomas. *Benjamin Franklin*. Newsweek, New York.

Foster. *George Washington's World*. Legion, New York.

Grun. *The Timetables of History*. Simon & Schuster

Harwood. *Shakespeare's Prophetic Mind*. Steiner Press.

Hauschka. *The Nature of Substance*. St. George Service. New York.

Kolisko. *Geology*. St. George/Steiner College Press.

Marcelle and Husimann. *Stories of the French Revolution*. Main Line Book Co.

Miers. *Abraham Lincoln in Peace and War*. Richard Brown.

Miller, John C. *The First Frontier Life in Colonial America*. Laurel, New York, 1966.

Peabody, James Bishop. *John Adams*. Newsweek, New York.

Podmove. *Robert Owen, A Biography*. M.S.G. House.

Sanderlin, George. *1776: Journals of American Independence*. Harper & Row, New York, 1968.

Scientific American. *Lives in Science*. Simon & Schuster.

Scott-Elliot, W. *The Story of Atlantis and the Lost Lemuria*. CreateSpace, 2013.

Sewell. *Brief Biographies of Famous Men and Women*. Permabooks.

Sutcliff, Rosemary. *Beowolf*. Dutton & Co., New York, 1962.

Tappan, Eva March. *American Hero Stories*. Houghton, New York, 1906.

Thomas. *The Vital Spark*. Doubleday.

Wachsmuth, Guenther. *The Evolution of Mankind*. Anthroposophic Press.

Wright. *Shakespeare's England*. Horizon.

Appendix

Source of the Force:
The Secret Behind Star Wars' Inspiration

I would like to share with you my personal experience of collaborating for three days in the early seventies with Marcia Lucas and a small team of Anthroposophy scholars on the script of *Star Wars* and my recent discoveries about how that foundational work affected the writing, editing, and expansions of the original Trilogy.

First of all, it seems fitting that my first encounter with the origins of *Star Wars*—a modern fairy tale ultimately about the return to spirit—would happen at Christmas time, a season in which humanity recalls its sense of spirit and hope.

I was a student at the Waldorf Institute at the time, and remember the day that I first met the characters of Luke Skywalker, R2-D2, C-3PO, and the entire *Star Wars* entourage. Yet, when I first encountered them, they were more like two-dimensional paper dolls in an unfinished script, before their true meaning had been breathed into them. For example, Luke Starkiller, as I met him, was a far cry from the Skywalker he turned out to be. You may be surprised to learn that the story, in its early form, was seen through the machinist eyes of two robots and was not yet the familiar, crowd-pleasing epic that would become one of the most famous and endearing movies in the world.

That was, of course, before my colleagues from the Waldorf Institute and I spent three days as part of a think-tank session with George Lucas' talented wife and professional film editor Marcia Lucas (née Marcia Griffin) to transform a story that was originally based on two robots into a sweeping modern fairy tale that even today still evokes a timeless sense of human destiny.

Meeting Marcia

At that time, like the characters, I was in development, too, as are all earnest students. In addition to being a student of Anthroposophy—a discipline of knowledge developed by Rudolf Steiner concerned with all aspects of human life, spirituality, and future evolution—I also managed the Waldorf bookstore, which was a treasure trove of spiritual knowledge.

That Christmas season had been busy, and I was just locking up the store and ready to head home when my teacher, Werner Glass, approached me.

Born in Austria, Werner was a beloved instructor at the Waldorf Institute and inarguably the most prominent Anthroposophist scholar in America. I can only say today that it was a great honor to be his student. That day, there was a glint of light-hearted cheer in his eyes. Thinking that he was simply going to wish me a merry holiday, I was surprised when he asked me to follow him.

"Where?" I asked, blindly following him like a faithful puppy.

Without answering, he led me into one of the more spacious classrooms, where four other students were already seated around a table, talking with the Institute's co-director, Hans Gebert. A woman I did not recognize seemed to be at the center of the conversation—a pleasant-looking brunette with a friendly yet sophisticated air.

When everyone saw Werner in the doorway, they looked up with a sense of expectation, as most students typically did when Werner walked into a room. He was like a father to us all. He motioned for me to take a seat, then sat down and began to explain the situation.

"I'm very pleased to introduce you all to Marcia Lucas," he said. "Her husband is a well-known movie director who is working on a screenplay for a science fiction film—a space opera of sorts—and they would like our Waldorf perspective. I don't know if you have heard of George Lucas?"

This was the first time I had ever heard George Lucas' name. I certainly hadn't seen his critically-acclaimed and commercially successful *American Graffiti*. I also didn't know that his wife, Marcia, was an accomplished film editor in her own right.

"Well, Marcia is familiar with Anthroposophy and the work of Rudolph Steiner, and she needs our help with the script, to make it more Waldorf-inspired so it will have good merit as both a movie and a spiritual story."

Marcia nodded and offered more context. She said that the "big screen" should be used to deliver important messages to audiences and tell a more spiritual story, one that has a good foundation in the truth, not just another director's dream.

This began to inspire me, as story-telling is at the center of our teaching curriculum in Waldorf schools. Movies are mass exposure to stories. Stories, like fairy tales, help inspire the psyches of those who witness them, similar to shared dreams. At the Waldorf school, the teacher will tell a story to the children, who learn it by heart and recite it back in class the next day. Once memorized, the stories are further interpreted through music, dance, drawing, painting, and any number of other creative responses.

Marcia needed our input, she told us, because the script was entering its third draft and lacked an element of spirituality. I could see that she was problem-solving, earnestly searching for a way to make the screenplay work.

"I'm sure we're up to the task," Werner said, looking at me.

For the past few minutes, I had been sitting there wondering, *"Why am I here? No one even told me about this meeting."* Then I looked around and realized that I was the most experienced student there. The others were too young, less studied in Anthroposophy, and certainly not up to this level of work. I was immensely relieved that Werner would be there to lead us through the session, and sat back, relaxed.

"The dialogue is a bit lacking," Werner said. "I told Marcia we could help with that as well."

With that, Werner rose from his seat and said, "Well, then. My family is waiting at home, and I must be off."

None of us could believe it. America's leading Anthroposophist was going to leave this important project in our hands?

Werner added, "Douglas is my right hand, and I will check in on your work throughout the next few days."

He then welcomed Marcia to the resources and hospitality of the Institute and politely left.

With Werner gone, we all looked at the Institute's co-director, Hans, to lead the session.

Hans stood up.

"Well, I must admit that science and mathematics are my true specialty," Hans said, in his characteristic fashion. "So I am afraid I will not be of much assistance to this group."

He politely bid us all adieu, then left.

At this point, I became a bit panicked. My leaders had left me in a great unknown!

Marcia Lucas, who I did not know at the time was one of the greatest film editors in the world, was looking expectantly at me.

I suddenly got the feeling Werner had said something to her about me, akin to his comment about me being his "right hand." I had a vague realization that both she and I were here solely because of Werner. Having been a brilliant actor at the London School of Theater, Werner had been the primary Anthroposophist in dealing with actors, directors, and producers at the Waldorf school in North Hollywood. She was here because of him, and I was here because he had brought a promising student to the table for this specialized project. Surely he knew what he was doing, so I decided to trust it.

"Well, then, let's get started," I said. "Tell us the story, Marcia."

As she spoke, I got up and went over to the classroom blackboard. Marcia had trouble articulating the story; it didn't flow easily. In colored chalk, I began to sketch out the storyboard.

"It's a story of two robots, you see—the movie is seen through their eyes," she said. "The robots are key elements of the story. They must be kept."

I understood that the robots were non-negotiable. We must somehow work with them.

"OK," I said. "Can you please read us the starting dialogue?"

She began. It was difficult for us to listen to. As an experienced editor, Marcia knew this. The characters didn't work. They weren't alive. She sincerely wanted to rewrite her husband's movie script to its full potential, but at this moment, it was stilted. Only later would I learn more about the context of their partnership—how George was a genius concerned with the theme of machines and technology, and Marcia was the humanistic side, focused on telling a meaningful story that would resonate with the audience. I did not know it then, but she was here, basically, to try to save the script.

I decided to be frank with her.

"First, the story is not archetypal," I said. "The author doesn't know the true nature and value of the characters he is set on gluing together."

Marcia began to take notes.

"The dialogue is unreal and trite. It serves only one purpose—to move to the next scene. So, the message of the story happens in the action between scenes."

She nodded, writing.

I continued. "There is no character development. No one will identify with these characters."

Then, on a positive note, I said, "However, your husband has tapped into the true spiritual reality of our time. His obsession with seeing the world through the eyes of two robots is genius, but a little confused. We can work with that."

Since everyone there, including Marcia, was a student of Anthroposophy, I began to do what Werner knew would come naturally to me as both a teacher and a student—apply the principles that I had studied to our current problem with the script.

"George has described the challenge of our times," I said, "The war with machines, symbolized in the two robot playmates of Luke Starkiller."

Now, an interesting side note about the names. Like Luke Starkiller, none of the character names that Marcia read to us were in their final form. In fact, I later recommended that the hero, Luke Starkiller, be changed to "Luke Skywalker," from American Indian and Tibetan traditions. Then, since Lucas is the name for "light," I also had the concept of a light saber, a weapon that both defends as a shield and attacks as a formidable force. (In Anthroposophist terms, the light saber represents the human spinal column.)

Those details would come later. Now, we had to focus on shaping the story itself.

"I think it needs to go back to the concept of a fairy tale," I said, explaining that all fairy tales begin with a reference of the story being outside of time and space and end with some reference to their own continuance. "I think what you may want is an adult science-fiction fairy tale that is spiritually accurate, yet engrossing and interesting."

Marcia agreed.

With her input, we decided to begin with Luke Starkiller. We tried to describe his character development in terms of the polarity that every person has in their soul—the left and right-hand paths of evil. In the end, it is the middle path, "the Force," that the Jedi warrior should choose. Yet, without exploring both the left and right paths, the Jedi is weakened by not knowing his enemy.

"So, each movie goer will be faced with making the same decision, no matter what their life is like?" said one of the students.

"Yes, that's the path of most fairy tales," I said. The question is: "Which of the three paths will you choose?"

Here again, I was impressed with George Lucas' brilliance. His obsession with machines underscored the biggest challenge of our age—the right-hand path of mechanical occultism as described by Rudolph Steiner, and the left-hand path of thinking that has turned evil. Had I seen his first film, *THX-1138*, I would have recognized this even more clearly.

"The two robots can represent thinking and willing," I proposed.

As the heroes of George's original story, both C-3PO and R2-D2 enable the audience to "see through the eyes of machines." In his relationship and interactions with them, Luke uses his robots to enhance his thinking (C-3PO) and willing (R2-D2) in an age of machines, but finally finds the middle path—of feeling.

"Let's explore the two extremes: the left-hand path of thinking, and the right-hand path of willing," I said.

We spent time talking it through. Both C-3PO and the Evil Emperor are on the left-hand path of "thinking" that has turned evil. For example, C-3PO can think but cannot act, and the Emperor needs Darth Vader to carry out his desired actions. In contrast, R2-D2 and Darth Vader are on the right-hand path of "willing." Having the capacity to will, they still must be told what to do.

"Darth Vader is the being we know as Ahriman," I added. "He represents the composite cleverness of all machines, incarnated into a human being."

"So, what about a middle path? Is there one?" one of the students asked.

"Excellent question," I said. "The middle path is what both the right-hand and left-hand paths miss. Unable to understand the middle path, both sides seek to destroy it. The Jedi masters such as Obi-Wan Kenobi and Yoda have developed themselves on the middle path, having already mastered the other two paths. They represent the desired balanced center between the two extremes."

Indeed, this dynamic of two poles of evil is the central motif of the first *Star Wars* trilogy.

Master of the Machines

Once we understood the story in context of this Anthroposophical framework, the next step was to focus on Luke's character.

"I think that Luke needs to develop his character by interacting with the two robots, both the left and the right hand," I said.

We then discussed each robot.

As a robot on the thinking side, C-3PO can speak many languages and is programmed for etiquette and translating, a truly inspired use for machines that we seldom see. He represents an evil that has been around as long as languages in every culture since the beginning of human intellectual development—the being named Lucifer, who incarnated in a physical body in China in 2000 BC. As the left-hand path of evil, Lucifer is a Promethean archetype who brings fire, language, philosophy, writing, and culture to humanity. Chained to a mountain, he suffered each day as a vulture ate out his liver until rescued by Heracles. By representing Lucifer/Prometheus, C-3PO would serve as a counter-pole for the incarnation four thousand years later in 2000 AD of Ahriman, the king of machines—otherwise known as Darth Vader.

Luke, who models the original Heracles (or the hero in all of us), eventually breaks the chains to free Prometheus, the fire-bringer, who is on the left-hand path. So, too, the Evil Emperor in *Star Wars* represents the power of fire (demonstrated as lightning from his hands and the evil wisdom of the Sith) that increasingly consumes him as he misuses it.

"Luke is situated between the two robots, between the two paths, like his twin sister. His lost spirituality is drawing him upward into spirit," I said.

All Jedi warriors have transformed blood: what was later called "midi-chlorians" in the blood. As they balance the forces of the left and right paths, they raise their consciousness, which then increases spiritual potential in the blood, a process that Steiner calls the "etherization of the blood." As Steiner taught, spiritual people charge their blood with a consciousness that connects them to spirit (the Force). However, unlike in the movie, the ability to access spirit or the Force isn't passed along through heredity.

So, after discussing all of these concepts and laying the groundwork for common understanding, here is the story of *Star Wars* that we mapped out:

> *Once upon a time, in a galaxy far, far away, Luke Skywalker (the archetypal human) finds his life embroiled, if not con-*

sumed, by machines. Luke is the master of those machines, because he has consciousness and, therefore, is pulled by the left and right. He is an orphan, as all modern humans find themselves, and knows that something great lives inside of him. He has hope in a hopeless world.

Luke's father has fallen prey to the evil right-hand path of machines that has transformed him into a part man, part machine abomination who wars against his own spirit and wishes to dominate the world, even if it means killing his son.

The left-hand path of personal black magic lives in the Evil Emperor, who also wishes to kill all Jedi and, most especially, the son of Darth Vader.

Luke is protected by the humble Jedi, Obi-Wan Kenobi. Eventually, this Jedi leads him to his teacher of the "middle way" (the Force) and sacrifices himself so that he can help him from the spiritual world. This middle path is like the path to the Higher Self.

On the path, just like Dorothy on the Yellow Brick Road, Luke gains some traveling companions. Just as the Wizard of Oz was a distillation of Masonic initiation rituals, Star Wars introduces the audience to parts of the soul. This is necessary to make the story archetypal, so that it will always be fresh.

For example, **Obi-Wan Kenobi** *represents the highest of the three parts of the soul, the* **consciousness soul**, *which merges spirit with matter, just as his Jedi powers give him the power of mind over matter.*

Chewbacca *represents the lower soul, the* **sentient or astral soul** *that must turn the animal in us into a human with spiritual characteristics.*

Han Solo *represents the* **intellectual soul** *that first begins to awaken to higher thinking. Although clever, Han lacks the ability to see the big picture like Obi-Wan.*

Between Luke's three companions, much like the Lion, Tin Man, and Scarecrow, each contributes a special quality to Luke along the way. Steiner calls these soul qualities "thinking, feeling, and willing."

At the center of the story, Luke represents the ego, or the thinking human being, and must master the three steps of the development of the soul.

A Return to Spirit

Now that we had built the underlying framework, which was the most Herculean part of our task, it was clear to me that we needed to develop these characters into archetypes. Knowing now what motivated each character, we could easily hear the words that each would naturally say and even envision their realistic reactions to the unfolding plot.

In doing so, we kept in mind a fundamental truth: good and evil are choices. The Evil Emperor and Darth Vader were not born evil; they chose their own paths. Luke, the archetypal human, also must make his choices and live with the good or evil that results.

Still, after all of this work we had done, one thing was missing.

"We still have one problem," I reminded Marcia. "Where is Luke going in the story?"

Sorely missing in the original version of the story, this issue had to be resolved so that everything else would make sense.

"Isn't Luke, essentially, the prodigal son?" I said. Others agreed that Luke was separated from his parents' home and longing to return. This is a universal element with which everyone could identify. Like Luke, each of us has our particular destiny. In our life, we embark on the search to find it and return to our kingdom in the spirit.

We further developed Luke's direction and role in the story as follows:

> *Luke knows he is special, but doesn't know why. Throughout the story, he must evolve into his mission of facing his true identity as Darth Vader's son, accept it, and decide what to do with it.*
>
> *Ultimately, Luke denies the power of the machines that try to gain control over him. Instead of the cold-hearted machine-human hybrids, Luke chooses love. He must come to this awakening only after receiving help from his companions.*
>
> *His sister Leia (who I said should be called Maya) represents his spiritual self. Although first drawn to her through*

physical desire, Luke transforms this attraction into spiritual love and links his destiny to hers, as the soul links to the spirit.

More sure about herself, Leia has been treated like the Princess she is. Luke has struggled to "catch up" to where she was, but in the end, their destinies are permanently entwined. Because he is on the spiritual path of self-development versus the physical path of earthly gratification, Luke doesn't "win the girl"—that part of the story is left to another character: Han Solo.

As part of his journey, Luke uses the middle path of the Force to conquer both the Evil Emperor and Darth Vader. The more the left and right-hand paths try to win Luke, the more they fall prey to the side effects of using evil for personal gain.

As the modern human, Luke conquers the evil machine-like foes with help from his companions and develops two powerful "forces" that the machines cannot control: human freedom and love. In this way, Luke learns to "see through the eyes of machines." He even sacrifices his human hand while denying his father's attempt to win him over to the Dark Side of the machines.

In the end, Luke loves his father and witnesses the death of Darth Vader, Ahriman, before his very eyes.

This is the same modern challenge that each of us faces:

Who is your parent?

What do you choose: the physical world of machines, or the middle path of the spirit—the Force?

A Beautiful Fairy Tale

Over the next two days, we built on our initial framework and polished the ideas to represent every possible perspective in our archetypal science-fiction, prodigal-son story. The script was turning into a beautiful fairy tale that I was certain had merit, whether or not it ever made it to the "big screen." I was very happy to work through these concepts, because I could see my own path to the spirit unfolding in the story. (Of course, Werner had known this would be part of my involvement!)

I also appreciated Marcia's priority of effective story-telling. In our modern times, I have seen a decline of storytelling in our culture. This is dangerous, for as archetypal stories vanish, our imagination weakens as the source of inner nourishment and soul inspiration. Movies have taken the place of storytelling, and actors have taken the place of the heroes and heroines found in all archetypal stories, whether myth, religion, legend, fairy tale, fable, or any other transcendental source. Yet, as we learned in developing *Star Wars*, if a story is not archetypal, it will not last the test of time. Still successful to this day, a full forty years after it was released, *Star Wars* has proven that to be true.

After our work was completed, I said goodbye to Marcia and wished her well with the movie. She thanked me and everyone else who had contributed their ideas to the marvelous fairy tale. I heard nothing more until 1977, when the movie was about to launch and generating a frenzied buildup of media attention.

I was working in the bookstore when Werner came in to tell me the news: Marcia and George Lucas were so happy with our help that they were offering all Waldorf schools in the United States a chance to show an advanced screening of the movie as a local fundraiser. This was a thrilling offer, because I knew that a good deal of money could be raised. Yet, staying true to its practice of opposing TV, movies, and technology in general, the Waldorf Institute politely declined the offer, to my deep disappointment.

I finally saw the Trilogy, after waiting impatiently for all three installments, and was happy that it stayed true to the fairy-tale idea we had developed in our Waldorf think tank.

As I watched the movies, I realized that *Star Wars* had affected the paths of those of us involved in the project. Just as we had mapped out a path for Luke, we were all on a journey to our own destinies. The archetypes we built had done their work!

For example, by working through the philosophical concepts, I saw my own path to the spirit reflected in the story, as Werner knew it would—the process had further emboldened my own understanding of the study of Anthroposophy. Also,

I remembered that Werner, who was like a scholarly father, had introduced me to Marcia as his "right hand," while Luke Skywalker had sacrificed his own right hand in the battle with his father. Both situations connected to the pursuit of spiritual knowledge. As a "right hand" substitute for Werner in the project with Marcia, I grew into my leadership role as a teacher. So, too, with the substitution of his right hand, Luke acquired more masterful poise as a Jedi warrior who had successfully denied the Dark Side and became more in touch with the Force.

George Lucas himself was on the path for his genius to be recognized with commercial and critical success. He would later open his famous Skywalker Ranch, which I think is a much better name than "Starkiller Ranch."

Yet, when his own right hand, Marcia Lucas, was symbolically severed in their 1983 divorce, he lost a part of the humanity that had been evident in the earlier movies, and some say lacking in the later versions of the *Star Wars* series.

For her part, Marcia Lucas would stand on stage to be ceremoniously honored, just like the characters in the ending of *Star Wars*. Looking tasteful and quietly elegant next to a glittery-gold presenter Farrah Fawcett at the 1977 Academy Awards, Marcia accepted an Oscar for best editing of a film that had started off an as unknown space opera and become a household name. At that ceremony, one of her editor colleagues would speak for her, and she would not have an opportunity to thank anyone publicly—not even her husband. Had they given her a chance at the microphone, I imagine that Marcia perhaps might have thanked the Waldorf Institute, although the process of being involved in this influential project was, for me, its own reward.

In fact, later, when working with producer Kathleen Kennedy during the writing of the *Indiana Jones* movies, I was quite aware of my participation in shaping small moments in the movies when true wisdom and light shine through the story. This is what I have tried to do in all of my writings: share the love of spirit that I try to live each day and bring that spirit into the souls of everyone I have the privilege to meet or touch in some small way—even through a simple story that is the ubiquitous retelling of the original story: the return to spirit.

Just a few days ago, with all of the resurgence of *Star Wars* memories and the recent release of the latest installment in the series, I googled Marcia Lucas' name and discovered that she and George had divorced in 1983. She had returned to using her maiden name, Marcia Griffin. When I worked with her, I had no idea that she was one of the greatest film editors in the world, her skills having been regularly in demand by the top directors, including Scorsese and Coppola. I was delighted to learn about her Academy Award and believe she is an unsung heroine in the history of *Star Wars*.

After all, how often does a mortal human being create something eternal—a story that lasts forever?

May the Force be with you, too!

The Enduring Legacy of
Han Solo and Indiana Jones

I greatly enjoyed being part of think-tank discussions with scriptwriter and film editor Marcia Lucas (George Lucas' wife at the time) about the characters and story development of *Star Wars* based on anthroposophical concepts that formed the spiritual core of the movie. After that, life went on. I went back to studying anthroposophy and working happily at the Waldorf Institute bookstore. The first *Star Wars* movie came out and, much to my delight, was a major international hit. All was well. I was satisfied that I had made a significant contribution and thought my brief connection with Hollywood was over.

It wasn't. In fact, it was just beginning. In the same way that Marcia Lucas and I had worked together to define a fairy tale space adventure within an anthroposophical framework, now I was about to enter a new kind of adventure. Hold on to your hat, Indiana Jones!

Here's how it happened. Not long after the first *Star Wars* movie came out, I was working in the Waldorf bookstore.

My boss and mentor, Werner Glas, stuck his head in the doorway and said, "Douglas, a friend of Marcia Lucas is on the phone, and she has too many questions for me to handle. Would you please speak with her and answer all of her questions?"

Then, he smiled radiantly at me, and headed back down the hall.

I began to feel a sense of excitement. I had met Marcia Lucas when she visited the Institute to discuss ideas for her husband's movie, *Star Wars*. At the time, I didn't realize her accomplishments as an editor, nor did I know the impact that the space opera would have on audiences around the world. The very fact that I had contributed some ideas to the *Star Wars* storyline and characters was a thrilling realization, especially when I had heard that people were standing in long lines just to see this incredible new movie that had opened in theaters. I was looking forward to speaking to any friend of Marcia's and helping out in any way I could.

I picked up the phone and began a conversation that lasted a long time. Kathleen, as she identified herself, was a direct and highly inquisitive person. Her questioning was unrelenting, and she didn't take partial answers. In fact, she wanted to know these answers as if her life depended on them. I naturally assumed, because of her insatiable questioning about anthroposophical principles, that she was interested in attending the Waldorf Institute as a student and taking one of the programs for teacher training. I answered as if her life really did depend on it.

Many times, I had taken phone calls similar to this in which someone would inquire about the course work, environment, or housing. Actually, that was standard protocol for running the Institute bookstore. Seldom, though, had one of the standard "student" calls been so direct, with such a broad range of modern themes to the questions.

"Who were Rudolf Steiner and HP Blavatsky? What is their relationship to Spiritism, telepathy, clairvoyance, poltergeists, possessions, exorcisms, Eastern masters, and living masters?"

So, I unpacked the whole history and development of theosophy and anthroposophy and made the distinction between spiritual realities and modern cartoons of these forces in the media. I can truly say that I filled her head with esoteric information, but at the same time, my limits were stretched by her questions like no Waldorf trainee before or after. I thoroughly enjoyed the breadth and depth of the conversation and could tell that Kathleen was getting it, from the anthroposophical view.

I was very happy that, in my mind, I had helped convince her that Rudolf Steiner (1861–1925), founder of anthroposophy and Waldorf education, and his followers were not pie-in-the-sky nutjobs who ignore science and direct observation of reality for a path of spiritual awakening. To the contrary, Steiner is the most applicable of all spiritual development paths, as evidenced by the numerous direct areas of work that have evolved from his insights into education, agriculture, architecture, medicine, and more.

In addition to answering Kathleen's questions, I also recommended books from our bookstore because I was, after all, a book salesman. I was shocked by the fact that she bought every book I referred to without hesitation, which was not the norm in our little bookstore. When I made reference to books that were not in stock here, she wrote them down. She asked where she could find these books, and I recommended the best bookstore for spiritual books, the Mayflower Bookshop in Berkley, Michigan. The Mayflower is still in operation in a little store so packed with books that one can hardly move about, yet, it has the best collection of spiritual-esoteric books in America, by far.

She took down the name enthusiastically. I gave her the number and told her to talk to my dear friend Robert Thibodeau, the proprietor.

The next round of questions focused principally on the Ark of the Covenant.

"Where is it? Was it real? What were its powers? What was it made of? Are there authentic pictures of it? Who stole it? What did the Templars have to do with it? Do the Jews have one now, and if so, where is it? Did the Queen of Sheba take it back to Ethiopia?"

Now, if you think those questions are a mouthful, you should have heard the answers. We talked for more than two hours, and the total of her book order was the largest I had ever sold. It took three boxes to hold all of the anthroposophical books she wanted. I started to think she might not be coming here, since she was having so many books shipped to her. I made it my business not to pry into other people's personal lives, so I didn't ask any direct questions about her background or whether or not she intended to join the Institute as a student. Anyway, there was no time for me to ask questions, because I was too busy answering them! I loved showing off my study in the very fields of knowledge she was asking about. And, of course, I was happy to sell books for the Institute.

I can honestly say that the depth of what I told Kathleen in that first telephone call, and two other similar calls, simply cannot be shared outside of esoteric circles. There are great and powerful secrets implicit in certain types of archetypal symbols and parables (stories) that shape human intellectual and spiritual development. I shared many of those ideas with Kathleen to try to drive to the heart of what "stories" embody for the collective consciousness of humanity. She was asking about the hidden meaning behind stories to try to find the core wisdom. This noble motivation inspired me, and I shared stories with her from obscure sources that explain the past with self-evident wisdom, frame the present as the eternal now, and predict the future from the eternal frameworks that move us from the past into the future. *The Ark of the Covenant* is one of those stories.

We followed all of the historic and legendary streams of the Ark, from its inception, to its theft, to its reinstatement and its travel to Africa, where it exists today as a continuous stream of consciousness from Moses. Wonders do indeed stream from its very presence, and only a few can endure its might in the underground temples dedicated to the Ark. A continuous priesthood has accompanied the Ark in an unbroken chain. All of these things can be found to be true, and I, or Robert from the Mayflower Bookshop, sold her a book on the topic to prove it.

I hadn't had this much fun in a long time. Helping people on the path of spiritual development is rewarding. Giving them the tools (books, in those pre-Internet days) to help themselves and pointing in the direction of growth that I and many others had taken was standard practice. Even today, my wife and spiritual partner Tyla and I strive to provide a path for others in their spiritual development. It is an endeavor that we commit to daily, whether it is through our website and newsletters at OurSpirit.com, online videos, books, or social media. We try to be as generous in our offerings to spiritual seekers as I hope I was with Kathleen so many years ago.

After the first conversation, I assumed Kathleen was overwhelmed with the knowledge and material, and might never call again, but she did. This time, she was even more intent on tracking down the truth, whether it lay in anthroposophy or someplace else.

I kept returning to Steiner because his opinion is so clear and helpful, but her questions seemed to go deeper, into the darker aspects of theology, so I drew upon my former experience as a Catholic priest, where I conducted many exorcisms with my mentor, Father William. At first I was slightly reluctant to share my firsthand experiences of what occurs between the boundaries of the physical and spiritual worlds, but I answered and told the truth, no matter how unbelievable it sounded. She did not seem to be skeptical, writing everything down and questioning me for clarification and detail as she drilled down layer by layer to hear about the darker side of the spiritual world.

We also had wide-ranging conversations about the caves in South America that Helena Blavatsky mentions, where the walls are lined with gold and the masters live in secret. Many have sought these caves to find the gold, but the entrance has always remained hidden to the uninitiated.

"But what would an adventurer gain from finding these caves?" she asked.

This was a sticking point that I remember quite well. These caves that Blavatsky spoke about are not physical; they are etheric. There would be nothing to take, no prize for the museum that had great power to rule over others. At that point, we discussed the alleged crystal skulls from South America, Shiva stones from India, the wish-fulfilling stone of Vajrayogini, magic crystals from Atlantis and Lemuria, the secret Halls of Wisdom beneath the Great Pyramid, the tomb of the first Emperor of China, and many other similar stories. All carried the same simplistic theme of physical stones being connected to spiritual development.

I emphasized downplaying the role of stones in relationship to the development of human consciousness, just like I did with George Lucas' Kyber stones. The plot of *Star Wars* was initially centered on two Kyber stones, one good and one evil. This plot was far too simple and materialistic to truly convey an understanding of the spiritual development of the human being. Consciousness does not depend on finding a physical object like a stone or an artifact, except in the ancient times of Atlantis, so I told her the story of the stones of Atlantis.

There were seven stones, each connected to the energy of one of the major six planets, with a central stone representing the sun. Each stone sat atop a pyramid in the shape of a six-pointed star. Each crystal was made of the substance that channeled a particular planet's energy as it joined with the energy of the other crystals. According to legends, this "harmony of the spheres" energy conduit powered the advanced technology of Atlantis.

The story of the crystals of Atlantis is taken from theosophical sources and is widely speculated upon. In those times, crystals were still radiant and forming. This active nature of the crystal made it a touch-point for the resonant harmonics created by the planets moving through the ethers. At that time in history, crystals did hold great power. In the future, crystals will release that same power through new technologies.

All these stories filled our second and third conversations, which I still hold as treasured memories. After each conversation, I packed up reference books and mailed them off. After the third conversation, the mysterious caller never called back. I wondered what had happened to her and asked Werner if Kathleen was going to come join us, he said he barely knew her and that, to his knowledge, she was not. I was saddened by that and had hoped to continue the lively discussions.

Time goes by, and we forget most of what we do. So it was for me, until one day I was in Michigan, watching TV with Robert at Mayflower Bookshop. On the show, producer Steven Spielberg was being interviewed. He had released the first of four Indiana Jones movies with Lucas and was discussing his new movie, *Poltergeist*. The interviewer asked him where he came up with such an unusual topic as poltergeists.

"From the Austrian scientist and philosopher Rudolf Steiner," said Spielberg.

I turned to Robert, both of us stunned. We could not believe what we had just heard! Spielberg went on but didn't say much more about Steiner, yet we had both clearly heard him credit

Steiner for the inspiration. This was amazing, because few people know about Steiner's teaching. To think that his anthroposophy inspired a Spielberg movie was shocking. We both had seen the movie and thought that the psychic in the movie resembled the Theosophist Madame Blavatsky. Several scenes, which were quite authentic, reminded me of my days as an exorcist. We thought the movie was amazing!

I turned to Robert and said that I had always wanted to help Spielberg do a movie, a great one that really gets to the heart of spiritual matters. I wanted to hang out with Spielberg and Lucas, both known to associate with Waldorf schools, and cross-pollenate archetypal icons for a spiritual future that could educate people through movies. I loved movies and found them to be just as demonic as Steiner said they were, but also a powerful tool of social development because they can display moral archetypes in a captivating way. They are "dreams of the future," if you will.

We had a group of thinkers in our Mayflower community who dreamt such thoughts and put our work into writing, education, music, art, and other cultural seeding. We longed for a platform to reach more people about the amazing powers of transformation available through self-development in many different streams of wisdom. Movies could deliver these messages to the world. I longed for the opportunity to unveil previously secret wisdom on the big screen.

I had often spoke to Robert and other esoteric friends about my dream to link up with Spielberg as I had the opportunity to do with Marcia Lucas before the *Star Wars* treatment became a screenplay. I simply wanted to know how much he knew about Steiner and how much he intended to display in movies. My friends and I discussed *Poltergeist*. We found anthroposophical ideas throughout the entire movie and especially clear representations of the electro-magnetic, sub-natural forces that bind human souls to the earth realm through television. The accurate depiction of possession was frightening and realistic, and the special effects and dynamic editing blew us all away.

Spielberg was going places that were inspired and gifted beyond anything before his time.

I eventually discovered the connection between Spielberg, Kathleen Kennedy, Marcia, and George Lucas and their blockbuster movies *Star Wars* and *Poltergeist*. I realized that Kathleen had acted as a creative proxy, reaching out to me and my colleagues for the knowledge to incorporate into his fabulous movies, just as Marcia had done with us at the Waldorf Institute. So, in that sense, I felt there was already a connection. I had, indirectly, influenced Spielberg's and Lucas' movies by providing the knowledge to Kathleen Kennedy and Marcia Lucas. I am filled with gratitude that these creative people found me in Michigan and gave me the time to share the arcane and occult.

Indiana Jones also came from this team, but did not get our full approval. We saw the movies and loved them, but found little coherence between the historical Ark of the Covenant and the entertainment version flush with Nazis. They were cheesy, not unlike parts of *Star Wars*. The entertainment value of the blockbuster feature was a new phenomenon of our time. Basically, we were seeing our new cultural heroes and heroines raised up to the silver screen like Greek gods raised into the starry sky.

Time passed. I had left the Institute and occasionally worked with Robert. One Saturday afternoon, I was working in his Mayflower Bookshop. The phone rang. I answered. A female voice on the other end said, "I understand this is where I can talk to the smartest anthroposophist around?"

If you knew Robert, you would understand my answer. "That's right, ma'am," I said. "You have a question, and we will give, get, or find the answer. I have a degree in anthroposophy. I may not be the smartest, but I actually have a college degree in these subjects.

"Well, I have some questions and need the entire background of the subject to form a picture of it. The many stories do not agree. What is the truth of the Holy Grail?" she asked.

As a side note, working at the Mayflower Bookshop involved answering the most far-out questions from the most far-out people in the English-speaking world. Robert had amassed the largest collection of rare books concerning every type of spiritual, religious, astrological, and historical topic. People traveled from all around the country to buy books at his store and to interact with Robert and his team of talented psychics, astrologers, readers, and the brilliant thinkers who frequented the scene. So, when you answer the phone at the Mayflower, you'd better be ready for anything. Being a little bit over-confident didn't hurt the Mayflower reputation.

Asking me about the Holy Grail is like asking an old man to talk about his aches and pains. I launched into a litany of descriptions framing the Celtic, Christian, Pagan, mythological, and archetypal nature of the grail. Then I described Steiner's views, both his cosmic and earthly descriptions. She asked me about books containing these ideas. I described the contents of each book on the topic. I was so proud and egotistic in my youth, and so anxious to show my intellectual prowess. Soon, a stack of books was mounting. Robert came out and asked what was going on. I pointed at the books. He smiled and returned to the front of the store.

We continued to talk and talk and stack up books on the Holy Grail. I was amazed to see just how many titles the Mayflower carried on the different versions of the grail. After two boxes of books, we ended the conversation, and I charged her for the books. I was shocked. Her credit card was in the name of Kathleen Kennedy.

"*The* Kathleen Kennedy, who works for Steven Spielberg?" I said.
"Yes," she said.

At that point, I almost passed out. The clouds of years cleared before my wisdom eye, and I realized this was the same Kathleen that I had spoken with years before. In fact, I had given her the very phone number of the Mayflower Bookshop phone that I now answered. The circuitous nature of destiny was dizzying.

I was dazed as I reviewed the ideas I had shared with her at that time and the two movies Spielberg had produced since then. Now, she was asking about the Holy Grail.

So, I had to ask: "Are these books getting to Spielberg to help develop new ideas?"

"Yes. I am his assistant, and I gather research for all of us to look at to stimulate ideas," she said frankly.

This was actually too much for my little mind to comprehend. I had unknowingly been sending books to the think tank of all movie think tanks and adding my two cents.

"These books will be looked at by a collective of people percolating ideas for movies," she said. "But honestly, we don't have the time to read them all, so we need you to point us in the direction of a simple version that is loaded with symbols, archetypes, and plots that resemble the true path," she added.

I was so glad the conversation ended shortly after she said that. I boxed up the books and hoped this would appease Robert for staying on the phone for so long. *We had been a part of the greatest movie think tank that has shaped humanity's collective consciousness!* I was numb at the thought of what I had unknowingly done. The very thing I wished to do but thought I was too insignificant to do had already happened (*Star Wars*) and was happening again. In some small way, I made a free offering of the heart that was taken up and developed into lasting modern icons. I was overwhelmed by what it must be like to be Spielberg or Lucas or Kathleen, knowing that they are shaping history and the perceptions that build human development directly into the subconscious realms of human aspiration and dreams.

Binding up the boxes and labeling them, I could hardly describe to Robert what had just happened. He was shocked and pleased. I asked a colleague to take over at the front desk and asked Robert to join me in his office. I told him what had just happened in detail, and the revelation that this had happened once before years ago. He was amazed, but not dazzled. Robert was already a famous personality himself, because of his high-profile astrological clients around the world who claimed he was one of the best. It took a lot to impress him. He was skeptical about ever meeting Spielberg or Lucas and that Kathleen Kennedy might do little with these books. He thought they would end up the same as the ones sent from the

Waldorf bookstore—barely influencing the plot line. In the gravity of his experience, he was right.

The next time Kathleen called the Mayflower, I talked with her deeply about the Holy Grail and about the underground "caves" in South America and the end of the story I called "Sun Seed." Kathleen seemed to be an honest and very practical student on the path. I held back nothing from her many penetrating questions. I answered as best I could, stacked up the books again, and mailed them.

This went on a number of times over a period of about a year. It was the same routine, and again I could not find exactly what the think tank wanted. They wanted something short and easily understood by young and old, slow and wise. This proved to be a huge problem for me, because the essence of the Holy Grail cannot be crammed into one short story. We needed to frame the cultural references and limit the topic.

After some time, the conversation went beyond buying books, and I had to take the calls as a "reading," which I was used to doing. We logged many hours talking about these subjects deeply. I was happy because I was being paid by the hour. Kathleen was happy to pay and ask questions, and I was happy to answer, be paid, and try to help in some small way. Still, I couldn't quite get it right.

Kathleen decided to come to the store, meet us, and have a face-to-face conversation about the Holy Grail. I looked forward to this meeting and hoped that the personal touch might bring forth the essence of what the think tank wanted to display in the movie. The opportunity was so grand, if I could just get the plot into a simple archetypal form.

We were honored the day Kathleen came to the Mayflower. We talked throughout the day, and she spent time looking through the amazing collection of rare books. She could now see why we had so much to offer in terms of books. At the end of the day, I could still see that look of dissatisfaction and incompletion on her face. I felt like a failure. We got up and went to the door. After hugging her goodbye, it suddenly hit me.

"Wait a minute. I get it," I said.

I suddenly had a clear picture in my mind. It was very simple and would incorporate many of the themes, but not a true and literal stream of the grail. It would be fictional, yet retain elements of truth that point in the right direction.

Kathleen came back, sat down, and took out her notebook. I explained the elements that must be in the story and synthesized all the stories into one.

Here is the vision I shared with her:

> *There need to be three knights who go to Jerusalem to find the grail. They are tasked with bringing it to the West and guarding it until the time comes for a "chosen one" to cross the bridge of death between the physical and spiritual, and reach the holy shrine of the grail carved in solid stone. Hide the grail in plain sight, so only the "pure of heart" knows which of the many grails is the one and only grail—the cup that Christ used at the Last Supper. This cup is humble, and anyone who drinks from it lives forever.*
>
> *The three knights drink from the cup to live and protect the grail. Two knights fall in battle defending the grail, and one knight retreats to the grail cave to watch over it. Only the pure of heart can make it over the "bridge of sighs" that takes the lives of all who try to cross without the proper moral development. They must know the question that frees the knight and then "knights" a new keeper of the grail.*
>
> *The moral question is, "Will the pure of heart give up their life for another?"*
>
> *This pursuit enables the seeker to cross the bridge, but then they must defeat the protector or assume his duties after the proper grail is discerned through purity. Once the grail leaves the purified realm of the grail cave, it heals the earth by falling into the deepest part, which brings restorative forces to Mother Nature.*
>
> *The Holy Grail is, thus, a living imagination of the etheric realm. The drama centers around efforts to defend Her just as others try to defile Her.*

This little story then became the simple plot of the movie *Indiana Jones and the Last Crusade*, which mixes crusaders with grail knights, adventurous archeologists, the CIA, Nazis, and Nubian Temples. Don't blink, or the spiritual plot of the movie may whiz right by you.

After the movie came out, I truly had to ask myself, "Was that what I was hoping for?" I didn't think so. The impact of the Holy Grail was incidental and marginalized, just as the Ark of the Covenant was perceived as a weapon in the first Indiana Jones movie, or as a golden skull inside a secret cave, or crystal skulls in a South American cave, or Shiva stones that assume the characteristics of the Stones of Atlantis. It is somewhat disappointing that the spiritual references were lost in the action-packed dynamics of adventure and mystery, but at least they were included.

Our response to seeing spiritual ideas trivialized was rather critical. The real mystery and power of the grail did not come through the plot of the movie. The reverent moment in the grail cave was beautiful and did stay true to the dynamics of a knight on the path of the Holy Grail, but all too soon, Indiana Jones crossed back over the bridge to save his father and ultimately see the Holy Grail fall into the bowels of the earth.

I was very happy about this particular point. I had focused on it as a critical element of truth that places the Holy Grail, as a physical object, deep within the earth. The true Holy Grail is not physical and shouldn't be an object that Nazis can find and utilize for evil, just like the Ark, or Shiva stones, or golden or crystal skulls. Spirit is displayed in the architecture, art, and relics of ancient cultures that held objects as sacred and filled with spirit. We should not over-materialize these spiritual forces by worship of objects that represent them. In that way, the ending of the movie was great. Indiana saves his dad, and the Holy Grail is committed to the heart of the earth. That part of the story was grand because it conveyed part of the true nature of the etheric Holy Grail, which is still active today.

After she had visited us that day in the bookstore, I only talked with Kathleen a few more times. We filled in some of the details of the short "fairy tale" version of the Holy Grail, as I came to call it. I also shared with her the "truth" about the caves in South America that Blavatsky said were lined with gold and home to the masters. This was in the form of a long story called "Sun Seed," about a seeker who finds his way to these caves and what he encounters there, as well as its relationship to sunspots and the shifting of the poles. Twelve masters must meet in the cave to create a new Ark that will keep the earth from great physical upheavals.

Years after *Indiana Jones and the Last Crusade*, the *Crystal Skull* came out, and I was sad to see that the story had devolved into using an alien craft, not a spiritual edifice, and that the last missing skull was necessary to activate the process instead of the last master who had to find his way to the Sun Ark. Again, rocks take the place of consciousness. Instead of bringing forth spiritual beings, they bring forth aliens. This was sadly disappointing and a far cry from the intention of the story as it was imagined. Only the outer husk of the story was used, then placed in the middle of muddle and action-packed suspense. In the noise, the spiritual message got lost.

Nowadays, it is our good fortune that so many amazing spiritual concepts have reached the movies. It is obvious that there are now plenty of people like me who want to see truth beautifully displayed through sweeping stories that connect the viewer with their humanity and enrich their place in the process of the whole.

I love a movie with a great story that keeps building capacities by reflecting upon the archetypes displayed. I hope that the never-ending stories and fairy tales inspire us to keep offering these soul archetypes to humanity. They will help all of us, as spiritual beings, to move through catharsis to the other side of suffering and to cross the bridge of sighs, where we will ultimately find wisdom at the end of the trail.

The Tree of Life

There are seven ethers, two of which are the Chemical and Life ethers that have fallen to Earth (Tree of Knowledge). Two others, the Unfallen Chemical and Unfallen Life ethers, are still raying in from the cosmos (Tree of Life). There is much confusion regarding these matters because, until now, they have remained a secret of the Mystery schools that draw the distinction between Christ (Lord of the Beings of Form who donated the human ego) and Ahriman (a fallen or "retarded" Being of Form who is actively working through the realm of the Archangels). This confusion is easily understood because the Tree of Knowledge (past) and the Tree of Life (future) look alike and initially consist of the same essential substances.

For instance, many people believe spiritual substance and beings live in the inner layers of the Earth. This is not quite correct. Christ, who descended into the core of the Earth, has established a golden core in the heart of the Earth that is similar to the core of the Sun, Christ's true throne of activity.

Christ redeemed the inner layers of the Earth, but evil is still rampant there. Likewise, the Etheric Christ lives in the super-etheric layers that wrap around the Earth like wings. Christ holds His temporary "court" in this realm, surrounded by the communion of saints: those perfected aspects of humanity that become the template for humans to use to spiritually advance. Christ's perfected bodies are also found there and can multiply endlessly for the use of worthy souls who can rise up to them.

The Tree of Life feeds this realm from the cosmos, helping it become a new star, birthed from the Earth's spiritual deeds offered by pious and pure souls to the spiritual world. Human hearts also glow with this same spiritual light—a sort of human sunlight.

The Unfallen Chemical (sound) ether and Unfallen Life (word) ether will someday be directly ingested as the nectar and ambrosia of the spiritual world. For humanity, this will happen in the far future, when spiritualized humans rise up into the atmosphere and directly experience the Unfallen Chemical and Unfallen Life ethers that come from the Sun. At this point of our evolution, the Earth's atmosphere screens solar rays and admit the parts of the Sun we call the Warmth and Light ethers and the fallen Chemical and fallen Life ethers. Presently, humans would be burnt alive if the solar rays were not screened by the ozone and the Earth's atmosphere. Even what we know as Light ether is not pure sunlight, for sunlight has all seven ethers beaming towards the Earth.

The issue concerning people who do not eat *(inedics)* is complex in that it could originate from a variety of sources. Most people imagine that permanently fasting is a spiritual endeavor, and the fasting person somehow derives nourishment from "higher" spiritual sources—"living off of the ethers." This would only be true if the person were spiritually strong enough to take part of their constitution (astral or etheric body) into the purified etheric realms, where higher spiritual beings reside, and there, to directly consume the Unfallen Chemical and Unfallen Life ethers.

If the inedic is spiritually developed enough, extreme fasting has been known to manifest in an "apocalypse," like the experience St. John the Divine describes in the *Book of Revelation*. The spiritual initiate may choose to follow the path of apocalypse (unveiling) that many other prophets and seers have taken. The initiate may have an "uncovering" of the soul and be "taken up" into the seventh heaven to the throne of the divine that is surrounded by elders and illuminated by seven lamps. If this process has truly happened to the person with inedia, it is evident to a clairvoyant. In modern times, it is not uncommon to hear of people who claim to live without food or water. Few of these people exist, but their authenticated existence demonstrates that living off the ethers is possible. In the future, humanity will live without food or drink and simply draw their life-force from air and sunlight.

In authentic cases of extraordinary spiritual manifestation, the person with inedia is typically "instructed" to write down what they have experienced, which tends to look quite similar to others' "revelations." Generally, the spiritual inedic undergoing a soul experience similar to an "apocalypse" will encounter Christ or Sophia in a timeless, spaceless realm where higher consciousness exists and hierarchical beings live. Often, the humble and devout person having this spiritual "unveiling" did not ask for the experience.

The Roman Catholic Church has encountered many people who were told to write down their spiritual experiences in a "new apocalypse," which usually resembles the well-known version in the Bible. Before making proclamations of authenticity, the Catholic Church studies these manifestations carefully for the signs of the "exact opposite" phenomenon—that of possession. Many cases of supposed "spiritual" manifestations are found to be possessions that require spiritual intervention. There are many more cases of stigmata rejected by the Catholic Church than accepted. Therefore, true revelation or spiritual manifestation must be judged by the "work" that comes from it, or the "strong virtues" that the person has come to embody.

The Catholic Church has accepted almost no writings of stigmatists as genuine revelations. It is the "work" that has arisen from the manifestation and "effects" of the stigmatist, prophet, or visionary that determines the authenticity of the case. Surviving without eating for any number of years, bleeding wounds, or supposed spiritual revelations are not "signs" that a person is being affected by the Unfallen Chemical and Life ethers that issue from the Tree of Life.

Currently, spiritual students should be trying to reach the etheric realm and find the Etheric Christ to help in the battle to resurrect the etheric body of the Earth and the human being. Ahrimanic, asuric, and sorathic materialistic thoughts are crucifying Christ in the etheric realm as materialists take their grey spider-thoughts into this realm of living light, wisdom, love, and spiritual nourishment. Christ is being crucified again! Descriptions of this Battle in Heaven usually are part of the message found in the "new apocalypse" writings of stigmatists and others who claim to live on "the ethers alone." Those who can live purely off of the Word of Christ, His love, and His ever-present bounty are happy to enlist in the battle and fight the darkness that is overtaking the etheric realms.

Christ started a fast immediately after being baptized in the Jordan by John the Baptist. He did so only once, and for forty days. During that fast, the three challenges of the astral (Lucifer), etheric (Ahriman), and physical (Asuric or Sorathic) doubles had to be tamed. Had Christ not tamed those three evil specters of Lucifer, Ahriman, and Sorath (leader of the Asuras), He would not have gained control of His physical body in this realm. The physical realm of maya, illusion, or delusion is the domain of Lucifer and Ahriman. If the temptations that come with fasting are not met and conquered, they come back to "haunt" the person attempting spiritual advancement.

It is interesting to note that the beautiful and sweet messages of "spiritual apparitions" take the apparitionist into a "light-filled realm" where angels sing and Jesus and Mary abide in love and harmony. The descriptions from those who have had apparitions often sound like they are looking into the realm of Shamballa, the super-etheric realm of higher life.

Spiritual influences work from the ego down into the three lower bodies. Apparitions, stigmata, possession, and revelation are all "issues" or "considerations" of the ego working on these lower bodies. Christ is the spiritual ego of humanity who has tamed these lower bodies through His passion and resurrection. Therefore, all spiritual phenomena should be measured against what Christ gave us as a model to follow.

Christ did not refuse food, but in fact He sanctified food through the Last Supper, making His body the body of the Earth, and His blood the enlivening force of human spiritualized blood. Each striving soul will encounter Christ on the path of spiritual development, and the personal relationship that they develop with Christ while on the Earth will hold the key to spiritual advancement. The amount of etherized blood of Christ in our bodies will be "weighed" when confronting the Lord of Karma (Christ) at the threshold of death.

Abstaining from eating or drinking could be seen as a rejection of Christ's body and blood. Christ redeemed all matter by His deed, and we must do the same in all aspects of our being. We are given the spiritual injunction to redeem the Earth and advance humanity's spiritual evolution. Rejecting food and water for the "ethers" is not an example Christ gave us, nor is "seeking a sign," going into trance, or being possessed by materialistic desires that look for God in the material world.

A manifestation of the Holy Trinity comes into being when we consciously *disenchant* matter by spiritually perceiving the revelation of the hierarchical donations of the past in the present moment. The donation of Christ's love in the present moment provides His perfected vehicles in the etheric realm through the Holy Spirit as the future design of human spiritual development. Humans are currently limited in space and time and must slowly come to spiritual consciousness and learn to conquer the limited perception of our self as a slave to our animalistic past that continues to limit our future with dead thinking.

Each of us directly encounters Christ, the Lord of Karma, each night as we go to sleep and cross the threshold between the physical and spiritual worlds. In the spiritual world, we benefit from having tried to unveil the mystery of Christ's body and blood working through earthly sense perception and the spiritual disenchantment of matter. To understand Christ's body is to understand the hierarchical donations of the past that created physical substance and the ethers that animate it. These mysteries are referred to as the *Father Ground of Being* or the *Mothers* who are the source of the seven ethers from which all things are made and sustained.

Cosmic and Earthly Nutrition Streams

The spiritual food in the super-etheric realm that feeds spiritual development can be imagined as a form of the unfallen ethers raying in from the cosmos. Contrary to this, there can also be a fixation or possession of the Chemical and Life ethers coming from the inner layers of the Earth, where evil is a living force. These two realms are opposite and work in different directions.

The Fallen Chemical and Fallen Life ether in the Earth draw the soul down into gravity and mirror images of the spirit. Through levity, the Unfallen Chemical and Unfallen Life ethers in the super-etheric realm of the atmosphere raise the soul up and into the light, where archetypal images of apocalypse are experienced and heavenly nourishment is provided from the spiritual world to the aspirant, who has developed the supersensible organs to commune in that realm. This process is called the "earthly and cosmic nutrition stream" that is explained in *The Gospel of Sophia: A Modern Path of Initiation* and found in most spiritual traditions.

It is this process of spiritual nourishment that creates the halo around the head of a saint as a manifestation of heavenly light and nourishment entering their body. This nourishment is sent from the divine and is the driving force with which an initiate shapes his spiritual future by creating free deeds of love. Often, this nourishment is experienced as visions, inspirations, and intuitions.

Every person who confronts the threshold between the physical and spiritual world through sleep, death, or initiation is given a choice to draw their forces from either gravity or levity—Ahriman or Christ. To know the difference between the two is to know the difference between the Tree of Knowledge of Good and Evil and the Tree of Life. One is found on the Earth and has a serpent wound around it (spinal column and brain), while the other remains unspoiled in the spiritual world (etheric realm). Fruit from one brings illness and death, while fruit from the other brings wisdom, love, and eternal life. Having the discernment to distinguish between the two trees is a major challenge for the spiritually striving soul. With both trees, we are dealing with spiritual beings. With the Tree of Knowledge, we are dealing with "retarded" spiritual beings who "decided" to remain behind in their evolution, and comparing them to the progressive spiritual beings who evolve upward through the hierarchy at the appropriate time. The downward-descending beings, who are moving backward in time, are the counter-image of the progressive spirits and are found wound around the Tree of Knowledge. The progressive spirits are found in the super-etheric realm, New Jerusalem, that is blessed by the fruits of the Tree of Life and the rivers flowing out from its base. The Tree of Knowledge draws us into the past, whereas the Tree of Life gives us the bright and blessed future joined with Sophia and Christ.

The path of spiritual development is a matter of balanced discernment. There are many paths and trails that the aspirant must travel as part of their individual karma, from fasting as a good way to go "up" to the spirit, to cosmic nutrition that is the result of the spirit coming "down" with the revelation of good news to the earth.

The Etheric Christ

What is even more profound than any of the above considerations is the direct experience with the Etheric Christ, who is resurrected in the etheric sphere around the earth. This experience often happens to those who are suffering, or about to go through great suffering. The experience is often accompanied by a glorious light that precedes the "appearance" of Christ. Some call the initial light the Holy Spirit, or Holy Sophia. Then, the cosmos announces the presence of Christ as He appears to the spiritual part of the aspirant's soul. This meeting with Christ in the etheric realm often reveals every spiritual milestone that has occurred to the aspirant throughout time. A sort of "time tableau" is witnessed that is the spiritual core of the aspirant being "unveiled" before the Lord of Karma. The apostle Paul was stricken with blindness when he encountered the etheric Christ on the road to Damascus, and it took time to be able to speak and see again. Christ sent him a teacher to explain to him what had happened in the encounter. Only afterwards was Paul able to understand the full ramifications of what had happened in his experience of the risen Christ.

A person having the experience of the etheric Christ may not understand much at all about what happened and may need decades to realize the full impact of the revelation. This is not accomplished through trance, astral travel, inedia, renunciation, or denial of the world. The experience of the "second coming" of Christ in the etheric realm integrates the person into the fabric of the entire world both physically and spiritually, showing the way to merge with Christ and Sophia. Many have had this "white light" experience wherein they "talk" with Jesus. A good number of these people had no prior experience of Christ or any religious ideas before they were "saved" by Jesus Christ in this realm of light that nourishes the soul and spirit.

There is a much easier way to steadily evolve spiritually towards the encounter with Christ in the etheric realm rather than the difficult and problematic routes of stigmata, inedia, renunciation, and austerities. For those poor souls who do have these experiences, we should look upon them with spiritual discernment and compassion for their suffering. Only in a few circumstances should we use these extreme measures as a model for our own spiritual development, unless we have experienced the phenomena firsthand and have the spiritual capacity to determine what is above, below, or on par with current human spiritual development.

A spiritual initiate can dissolve space and time and still maintain consciousness. It is this capacity that allows her to enter the spiritual world and remain conscious when the forces of sleep, dream, and trance would overwhelm a less developed individual. No physical "signs" are given as a standard of spiritual development on the slow and steady path of spiritual development. A person experiencing a valid revelation, apparition, stigmata, or extraordinary manifestation is not any more developed than one who is not. This is the common confusion of those who "need a sign" and are not able to manifest the spiritual world in the physical world themselves.

Miracles happen every day, and each of us can be a healer who helps all those with whom we have contact. We can be "all things to all people" and leave room for the miraculous working of the divine. We can fast regularly to fully understand the physical nature and not be bound by it. We can attempt to relive Christ's passion and resurrection. We can look to the "heavens" with confidence for intervention from Christ, Sophia, and the communion of saints and masters who wish to help us evolve.

In the process of self-development, we can move through the inner layers of the Earth to the golden core where Christ's love helps turn our Earth into a new sun. We then can begin to show the "signs of Christ" in our virtuous activities that help Christ fulfill His mission of Love that heals the Earth and humanity. When we have developed discernment, we will know the difference between surrendering to Christ and surrendering to Ahriman, Lucifer, or Sorath.

We are called to the resurrection of the etheric Earth to create a glorious new Sun of Love and Wisdom. The battle to re-crucify Christ in the etheric realm by the adversarial forces is raging, and true followers of Christ must find new courage and strength to lead others out of darkness and into the light, from gravity to levity. It is through this direct, conscious interaction with living spiritual beings that we create our own fate and find the way to imitate the resurrection of Christ from the forces of death and hatred that threaten to enslave materialists.

Christ's living presence is the sword of love that strikes down ignorance and evil and raises the pure of heart into the divine realms. The battle in heaven still wages to this day. The only question is, whose side are we aligned with?

Armed with the power and understanding of the ethers and the etheric formative forces, the aspirant can study the Eternal Curriculum and resurrect the Wisdom Child that exists in every soul. Through study of the "new song" of the Book of Revelation, the etheric body, we sing together the true history of the Cosmic Christ and embody of Wisdom of Sophia that descended with Christ to redeem the Earth and humanity. Through diving into our own etheric bodies, we can find the Wisdom Child in our spiritual souls and raise her up into the light of the unfallen ethers to receive the ever-abundant nourishment from the spiritual world.

www.ingramcontent.com/pod-product-compliance
Lightning Source LLC
Chambersburg PA
CBHW050125170426
43197CB00011B/1719